The Sustainable Business Blueprint

Understanding how to build and manage a sustainability business plan has become a business imperative as investors demand, regulators require, and stakeholders increasingly expect companies to report their financial economic sustainability performance (ESP) and non-financial environmental, social, and governance (ESG) sustainability information. This book provides both the rationale for and key practical steps in how to approach business sustainability factors of planning, performance, risk, reporting, and assurance.

This comprehensive book covers all the areas that a business would need to embed, articulate, and execute a strategy of profit-with-purpose in promoting shared value creation for all stakeholders. It addresses drivers, sources, and international guidelines (GRI, IIRC, SASB, FASB, PCAOB, IAASB, ISSB) for prioritising business sustainability factors, and establishing the link between ESG performance and financial performance. It presents key performance indicators (KPIs) of ESP and ESG dimensions of sustainability performance. It also provides templates for performance, risk, and disclosure; presenting cases and examples of why to disclose ESG performance, what to disclose, and where and how to disclose ESG performance information.

For businesses wanting a detailed understanding of how to deliver on these important areas, including boards of directors, senior management, financial officers, internal auditors, external auditors, legal counsel, investors, and regulators, this book is an invaluable resource.

Zabihollah (Zabi) Rezaee is the Thompson-Hill Chair of Excellence and Professor of Accounting at the Crews School of Accountancy of the University of Memphis. He has served a two-year term (2004–2006) on the Standing Advisory Group (SAG) of the Public Company Accounting Oversight Board (PCAOB) and is Honorary Advisor of the Accounting and Financial Reporting Council (AFRC) in Hong Kong (December 2019–September 2025).

"Zabihollah Rezaee, an academic expert in the field of business sustainability, provides an exploration of environmental, social and governance factors together with economic financial performance and ethics. His analysis offers readers insights into the complex interplay between sustainability and operating a contemporary business from strategic planning to disclosure and assurance."

Brigitte W. Muehlmann, *Ph.D., CPA,*
Professor of Accounting, Babson College

"This book by Dr. Zabihollah Rezaee is an excellent practitioner book that addresses important and emerging issues of sustainability including strategic planning, performance, risk, reporting, and assurance. It has chapters on shareholder and stakeholder primacy in the context of a corporate mission of profit-with-purpose and discusses how business organizations can focus on achieving financial economic sustainability while generating a desired rate of return for their shareholders and simultaneously producing a positive social and environmental impact."

Dr. Kenneth Lambert, *Professor and Interim Director,*
Crews School of Accountancy

"In this book, Dr. Rezaee competently examines an integrated and strategic approach to business sustainability planning, performance, risk, reporting, and assurance, including the fiduciary roles of those charged with governance. Specifically, Dr. Rezaee conveys his deep understanding of the emerging ESG landscape by revealing *what his mind has grasped*, while suitably highlighting for the reader *what has grasped his mind…*"

Dr. Sridhar Ramamoorti, *University of Dayton*

The Sustainable Business Blueprint

Planning, Performance, Risk, Reporting, and Assurance

Zabihollah Rezaee

Routledge
Taylor & Francis Group
LONDON AND NEW YORK

Designed cover image: Getty Images

First published 2025
by Routledge
4 Park Square, Milton Park, Abingdon, Oxon OX14 4RN

and by Routledge
605 Third Avenue, New York, NY 10158

Routledge is an imprint of the Taylor & Francis Group, an informa business

British Library Cataloguing-in-Publication Data
A catalogue record for this book is available from the British Library

ISBN: 978-1-032-56764-8 (hbk)
ISBN: 978-1-032-57127-0 (pbk)
ISBN: 978-1-003-43794-9 (ebk)

DOI: 10.4324/9781003437949

Typeset in Adobe Garamond
by codeMantra

Contents

About the Author

Zabihollah (Zabi) Rezaee is the Thompson-Hill Chair of Excellence and Professor of Accounting at the Crews School of Accountancy of the University of Memphis. He served a two-year term (2004–2006) on the Standing Advisory Group (SAG) of the Public Company Accounting Oversight Board (PCAOB) and is the Honorary Advisor of the Accounting and Financial Reporting Council (AFRC) in Hong Kong (December 2019–September 2025). He is the senior editor of the *Journal of Forensic Accounting Research* (*JFAR*) one of the AAA journals. He has also published fourteen books, several of them are on business sustainability including the one that won the 2013 Axiom Gold Award in the category of Business Ethics. He holds ten professional certifications including CPA and his PhD is in accounting. He has published over 275 articles in well-recognised academic and practitioner journals and made more than 300 presentations nationally and internationally. He has served as an expert witness in several court cases and testified before a federal judge. He is ranked highly among the best scientists in the United States and worldwide.

Preface

Business sustainability has gained considerable attention from investors, regulators, standard-setters, business organizations, academics, and the accounting profession in recent decades. Business sustainability focuses on achieving financial economic sustainability performance (ESP) to create shareholder value and desired financial returns for shareholders while generating non-financial environmental, social, and governance (ESG) sustainability performance to protect the interests of other stakeholders (e.g., employees, customers, suppliers, society, and the environment). The purpose of this book is to examine an integrated strategic approach to business sustainability factors of planning, performance, risk, reporting, and assurance, as well as the roles and responsibilities of all corporate gatekeepers (the board, management, accountants, regulators, and investors among others) in creating shared value for all stakeholders. Business sustainability is no longer about greenwashing and branding as it has become a business imperative as investors demand, regulators require, and companies report their sustainability information in areas of financial ESP and non-financial ESG sustainability performance with the ethics component is integrated into both ESP and ESG dimensions. Business organizations worldwide are moving away from short-term planning to long-term strategic planning; seeking financial returns alongside positive social and environmental impacts.

The achievement of both financial ESP and non-financial ESG sustainability performance contributes to the creation of shared value for all stakeholders. Stakeholders are those who have vested interests in a firm through their investments in the form of financial capital (shareholders), human capital (employees), physical capital (customers and suppliers), social capital (the society), environmental capital (ecological), and regulatory capital (government). Business organizations that focus on their non-financial ESG sustainability performance, conduct their business ethically and manage their activities more effectively with good corporate governance, are more financially sustainable in the long term and add to their bottom-line earnings. The primary purpose of business organization has transformed from profit maximization and wealth enhancement for shareholders to stakeholder shared value creation. Global businesses now employ the stakeholder primacy model and stakeholder governance as opposed to the shareholder primacy model and shareholder governance to achieve the mission of profit-with-purpose: securing financial returns for shareholders while having social and environmental impacts.

Several recent initiatives have promote the move toward integrated sustainability reporting by public companies. Corporate disclosures, both mandatory on ESP information and voluntary on ESG sustainability performance information, are vital to the financial markets and value-relevant to investors and other stakeholders. The type and extent of sustainability reports have recently received considerable attention as many firms worldwide disclose information on various ESG dimensions of their sustainability performance. Integrated sustainability reports are intended to provide investors and other stakeholders with relevant, useful, transparent, and reliable information in making sound investment decisions and have thus become the backbone of the financial markets. The credibility and objectivity of sustainability reports should be assured by the third-party assurance providers.

This book consists of 10 chapters covering all four sustainability factors of planning, performance, risk, and disclosure with a keen focus on their implications for business organizations. Anyone who is involved with business sustainability and corporate governance, the financial reporting process, investment decisions, legal and financial advising, audit functions, and corporate governance education will be interested in this book. Specifically, corporations, their executives, the boards of directors, board committees, internal and external auditors, accountants, lawmakers, regulators, standard-setters, users of financial statements (investors, creditors, and pensioners), investor activists, business schools, and other professionals (attorneys, financial analysts, and bankers) will benefit from this book. This book offers guidance for proper measurement, recognition, and reporting of all sustainability key performance indicators. The ever-increasing erosion of public trust and investor confidence in the sustainability of large businesses, the widening concern about social responsibility and environmental matters, overconsumption of natural resources, the global government bailout of big businesses, and the perception that government cannot solve all problems of businesses underscore the importance of keen focus on the sustainability factors of planning, performance, risk, and disclosure. This book also highlights how people, business, and resources collaborate in a business sustainability and accountability model. This book covers a variety of issues relevant to business sustainability and their implications for organizations of all types and sizes. I hope you find this book relevant and useful to gain and maintain your business and personal sustainability.

Zabihollah (Zabi) Rezaee
March 30, 2024

Acknowledgments

I acknowledge the Securities and Exchange Commission, the Public Company Accounting Oversight Board, the American Institute of Certified Public Accountants, the big four accounting firms and corporate governance organizations, American Accounting Association, Global Reporting Initiative (GRI), International Integrated Reporting Council (IIRC), Sustainability Accounting Standards Board (SASB), United Nations, International Sustainability Standards Board (ISSB) and other sustainability standards-setting organizations for permission to quote and reference their professional standards and other publications.

The encouragement and support of my colleagues at the University of Memphis are also acknowledged. Especially, my graduate assistants, Ms. Nastaran Kazemeini and Mr. Mahdi Tarokh for providing invaluable assistance. I thank the members of the Taylor & Francis Group and Business, Management, Economics Routledge Publisher Team for their hard work and dedication in editing the book, including, Rebecca Marsh, Lauren Whelan, and Ruth Bourne.

My sincere thanks are due to my family, my wife Soheila, and my children Rose and Nick. Without their love, enthusiasm, and support, this book would not have come to fruition when it did. I am dedicating this book to the loving memory of my father, Fazlollah Rezaee; my mother Fatemeh Rezaee; sister Monireh Rezaee; and my younger brother Heshmat (John) Rezaee.

Chapter I

Introduction to the Sustainable Business Factors of Planning, Performance, Risk, and Disclosure

I. INTRODUCTION AND BOOK OBJECTIVES

The purpose of this book is to examine an integrated and wholistic approach to the business sustainability factors of planning, performance, risk, and disclosure, as well as the roles and responsibilities of all corporate gatekeepers (the board, management, accountants, regulators, and investors among others) in creating shared value for all stakeholders. The 2020 COVID-19 pandemic, recent perceived social unrest, and focus on climate change, global warming, and human capital management, have brought business sustainability to the center stage of corporate culture, business environment, and corporate governance. Business sustainability is no longer about greenwashing and branding. It has become a business imperative as investors demand, regulators require, scholars research, and companies report their sustainability performance. Sustainability has become an economic and strategic imperative with significant opportunities and risks for investors and businesses in creating shared value for all stakeholders. This book defines business sustainability as a process of generating financial economic sustainability performance (ESP) to

DOI: 10.4324/9781003437949-1

create shareholder value while achieving non-financial environmental, social, and governance (ESG) sustainability performance in protecting the interests of other stakeholders, including creditors, customers, employees, suppliers, government, society, communities, and the environment.[1] Business organizations worldwide are now adopting the corporate mission of profit-with-purpose to generate a desired rate of returns for shareholders while having some social and environmental impacts. Shared value creation for all stakeholders can be promoted within the wealth-maximization framework in pursuing the goal of profit-with-purpose for corporations. Corporations can balance the wealth maximization for shareholders under the shareholder primacy model while achieving the welfare maximization for all stakeholders under the stakeholder primacy model discussed in Chapter 2. The focus on the profit-with-purpose mission, combined with public pressure to engage on social, environmental, and political topics (e.g., human capital, diversity, immigration, gun control, gender pay equity, climate change), encourages business organizations worldwide to advance towards business sustainability.

Global competition and business continuity have been the main drivers of moving away from short-term profit maximization planning to long-term strategic and sustainable planning in achieving ESP and ESG sustainability performance, with the ethics component is integrated into ESP and ESG dimensions. Several initiatives have recently been taken that promote public companies' move toward sustainability planning, performance, reporting, and assurance. For example, the Sustainability Accounting Standards Board (SASB) and the International Integrated Reporting Council (IIRC) have merged to create the Value Reporting Foundation (VRF) that promotes the relevance of sustainability disclosures to investors and focuses on producing material and useful sustainability information by business organizations in all industries including the integrated thinking principles, the integrated reporting framework, and the SASB Standards.[2] The Global Reporting Initiative (GRI) and the SASB have joined in issuing a practical guide to sustainability reporting from a market participant's perspective, including sustainability materiality, disclosures, and audiences. The International Sustainability Standards Board (ISSB), a non-profit organization, was created by the International Financial Reporting Standards (IFRS) in 2021. By August 2022, it has integrated the VRF, GRI, SASB, and IIRC as a primary sustainability organization in establishing sustainability accounting and reporting standards.[3] The regulators worldwide, including the Securities and Exchange Commission (SEC) in the United States, have required more robust and relevant disclosures of sustainability-related disclosure issues, including climate change and human capital.[4] The European Union (EU), in January 2023, adapted the Corporate Sustainability Reporting Directive (CSRD) that requires companies to disclose historical and forward-looking information about sustainability factors of planning, reporting, risk, and other matters, including environmental, social, employee, human rights, and governance.[5] These initiatives will extend sustainability reporting beyond metrics, disclosures, and ratings to assigning monetary values to an organization's ESG issues and their integration into ESP and financial statements. This introductory chapter presents a synopsis of business sustainability's importance, relevance, drivers, and factors, including planning, performance, risk, and disclosure.

II. BUSINESS SUSTAINABILITY FACTORS

Business sustainability is defined as a process (journey) of achieving both financial ESP and non-financial ESG sustainability performance with an ethics component integrated into ESP and ESG in creating share value for all stakeholders. The four critical sustainability factors are sustainability planning, performance, risk, and disclosure, enabling business organizations to create shared value for all stakeholders, including shareholders.[6] The financial ESP sustainability performance consists of long-term earnings, economic growth, innovation, and related cash flows. The non-financial ESG sustainability performance consists of business activities that generate ethical, accountable, social, and environmental impacts. The achievements of both financial ESP and non-financial ESG sustainability performance have contributed to creating shared value for all stakeholders. Stabilizability risk assessment and reporting have become integral components of corporate reporting.

II.1 Sustainability Planning

Business sustainability is a relatively broad concept related to the benefits of internal and external stakeholders. These stakeholders are those who have vested interests in a firm through their investments in the form of financial capital (shareholders), human capital (employees), physical capital (customers and suppliers), social capital (the society), environmental capital (ecological), and regulatory capital (government). Stakeholders have a reciprocal relation and interaction with a firm in the sense that they contribute to the firm's value creation, and in return, their well-being is also affected by the firm. Sustainability planning involves developing goals, strategies, and practices to establish the right balance between "shareholder value maximization," where management attempts to improve earnings for shareholders, versus the broader "stakeholder/society value creation," where management maximizes the sum of the various stakeholders' surpluses (e.g., creditors, employees, customers, suppliers, society, and the environment) in creating shared value for all stakeholders. Sustainability planning focuses on activities and processes that are sustainable in the long term without causing significant short-term negative impacts on economic resources, society, and the environment. Sustainability planning consists of (1) evaluation and assessment of business activities and priorities; (2) establishment of goals and objectives; (3) stakeholder engagement and communication; (4) implementation and monitoring; and (5) reevaluation, reassessment, and adaptation that will be discussed in detail in Chapter 4.

II.2 Sustainability Performance

Sustainability performance consists of financial ESP and non-financial ESG sustainability performance, with the ethics component integrated into both ESP and ESG dimensions of sustainability performance. The focus on sustainability efforts indicates that companies that achieve non-financial ESG sustainability performance, including social and environmental performance, manage their activities more effectively with effective corporate governance, conduct their business ethically, and are more financially sustainable in terms of ESP can stay in business longer to contribute to their bottom-line earnings. The voluntary or mandatory ESG performance disclosures demonstrate that "sustainability-centric" companies that focus on achieving financial ESP and non-financial ESG sustainability performance have more incentives to disclose information that will differentiate themselves from "non-sustainability-centric" companies that often do not focus on financial ESP and non-financial ESG to avoid a bad reputation. Therefore, disclosure of voluntary non-financial ESG sustainability performance may signal management's commitment to transparency of both financial ESP and non-financial ESG sustainability performance and thus can reduce information asymmetry and increase firm value. The sustainability risk factor determines stakeholder exposure to risks associated with failure to achieve sustainability performance.

Sustainability performance has received the attention of investors, and several dimensions of sustainability performance focused on social and environmental initiatives have gained widespread global acceptance. These initiatives include important sustainability matters, such as global warming, climate change, ethical workspace, customer satisfaction, just and safe working conditions, non-discriminatory fair wages, workplace diversity and inclusion, safe and quality products, concern for the environment, and fair and transparent business practices and environmental preservation, clear air and water, minimum age for child labor. It is, however, important to realize that each industry has its own applicable set of financial and non-financial key performance indicators (KPIs) relevant to both financial ESP and non-financial ESG sustainability performance. Each business organization must carefully identify its profit-with-purpose mission of generating profit for shareholders while protecting the interests of other stakeholders, including social and environmental responsibilities and impacts in the context of its business culture and environment. The proper and relevant list of financial ESP and non-financial ESG sustainability KPIs should be determined according to corporate mission and strategy, industry best practices, legal regimes, corporate culture, diversity, political infrastructure, and managerial philosophy. Chapter 5 describes ESP and ESG sustainability performance dimensions in depth.

II.3 Sustainability Risk

The four sustainability factors are planning, performance, risk, and disclosure. Sustainability planning and performance factors were discussed in the previous sections.

A synopsis of the sustainability factor of risk is presented in this section and thoroughly discussed in Chapter 7. Sustainability risks present the likelihood that an organization is not achieving its financial ESP and non-financial ESG sustainability performance targets. Strategic, operations, compliance, financial, and reputation are important sustainability risks. The most important risk relevant to business sustainability is strategic risk, which reflects the failure of strategic plans to achieve sustainability goals. These risks should be identified, assessed, managed, and minimized to achieve sustainability goals. Operations risks of disruptions in the sustainability supply chain are also relevant to financial ESP and non-financial ESG dimensions of sustainability performance. Integrating all sustainability performance dimensions into operating activities across operational units, operation technology, supply chain, information technology, and other functional areas minimizes operational risks. The financial risk of issuing materially misstated financial reports is detrimental to the sustainability of corporations. The company's reputation and related risks should be evaluated continuously, and damage to the reputation should be minimized. These and other sustainability risks are further described in detail in Chapter 7.

II.4 Sustainability Disclosure

Traditionally, organizations have reported their performance on economic activities and affairs, and their focus on financial results has become complicated, and less value-relevant to all stakeholders, including shareholders. In recent years, stakeholders, global organizations, and the public have increasingly demanded information on financial ESP and non-financial ESG sustainability key performance indicators (KPIs) in the accountability and integrated sustainability reporting platform. Firm performance is measured by ESP performance and related financial earnings and by the mechanisms in which business success and sustainability are measured in terms of non-financial ESG sustainability key performance indicators.

Sustainability disclosures cover sustainability reporting, assurance, ranking, rating, and indexing. Sustainability reporting refers to the continuous process of promoting, measuring, recognizing, enforcing, reporting, and auditing sustainability performance in both financial ESP and non-financial ESG dimensions of sustainability.[7] Sustainability performance and integrated reporting generated a new interest during the recent financial crisis and resulting global economic meltdown and in the aftermath of the 2020 global COVID-19 pandemic, which has sparked widening concerns about whether big businesses are sustainable in the long-term in contributing to the economic growth and prosperity of the nation.

The ever-increasing erosion of public trust and investor confidence in conventional financial reporting focusing on economic activities necessitates expanding corporate reporting to the integrated reporting of both financial ESP and non-financial ESG performance. The widening concern about social responsibility and environmental matters, along with the overconsumption of natural resources, the global government bailout of big businesses, and the perception that the government cannot solve all problems in the business world, underscore the importance of integrated sustainability reporting and assurance. The United Nations Global Compact, in its 2013 *Global Corporate Sustainability Report*, underscoring the importance of business sustainability, calls on corporations worldwide to integrate ten sustainability principles pertaining to the environment, human rights, fair labor, and anti-corruption into their strategies and operations.[8] Chapters 8, 9, and 10 present detailed sustainability disclosures, including ranking, indexing, rating, reporting, and assurance.

III. BUSINESS SUSTAINABILITY INITIATIVES

Recent events, including the 2020 global COVID-19 pandemic, the perceived social injustice, environmental consciences, and the global financial crisis of 2007–2009, have made business organizations adopt initiatives to improve their performance in both ESP and ESG dimensions of sustainability. At the same time, corporations are expected to effectively communicate their sustainability factors of planning performance and risk to all their stakeholders through sustainability reporting. This section discusses sources and drivers of recent moves toward business sustainability performance, integrated/sustainability, sustainability disclosure, risk assessment, reporting, and assurance. Responding to increasing interest in and demand for business sustainability factors of planning, performance, risk, and disclosure, many public companies now voluntarily manage, measure, recognize, and disclose their commitments and related transactions relevant to financial ESP and non-financial ESG dimensions of sustainability performance. Many business organizations have voluntarily pledged to minimize environmental and social harms beyond the mandatory requirement of laws, rules, and regulations. For example, Google plans to operate on carbon-free energy by 2030, and Nike has linked executive compensation to progress in achieving diversity and inclusion.

Whether mandatory or voluntary, sustainability initiatives are intended to promote both financial ESP and non-financial ESG sustainability performance in maximizing corporate social benefits and environmental impacts while minimizing the potential conflicts of interest among corporations, society, and the environment. The corporate mission of profit-with-purpose should be aligned with the goals of society and the environment to minimize the differences between private and social costs and benefits. There are many examples of potential conflicts of interest between corporation activities and society, and some can be linked to social injustice and unrest, poor quality of education, child labor in developing countries, environmental issues (pollution, acid rain, global warming), and wages paid by multinational corporations in poor countries. Business sustainability initiatives can raise companies' awareness of their business activities' social costs and benefits. The Organisation for Economic Co-operation and Development (OECD) defines the purpose of a corporate social responsibility (CSR) program as "To encourage the positive contributions that multinational enterprises can make to economics, environmental, and social progress and to minimize the difficulties to which their various operations may give rise."[9]

This definition focuses on two important aspects of a CSR program: creating social value through corporate activities (social value-added activities) and avoiding conflicts between corporate goals and societal goals (societal consensus). These two aspects of CSR programs are voluntarily integrated into business sustainability strategies, decisions, performance, and reporting. Business organizations have several reasons to take on voluntary sustainability strategies and initiatives. For example, the increasing move toward industry consolidation and globalization reduces the efficacy of formal domestic regulation in addressing businesses' social and environmental impacts, and regulators may face political challenges in addressing growing social and environmental issues (climate change, diversity). However, voluntary sustainability initiatives could be less effective because of a lack of management incentives and commitments to mitigate corporate harms to society and the environment, and sustainability becomes a greenwashing strategy by management.

There are several mandatory and voluntary initiatives and guidelines for sustainability factors of planning, performance, risk, and disclosure, including the reporting frameworks released by the Global Reporting Initiative (GRI), sustainability reporting guidelines of the Sustainability Accounting Standards Board (SASB), integrated reporting promoted by the International Integrated Reporting Council (IIRC) and the Value Reporting Foundation (VRF), which is the joint efforts of the IIRC and SASB, and the International Sustainability Standards Board (ISSB) that attempts to standardize the sustainability reporting and assurance process by bringing comparability and consistency to global sustainability reporting. These sustainability initiatives have collectively promoted the relevance of sustainability disclosures to investors and focus on producing material and useful sustainability information by business organizations in all industries. In the latest survey from Callan Institute, almost 50% of respondents indicate that they have added ESG into their investment decisions, which is a 7% increase from the prior year; about 40% of survey respondents who did not implement ESG were considering it, and the most common investors that incorporated ESG were public plans, foundations, and endowments.[10] Some common reasons for incorporating ESG factors include aligning the portfolio with company values, fiduciary responsibility, and stakeholder interests. Furthermore, 39% of the respondents who incorporated ESG into the investment decision-making process indicate that they will broaden their approach to ESG in the next 1–3 years, implying a continued progression of implementation.[11] Corporate disclosures, mandatory or voluntary, are the backbone of financial markets worldwide. Sustainability initiatives and drivers, both voluntary and mandatory, enable business organizations to standardize the sustainability performance reporting and assurance by accomplishing the following:

a. Move away from the shareholder primacy model and toward the stakeholder primacy model presented in Chapter 2.
b. Promote the corporate mission of profit-with-purpose and shared value concept for all stakeholders presented in Chapter 3.

c. Create uniformity in objectively measuring all five environmental, ethical, economic, social, and governance dimensions of sustainability performance presented in Chapter 5.
d. Establish globally accepted and widely used sustainability key performance indicators (KPIs) for all five environmental, ethical, economic, social, and governance dimensions of sustainability performance presented in Chapter 5.
e. Provide a comprehensive framework in core principles and objectives of sustainability that guide standard-setting efforts in modernizing and standardizing sustainability reporting and assurance presented in Chapters 8 and 9.
f. Offer a common language of the standardized sustainability reports that improve the ability of standard setters to communicate ideas and intentions with key stakeholders.
g. Establish a globally accepted reporting framework and standards for sustainability disclosures, as presented in Chapter 8.
h. Make management steward all sustainability capitals, including financial, strategic, reputation, human resources, environmental, and social, as presented in Chapter 6.
i. Develop a framework for proper assessment and management of all aspects of sustainability risks, including financial, reputational, manufacturing, and compliance, as presented in Chapter 7.
j. Create the uniform sustainability disclosure guidelines presented in Chapter 8.
k. Establish standardized sustainability assurance processes as presented in Chapter 9.
l. Establish a sustainability disclosure index and ratings to establish comparability analyses of sustainability initiatives, goals, performance, and achievement among industries and companies as presented in Chapter 9.
m. Present contemporary issues in business sustainability, including sustainability supply chain and sustainability in not-for-profit organizations, as presented in Chapter 10.

III.1 Mandatory Business Sustainability Initiatives

There has been much confusion and disagreement about the role of regulators and regulations worldwide in promoting ESG sustainability and whether business organizations and their boards of directors and executives should be required to achieve ESG sustainability beyond creating value for their shareholders. Many countries have adopted mandatory sustainability initiatives relevant to their non-financial ESG sustainability performance in the past several decades. These countries include Australia, Austria, Canada, Denmark, France, Germany, Hong Kong, Malaysia, Netherlands, Sweden, the United Kingdom and the United States. These countries have adopted mandatory reporting on financial ESP and non-financial ESG sustainability performance.[12] Corporate mandatory disclosures are intended to provide investors and other stakeholders with relevant, useful, transparent, and reliable information for making sound investments and other policy decisions. Agency theory suggests that moral hazard occurs in the presence of information asymmetry where the agent (management) acting on behalf of the principal (shareholders) knows more about its actions and corporate performance information than the principals who use information in making decisions. This information asymmetry can occur because of the lack of proper monitoring of the agent by principals, the interests of the agent are not aligned with those of the principals, the agent has incentives and may not act in the best interest of principals and/or withhold important information from the principals and most importantly lack of sufficient monitoring of the agent through effective, efficient, scalable, and proactive regulations and mandatory initiatives.

Effective implementation of mandatory business sustainability initiatives enables business organizations to address their environmental, social, and economic concerns and contribute positively to the well-being of shareholders, the planet, and society. Management may not, on a voluntary basis, provide sufficient relevant sustainability information to all stakeholders; thus, mandatory disclosures may be desirable to minimize opportunities for information asymmetry. Public companies worldwide are required to disclose a set of financial information to their shareholders when the public holds their securities/stocks. The primary purpose of corporate disclosure is to provide stakeholders (e.g., shareholders, creditors, employees, suppliers, and customers) with adequate, reliable, and useful information to make appropriate decisions. Financial information on ESP is intended to help investors protect their interests, minimizing management incentives for providing materially misstated financial information to investors and enhance their confidence in the financial reports and markets, mitigating the information asymmetry, and ensuring that stock prices fully reflect all value-relevant information in an efficient capital market.

Business sustainability encourages management to manage business operations to achieve sustainable performance to meet the needs of various stakeholders. For example, shareholders and creditors provide financial capital, and they expect and believe that the company's purpose is to maximize profit to generate a desired return on investment for investors. Employees provide human capital and expect to be properly compensated and have an ethical work environment. Customers may expect that the company provides not only the advertised product or service but also gives back to society meaningfully. Customer satisfaction, business reputation, environmental initiatives, social responsibility, and brand value are often considered intangible business assets that cannot be described and measured adequately in purely economic and financial terms. However, these assets and their value should be linked to their related economic value over the long term to ensure business sustainability. Shareholders are better off in the long term if they recognize the various financial benefits derived from the ESG sustainability performance and related intangible business assets generated through sustainability efforts and development. Thus, management should be motivated to generate financial ESP performance for shareholders while protecting the interests of other stakeholders by achieving ESG sustainability performance. Mandatory disclosures are disclosures of financial ESP information required by laws or regulations. This sustainability information can be found within financial filings such as 10-K, annual reports, and management disclosure and analysis. Management should also disclose non-financial ESG information, including health and safety disclosure, human capital management information, climate change, and pollutant release/emissions disclosure.

Regulators worldwide have addressed ESG-related disclosure requirements and established mandatory sustainability initiatives relevant to climate change, human capital, and board and workforce diversity, equity, and inclusion. Examples of globally accepted mandatory business sustainability initiatives are "Waste Reduction and Recycling," "Carbon Footprint Reduction," "Water Conservation," and "Compliance with Environmental Regulations." Business organizations should tailor these mandatory sustainability initiatives to their specific industry, size, and operations and update their sustainability initiatives to stay current with ever-increasing standards and best practices. Laws, rules, regulations, and industry standards can drive mandatory initiatives. The risk of noncompliance with mandatory sustainability initiatives can be very costly as the risk of ESG-related litigation compliance regulatory actions and shareholders' demand continue to grow. Companies should effectively and comprehensively review their ESG-related strategy, risk, and disclosure. The global sustainable finance market is expected to grow because of new central banks and regulatory actions and the implementation of more rigorous criteria for ESG-labeled products. Companies should consider relevant opportunities to participate in this market. Financial regulators focus on climate risk management and climate change's effects on financial stability. Financial institutions should assess their current approach to climate risks and opportunities and prepare for new requirements and supervisory expectations. The following subsections present mandatory sustainability initiatives in the United States, Europe, and Asia.

III.1.1 United States

Regulations in the United States require that corporate directors focus on business activities that increase corporate value for the benefit of shareholders and few or no other purposes, such as achieving ESG performance. Regulations and rules of the Securities and Exchange Commission (SEC) on firm valuations and corporate ESG policies have drastically changed in the past 50 years due to globalization, technology advancements, and other industry-specific developments and investor sentiments. A study on SEC regulations and their relationship with firm value was done to identify the benefits and detriments of these increasingly stringent market rules.[13] The SEC concept on disclosure reform was released on 22 April 2016, which includes 11 pages of discussion of sustainability disclosure and poses the following questions:[14]

1. How does sustainability disclosure fit within the existing regulatory requirements (Regulation S-K)?

2. What is the current cost of sustainability disclosure?
3. What are the challenges with line-item requirements?
4. How can a market standard for sustainability disclosure benefit companies?
5. Should the focus be on ESG sustainability disclosures or just environmental and climate change matters?
6. How can the SEC work with the SASB in developing sustainability disclosure guidelines for many industries.

The use of ESG-related disclosures has gone from a simple concept to a mainstream global investment priority The SEC also created a sample comment letter detailing the potential comments from the Division of Corporation Finance that could be sent to companies related to their disclosures. Examples of comments from the Division include disclosures of transition and litigation risks concerning climate change and the effects on the corresponding company, changes in legislation and capital expenditures dealing with climate change, and consequences for business operations.[15]

Most recently, the SEC has worked with the SASB to integrate ESG sustainability reporting into the SEC filings of 10K and 10Q annual and quarterly corporate reports. Specifically, the SEC has proposed new climate disclosure regulations and has also set up a task force designed to scrutinize ESG disclosures in the following areas:[16]

In 2021, the SEC considered releasing its proposed Climate Risk Disclosure Requirements rule by registrants. On 21 March 2022, the SEC released its proposed rule changes requiring registrants to disclose certain climate-related information in their registration statements and periodic reports. The proposed disclosures contain information about climate-related risks that are reasonably likely to impact registrants' financial results and conditions, including disclosure of a registrant's greenhouse gas emissions.[17] The SEC, in March 2024, released its final rules that require public companies to: (1) disclose information related to their climate-related risks, impacts, and strategies including greenhouse gas emissions, climate-related risks to operations and supply chains, and the potential financial impacts of climate change on the company's business; (2) integrate climate-related disclosures into existing SEC reporting frameworks, such as Form 10-K, Form 20-F, and Form 40-F; and (3) disclose information about their governance structures, internal controls, and management processes related to climate-related risks and opportunities to enable investors to evaluate how companies are managing and addressing climate-related issues at the board and executive levels.[18]

- SEC plans further rules for human capital management (HCM) and board diversity disclosure. In August 2020, the SEC adopted rules to modernize human capital disclosure.[19] In July 2023, the Financial Accounting Standards Board (FASB) issued a proposal to mandate that companies disaggregate the reporting of major operating costs, thus requiring public companies to disclose employee compensation costs included in the income statement.[20]
- In February 2021, Nasdaq filed an amended proposal with the SEC to increase board diversity, which was subsequently approved. Nasdaq's board diversity

rule requires companies listed on the Nasdaq exchange to disclose board-level diversity statistics annually or explain why they do not have diverse directors.[21]

- Proposed US legislation would increase disclosure mandates. The US Senate and House of Representatives are considering multiple bills that could increase companies' obligations to disclose ESG-related metrics.

In the Spring 2021 Unified Agenda of Regulatory and Deregulatory Actions, the SEC announced several rulemaking actions and areas to protect investors and improve markets and capital, including disclosures surrounding climate, cybersecurity, and diversity.[22] Several sustainability-related bills are currently under legislation that would provide more guidelines for investors and boards of directors to focus on the achievement of both financial ESP and non-financial ESG sustainability performance, including the following:

- **ESG Disclosure Simplification Act**. This bill would require companies to disclose their views about the link between ESG metrics and long-term business strategy and require the SEC to define ESG metrics and companies to disclose those metrics.
- **The Shareholder Protection Act**. This bill would require public companies to disclose their political spending activity. Over the years, shareholder proposals requiring political and lobbying disclosures have consistently been rejected by shareholders. Last year, roughly 74% of Fortune 250 shareholders rejected these proposals.
- **Corporate Human Rights Risk Assessment, Prevention, and Mitigation Act of 2019**. This bill would require identifying any human-rights risks or impacts in the operations and value chain of the issuer and ranking them based on severity.
- **Accountable Capitalism Act**. This bill opens the opportunity to produce economic growth on a broad scale for shareholders and workers alike, thus reducing the chances to maximize shareholder value and wealth for only the top percentage of rich households. This act provides for obtaining a charter, restricting sales of company shares, improving board approval, and ensuring corporations are being run legally and ethically.[23]
- **Climate Risk Disclosure Act of 2019**. This bill would require public companies to disclose information about the financial and business risks associated with climate change in their annual reports and require the SEC to establish climate-related risk disclosure metrics and guidance.
- **New Climate Disclosure**. The White House and the Securities and Exchange Commission have implemented measures to address climate-related disclosure. On May 20, 2021, President Biden issued an executive order called "Climate-Related Financial Risk." This would require the US government and its respective bureaucratic agencies to incorporate climate risk into regulation processes. The goal of this was to also have a reduced emissions economy.[24] The SEC has

put out a sample letter to companies to give guidance on how to disclose key climate-related material that affects their business.[25] In addition, Acting Chair Allison Herren Lee put out a statement on March 15, 2021, encouraging public input from investors and market participants regarding the disclosure of climate-related information by providing questions for the public to consider when analyzing important ideas surrounding climate change from an outsider's point of view.[26] Much of the sustainability-related rules and regulations in the United States focus on addressing adequate disclosure of climate change, human capital, and diversity issues.

III.1.2 European Union

In the past decade, regulators in Europe (EU) have made important steps toward promoting business sustainability and ESG dimensions of sustainability performance by improving the type, extent, nature, completeness, and comparability of listed firms' ESG disclosures. Specifically, on October 22, 2014, The European Commission adopted Directive 2014/95/EU, which requires that starting from fiscal year 2017, EU companies provide disclosures of non-financial ESG sustainability information. Companies and their stakeholders, including investors and society, are expected to benefit from this increased transparency of non-financial ESG sustainability information. The EU Directive provides non-binding guidelines in facilitating the disclosure of non-financial information by large public companies (firms with over 500 employees and yearly sales of over €40 million or net income of over €20 million).[27] This regulation also allows large companies to disclose non-financial information as a separate report or an integrated report along with financial information. It is possible that different implementation approaches chosen by the various EU countries could determine how the implementation of mandated ESG disclosure affects ESG disclosure levels, ESG disclosure quality (comparability and credibility), and the value-relevance of ESG information. For example, while some EU countries require sustainability disclosure in annual financial reports, others allow disclosures to be made in standalone sustainability reports, and certain EU countries could require more extensive auditor involvement (e.g., Belgium, Denmark, France).

On November 27, 2019, the European Parliament and the Council of the European Union passed disclosure regulations relevant to ESG information for the financial sector.[28] The UN General Assembly adopted a new global sustainable development framework: the 2030 Agenda for Sustainable Development (the "2030 Agenda"), which includes the Sustainable Development Goals (SDGs) at its core.[29] The European regulations on ESG disclosures took effect on March 10, 2021 and have enhanced the reliability and transparency of ESG disclosures and their valuable contribution to investment decisions and other proposals.[30] This regulation aims to reduce information asymmetries in principle-agent relationships with regard to the integration of sustainability risks, the consideration of adverse sustainability impacts, the promotion of environmental or social characteristics, and sustainable investment by requiring financial market participants and financial advisers to make pre-contractual and ongoing disclosures for investors when they act as agents of those end investors. Regulators in the UK and the EU have proposed additional ESG disclosures to promote sustainable economic activity. For example, the UK's Financial Conduct Authority (FCA) published a consultation paper in March 2020, proposing that certain UK firms make climate change disclosures.[31] Disclosure policies of enterprises should include, but not be limited to, material information on (1) the financial and operating results of the enterprise; (2) enterprise objectives; (3) major share ownership and voting rights, including the structure of a group of enterprises and intra-group relations, as well as control enhancing mechanisms; (4) remuneration policy for members of the board and key executives, and information about board members, including qualifications, the selection process, other enterprise directorships and whether each board member is regarded as independent by the board; (5) related party transactions; (6) foreseeable risk factors; (7) issues regarding workers and other stakeholders; (8) governance structures and policies, in particular, the content of any corporate governance code or policy and its implementation process. Enterprises should install high-quality standards for accounting and financial and non-financial disclosure, including environmental and social reporting. In addition, the standards or policies under which information is compiled or published should be reported. These standards have increased ESG reporting with positive effects on corporate governance. A survey conducted by Pay Governance LLC in January 2021 reveals that (1) 29% of companies have incorporated ESG metrics into their incentive compensation plans in 2021, which is an increase from 22% in 2020; (2) the majority of companies that incorporated ESG metrics use a balanced scorecard approach, with 48% of companies using it in 2020 and 53% using it in 2021; and (3) The most common ESG metric used in incentive plans were "social" metrics. In 2020, 84% of companies used the social metric and 87% of companies used it in 2021.[32]

To further improve ESG disclosure, on November 27, 2019, the European Parliament and the Council of the European Union passed disclosure regulations relevant to ESG information for the financial sector.[33] Regulators in the UK and the EU have recently proposed additional ESG disclosures to promote sustainable economic activity. For example, the UK's Financial Conduct Authority (FCA) published a consultation paper in March 2020, proposing that certain UK firms make climate change disclosures.[34]

European Commission directive: (1) requires companies to disclose their environmental, social, governance, and diversity sustainability performance; (2) is effective for the 2017 reporting year and onwards; (3) is moving from internal and self-assessed sustainability reporting to more standardized, normalized and monitored governmental process by 2024; and (4) affects over 6,000 companies. Companies must report:

- Environmental performance.
- Social and employee-related matters.

- Human rights policies.
- Anti-corruption and bribery issues.
- Diversity on the board of directors.

Covered organizations will need to include information about their suppliers.

Asset managers and investment advisers will be required to take the following steps to comply with the disclosure regulation:

- **Policies and procedures.** To produce the required disclosures, in-scope firms will need to consider and document the relevance of ESG to their investment policies. In addition, when preparing or updating their staff remuneration policies (including, where required, public or investor disclosures with regard to their remuneration practices), managers will be required to specify how these policies are consistent with the integration of sustainability risks. This will involve making a series of strategic business and investor relations decisions.
- **Website disclosures.** All managers will be required to publish information on their websites about their policies on integrating sustainability risks in their investment decision-making processes. Additional public disclosure obligations will apply to larger firms (with 500 employees or more). They will include descriptions of investment due diligence processes for assessing adverse impacts of investment decisions on sustainability factors, a description of the principal adverse sustainability impacts, policies on their identification and prioritization, any action taken or planned with regards to such sustainability impacts, as well as information on the manager's shareholder engagement policies. Firms that choose not to take sustainability risks into account when making their investment decisions will be required to provide clear reasons for their decision.
- **Pre-contractual disclosures.** Disclosures on the manner in which sustainability risks are integrated into investment decisions and advice and the results of the manager's assessment of the likely impacts of sustainability risks on the returns must also be included in the "pre-contractual disclosures," such as the investment management agreement relating to a separately managed account, or the private placement memorandum or prospectus of a fund. If a manager does not consider sustainability risks to be relevant, the pre-contractual disclosures must include a clear explanation of the manager's rationale.
- **Sustainable investments.** Additional detailed disclosure obligations will apply to investments marketed as sustainable investments (meeting the requirements of the Taxonomy Regulation) or other products promoting specific ESG characteristics.

In January 2023, the EU Corporate Sustainability Reporting Directive (CSRD) was released, which would require mandatory sustainability reporting for European companies and their counterparts and trading partners worldwide.[35] The CSRD is designed to complement existing sustainability-focused regulations and voluntary frameworks and standards of the Global Reporting Initiative (GRI) and the International Sustainability Standards Board (ISSB) and has a global implication. For example, US-domiciled public and private companies with significant EU revenue are now subject to CSRD's reporting requirements. The CSRD requires covered companies to disclose historical and forward-looking information relevant to sustainability matters, including ESG issues and information about sustainability risk management, metrics, and value chain due diligence for EU companies starting July 2023 and onwards. The first sustainability reports in compliance with CSRD requirements covering non-EU companies are not due until 2029, and early compliance is encouraged. Specifically, the CSRD applies to:

1. Large EU-domiciled companies.
2. All EU-listed companies, wherever incorporated.
3. Any public or private company headquartered outside the EU that has consolidated annual "net turnover" in the EU exceeding €150 million in each of the last two fiscal years.
4. An EU branch with net revenue exceeding €40 million in the last fiscal year or an EU subsidiary that meets two of the following criteria for the last fiscal year: (1) average of more than 250 employees during the year and (2) annual net turnover of more than €40 million balance sheet over €20 million.

III.1.3 Asia

Like Western countries, business organizations in Asia have traditionally reported their performance on financial ESP with less focus on non-financial ESG sustainability performance.[36] In recent years, in Asia, investors, regulators, and the business community have increasingly demanded information on both financial ESP and non-financial ESG sustainability performance information. Sustainability factors of planning, performance, and risk have become a greater priority in the aftermath of the 2017–2019 financial crises and the 2020 COVID-19 pandemic resulting in global economic meltdown, encouraging business organizations to maintain their financial ESP and non-financial ESG sustainability performance. The United Nations Global Compact, in its 2013 *Global Corporate Sustainability Report*, underscoring the importance of business sustainability, calls on corporations worldwide to integrate ten sustainability principles pertaining to the environment, human rights, fair labor, and anti-corruption into their strategies and operations.[37]

Sustainability performance information can be disclosed voluntarily in some Asian countries and is mandatory in other countries (required by Hong Kong listing standards for their listed companies since 2015.)[38] In September 2015, the United Nations (UN) proposed a holistic framework of the Sustainable Development Goals (SDGs) to design indicators and an integrated monitoring framework to address all three dimensions of economic development, social inclusion, and environmental sustainability.[39] Asian companies are expected to keep moving toward improving their sustainability factors of performance, risk, and disclosure as investors demand and regulators require disclosure of sustainability information.

The Hong Kong Stock Exchange code provisions for ESG sustainability reporting are detailed in the *Environmental, Social, and Governance (ESG) Reporting Guide* of the Hong Kong Stock Exchange Listing Rules for listing companies. The guide identifies general disclosure and key performance indicators in four ESG areas: workplace quality, environmental protection, operating practices, and community involvement, in addition to corporate governance, which the main board listing rules cover. The Exchange allows the company to specify the subject areas, aspects, and indicators that are relevant and material in the context of its corporate strategy. As of January 1, 2016, the listing rules open the option for the companies to consider offering assurance on the ESG reports.

More firms in China are expected to disclose their overall ESG strategies, activities, and performance. Asian countries have their own sustainability programs and initiatives influenced by their cultural, political, economic, and legal infrastructure. In December 2008, the Shanghai and Shenzhen Stock Exchanges required a subset of Chinese listed firms to issue ESG sustainability reports.[40] Business sustainability initiatives in Asia are gaining attention because corporations' goals have refocused from socialism to capitalism, maximizing profit for shareholders and creating shared value for all stakeholders, including shareholders, society, and the environment. The financial ESP and non-financial ESG dimensions of sustainability performance are becoming a strategic imperative in Asia and being integrated into corporate culture, business environment, and managerial decisions and operations. Currently, sustainability performance disclosures and sustainability reporting and assurance in many Asian countries, except for Hong Kong, Malaysia, and a few others, are voluntary, and sustainability reports are not consistently prepared. These sustainability reports are often not assured by third-party assurance providers. Assurance providers play an important role in assuring sustainability reports, and their objectivity, independence, reliability, transparency, usefulness, and credibility of sustainability reports are important to both internal and external users of ESG sustainability reports and can be enhanced by assuring sustainability reports.

The Chinese central government has played and will continue to play an important role in promoting ESG/CSR sustainability practices in China, which is working to align the nationwide CSR sustainability programs with the country's development policy.[41] The Hong Kong Stock Exchange (HKEX) 2015 issued the *Environmental, Social, and Governance (ESG) Reporting Guide* that requires listed companies to disclose ESG information on a comply-or-explain basis effective from financial years ending on or after December 31, 2015.[42] the Hong Kong Stock Exchange code provisions for sustainability reporting are detailed in Appendix 24: Environmental, Social, and Governance (ESG) Reporting Guide of the Hong Kong Stock Exchange Listing Rules for the Main Board, listing companies HKLR. Appendix 27 has come into effect since January 2016, and the HKEX issued "7 recommendations" in ESG disclosure in May 2018, followed by other updates in November 2018.

The "Environmental" subject area includes three aspects: emissions (A1), use of resources (A2), and the environment and natural resources (A3). The "Social" subject area includes eight aspects: employment (B1), health and safety (B2), development and training (B3), labor standards (B4), supply chain management (B5), product responsibility (B6), anti-corruption (B7) and community investment (B8). Each "aspect" contains both "comply or explain" items and "recommended disclosure" items. The growing popularity of ESG disclosures is partly due to global market competition and mainly from the future sustainability benefits. China is the world's largest developing country and has been the leader in introducing many sustainability policies, such as ESG guidelines.

III.1.4 OECD Guidelines

The Organisation for Economic Co-operation and Development (OECD) defines the purpose of a CSR program and ESG business sustainability as "To encourage the positive contributions that multinational enterprises can make to economics, environmental, and social progress and to minimize the difficulties to which their various operations may give rise."[43] This definition focuses on two important aspects of ESG sustainability programs, including creating social value through corporate activities (social value-added activities) and avoiding conflicts between corporate goals and societal goals (societal consensus). These two aspects of business sustainability and CSR programs should be integrated into business sustainability strategies, decisions, performance, reporting, and assurance.

Guidelines established by the OECD are recommendations addressed by various governments, specifically toward multinational enterprises involving sustainability, and are viewed by many as a prerequisite for conducting global business with trading partners. The OECD Guidelines have a main objective to ensure that each enterprise's operations follow government policies to strengthen the basis of mutual confidence between the enterprises and society, improve the foreign investment environment, and enhance enterprises' contribution to sustainable development. The OECD Guidelines have contributed to business sustainability in important ways, such as by developing standards that cover sustainable areas involving the environment, carbon footprint, fraudulent reporting risks and corruption, consumer interests, desires, corporate governance mechanisms, and diversity. The common goal of businesses to adhere to the OECD Guidelines is to encourage positive contributions to business sustainability for the economy, environment, and social progress and to minimize sustainable difficulties. In reaching this goal, governments can help by providing effective domestic policy frameworks to include sustainability, long-term stability, an impartial system of courts and laws, appropriate regulation, and efficient and honest public administration. Governments can also aid by promoting the appropriate sustainability standards and policies to support the development while engaging in ongoing current reforms to ensure that the public sector contributes actively, efficiently, and effectively. Businesses and governments adhering to the

OECD Guidelines are more committed to continuously improving sustainability policies with an aim and perspective to improve the welfare and living standards of all people and future peoples.

The *OECD Principles of Corporate Governance* published in 2023 is the international standard for corporate governance that enables policymakers to evaluate and improve the legal, regulatory, and institutional framework for corporate governance with a keen focus on sustainable growth and financial stability.[44] These OECD corporate governance principles:

1. Contribute to economic, environmental, and social progress to achieve sustainable development.
2. Respect the internationally recognized human rights of those affected by their activities.
3. Encourage local capacity building through close cooperation with the local community, including business interests, and develop the enterprise's activities in domestic and foreign markets, consistent with the need for sound commercial practice.
4. Encourage human capital formation, particularly by creating employment opportunities and facilitating employee training opportunities.
5. Refrain from seeking or accepting exemptions not contemplated in the statutory or regulatory framework related to human rights, environmental, health, safety, labor, taxation, financial incentives, or other issues.
6. Support and uphold good corporate governance principles and develop and apply good corporate governance practices, including throughout the enterprise groups.
7. Develop and apply effective self-regulatory practices and management systems that foster a relationship of confidence and mutual trust between enterprises and the societies in which they operate.
8. Promote awareness of and compliance with company policies by workers employed by multinational enterprises through appropriate dissemination of these policies, including through training programs.
9. Refrain from discriminatory or disciplinary action against workers who make bona fide reports to management or, as appropriate, to the competent public authorities on practices that contravene the law or the enterprise's policies.
10. By incorporating risk-based due diligence into their enterprise risk management systems to identify, prevent, and mitigate actual and potential adverse impacts and account for how they are addressed. The nature and extent of due diligence depend on the circumstances of a situation.
11. Avoid causing or contributing to adverse impacts on matters covered by the Guidelines through their own activities and address such impacts when they occur.
12. Seek to prevent or mitigate an adverse impact where they have not contributed to it when the impact is directly linked to their operations, products, or

services by a business relationship. This is not intended to shift responsibility from the entity, causing an adverse impact on the enterprise with which it has a business relationship.

13. In addition to addressing adverse impacts in relation to matters covered by the Guidelines, encourage, where practicable, business partners, including suppliers and sub-contractors, to apply principles of responsible business conduct compatible with the Guidelines.
14. Engage with relevant stakeholders to provide meaningful opportunities for their views to be taken into account in planning and decision-making for projects or other activities that may significantly impact local communities.
15. Abstain from any improper involvement in local political activities.

The OECD Guidelines further encourage enterprises to (1) Support, as appropriate to their circumstances, cooperative efforts to promote Internet freedom through respect of freedom of expression, assembly, and association online and (2) Engage in or support, where appropriate, private or multi-stakeholder initiatives and social dialogue on responsible supply chain management while ensuring that these initiatives take due account of their social and economic effects on developing countries and of existing internationally recognized standards.[45]

In summary, mandatory sustainability initiatives require companies to report:

- Environmental performance.
- Social and employee-related matters.
- Human rights policies.
- Anti-corruption and bribery issues.
- Waste Reduction and Recycling.
- Carbon Footprint Reduction.
- Water Conservation.
- Compliance with Environmental Regulations.
- Diversity on the board of directors.

III.2 Voluntary Initiatives

Business organizations can take voluntary initiatives to address their sustainability challenges by establishing a comprehensive conceptual framework to guide them in developing their sustainability factors of planning, performance, risk, and disclosure. Voluntary sustainability initiatives refer to business organizations' programs, strategic plans, actions, or projects to address their ESP and ESG sustainability performance. Regulations do not mandate these initiatives but are voluntarily adopted by companies that recognize the importance of sustainability and responsible and ethical practices. Several organizations worldwide, including the Global Reporting Initiative (GRI), International Integrated Reporting Council (IIRC), Sustainability Accounting Standards Board (SASB), and the United Nations Global Compact,

Value Reporting Foundation, have issued guidelines and guiding principles regarding voluntary disclosure of sustainability performance information. The effective implementation of these voluntary initiatives can demonstrate corporations' commitments to sustainability, improve corporate credibility and reputation in having social and environmental impacts, and prevent excessive government mandatory sustainability initiatives. Over 20,000 public companies have used these guiding principles in producing standalone integrated sustainability reports. Several organizations that are currently promoting sustainability in general and climate change in particular are:

The Global Reporting Initiative (GRI), 2013 G4 sustainability guidelines, promotes integrated reporting for ESP and ESG sustainability performance dimensions, incorporating the ethical dimension into other dimensions. In 2016, the GRI established the Global Sustainability Standards Board, which develops sustainability standards http://www.globalreporting.org/.

The International Integrated Reporting Council (IIRC) developed the International Integrated Reporting Framework in 2013. Sustainability Accounting Standards Board (SASB) has developed sustainability accounting standards intended to assist public companies in disclosing material sustainability issues for the purpose of mandatory filings to the SEC, such as Form 10-K and 20-F, through the first quarter of 2015.

This subsection summarizes these sustainability-related voluntary guiding principles and guidelines and their issuing organizations.

III.2.1 Global Reporting Initiative (GRI)

Global Reporting Initiative (GRI) is an international independent standard organization, and its sustainability reporting and disclosure standards are the most widely used standards for reporting on non-financial ESG sustainability performance. The GRI was launched in 1997 to bring consistency and global standardization to sustainability reporting. The evolution of GRI guidelines began with an initial focus on incorporating environmental performance into corporate reporting with its first publication, *Sustainability Reporting Guidelines*, in 2000. The GRI was originally created in response to the worldwide demand for comparable sustainability reporting. These GRI *Sustainability Reporting Guidelines* are updated periodically to reflect new sustainability reporting and guidance developments. Guideline G4, released in May 2013, is the fourth update so far.[46] The G4 Guideline presents Reporting Principles, Standard Disclosures, and an Implementation Manual for sustainability reporting on economic, governance, social, and environmental sustainability performance metrics by all organizations regardless of their type, size, sector, or location.[47] It focuses more heavily on materiality considerations in the reporting process and final report. The intention is to make sustainability reports "more relevant, more credible, and more user-friendly" by encouraging companies to center their reports on the organization's goals and their impact on society and other stakeholders. In this guideline, the GRI promotes sustainability reporting as a standard practice of disclosing sustainability-related issues relevant to companies' businesses and stakeholders.

GRI global sustainability reporting standards have been developed through multi-stakeholder participation, and they address both comprehensive ESG reports, material sustainability topics, and selected disclosures. GRI standards are based on a multi-stakeholder approach to report material sustainability topics and provide disclosure guiding principles guidelines for companies to communicate their ESG sustainability performance, including environmental issues of climate change and global warming, social issues of human rights, workplace environment, and governance issues of board diversity and independence and commitments to sustainability. GRI establishes a due diligence and transparent sustainability reporting process that can be applied globally to promote sustainable development, advance sustainability performance, guide effective and efficient sustainability reporting, and enable appropriate use of sustainability information to improve ESG sustainability performance.

The G4 Guideline is broken into two parts: (1) "Reporting Principles and Standard Disclosures," which contains the criteria necessary for an organization to prepare its sustainability report "in accordance" with the Guideline, and (2) the "Implementation Manual," which instructs practitioners how to apply the Reporting Principles, how to prepare disclosure information, and how to interpret various concepts in the guideline.[48] There are also two components – Core and Comprehensive – for the "in accordance" process of identifying material to be disclosed under the concept "Aspects," which refer to information with the most influential economic, environmental, and social impacts or have a marked effect on the decisions and perceptions of stakeholders. The "Core" information should be disclosed in all cases and is meant to serve as a background for disclosing the impacts of its performance in economics, governance, social, and environmental sustainability dimensions. The "Comprehensive" option requires additional standard disclosures on strategy and analysis, governance, and ethics and integrity, along with more extensive reporting on all indicators related to the material aspects identified earlier in the process, rather than the minimum of one required to be in accordance with the Core requirements.[49]

The Global Sustainability Standards Board (GSSB) was established by the GRI in 2020 to develop globally accepted standards for sustainability reporting. The standards issued by GSSB were among the first globally accepted standards for sustainability reporting. These GSSB standards were established as independent operating entities under the auspices of GRI. The GSSB is made up of 15 members representing a range of expertise and multi-stakeholder perspectives on sustainability reporting. The GSSB operates under the GSSB terms of reference to oversee the development of the GRI Standards according to a formally defined due process.[50] The GSSB works exclusively in the public interest and according to the vision and mission of GRI. The GRI Sustainability Reporting Standards are the product of more than 15 years of robust, global, multi-stakeholder development, governed by a formally defined due process protocol, overseen by the Due Process Oversight Committee (DPOC). The due process protocol ensures that the GRI Standards promote the public interest and align with GRI's vision and mission. It also ensures that GRI Standards move through a communicated development process. The GRI reporting process involves multiple stakeholders, follows due diligence, and focuses on the material topics. It starts with project identification, prioritization, and commencement; continues with content development, public exposure, and consideration of feedback; and concludes with the final release of Standards.[51]

The GRI launched its 2021 Universal Standards in October 2021, which represent the most important update on ESG sustainability reporting, from providing GRI guidance to setting standards for sustainability.[52] The 2021 Universal Standards strengthen the basic foundations of all sustainability reporting through GRI, focusing on transparency, due diligence, and material topics that impact the economy, environment, and people for global organizations of all types and sizes. The 2022 updated GRI standards include a consolidated set of GRI standards, including GRI 1 Foundations, GRI 2 General Disclosures, GRI 3, Material Topics, GRI 11, Oil and Gas Sector, GRI 201 Economic Performance, GRI 202 Market Presence, GRI 203 Indirect Economic Impacts, GRI 204 Performance Practices, and GRI 205 Anti-corruption.[53]

III.2.2 International Integrated Reporting Council (IIRC)

The International Integrated Reporting Council (IIRC) is a global coalition of investors, public companies, regulators, standard setters, nongovernmental organizations (NGOs), the accounting profession, and academia. In April 2013, the International Integrated Reporting Council (IIRC) released the draft of its framework consultation on integrated reporting intended to provide guidelines on communication with stakeholders.[54] The IIRC's proposed framework addresses fundamental concepts of integrated reporting and its guiding principles on an organization's strategy, governance, performance, and prospects. In its December 2013 Integrated Reporting Framework, the IIRC promotes a more integrated approach to corporate reporting by improving the quality and quantity of information disseminated to providers of financial capital, including shareholders and other stakeholders.[55] In January 2021, the IIRC published its <IR> Framework, which takes a principles-based approach in preparing integrated sustainability reporting. The framework attempts to strike an appropriate balance between flexibility and prescription to be tailored to an organization's specific culture and environment while enabling sufficient comparability and standardization across organizations in preparing their sustainability reports.

The IIRC promotes integrated sustainability reporting to enhance communication about value creation in corporate reporting. The IIRC's mission is to establish integrated reporting and thinking within mainstream business practice as the standard of sustainability reporting for business organizations in the public and private sectors. The goals of the IIRC are to establish a globally integrated sustainability process to align capital allocation and corporate behavior to wider goals of financial stability and sustainable development.[56] The IIRC has established the Integrated

Reporting Framework that is intended to enable companies to produce comprehensive, concise, standardized, transparent, and investor-focused sustainability reports. The integrated reporting framework enables companies to report their sustainability performance by focusing on six "capitals" (financial, manufactured, human, natural, intellectual, social and relationship), as discussed in depth in Chapter 6.

III.2.3 Sustainability Accounting Standards Board (SASB)

The Stainability Accounting Standards Board (SASB) is an independent, non-profit organization that aims to establish and release sustainability accounting standards to enable public corporations to disclose material, decision-useful sustainability information to investors.[57] Standards published by the SASB go through a rigorous, industry-driven process that includes evidence-based research focusing on materiality and stakeholder participation. The SASB develops sustainability accounting standards to enable public companies to disclose material, relevant, and decision-useful ESG information to investors by integrating ESG information into their mandatory filings with regulators (e.g., the SEC). In October 2013, the SASB released its Sustainability Conceptual Framework, which consists of objectives, key definitions, sustainability accounting, and disclosures characteristics, methodology for assessing the materiality of sustainability issues, and structure and harmonization of sustainability accounting standards.[58] The SASB has developed sustainability accounting standards relevant to disclosing material sustainability issues for 88 industries in 10 sectors, launching the process for mandatory filings to the Securities and Exchange Commission (SEC) that enables comparisons between companies, which can be useful for investment decisions and capital allocations. Standardizing and harmonizing SASB standards with existing disclosure standards help public companies avoid additional costs and align SASB's work with global corporate transparency efforts.

In 2017, the SASB established a standards-setting group consisting of nine individuals to revise its conceptual framework to ensure that its standards are relevant and enable the disclosure of useful sustainability information to investors.[59] Consistent with the conceptual frameworks of the Financial Accounting Standards Board (FASB) and the International Accounting Standards Board (IASB), the SASB's Conceptual Framework established the basic principles, objectives, and definitions that guide its technical staff in setting sustainability accounting standards. The proposed SASB's conceptual framework is still under revision and intended to better articulate SASB's approach to setting sustainability accounting standards.

The SASB's framework has substantially changed several aspects of the previous framework. First, the definition of materiality is changed by specifying that SASB "applies the definition of 'materiality' established under the US securities law," suggesting that information is material if there is a "substantial likelihood that the disclosure of the omitted fact would have been viewed by the reasonable investor as having significantly altered the 'total mix' of information made available." Thus, any sustainability disclosure is deemed material when it influences a reasonable investor's decision in providing decision-useful and relevant information. Second, there are more guidelines and clarity on the characteristics of decision-useful information with the intent to provide more clarity in articulating principles that guide standards. Finally, the SASB's rules and procedures are revised, which affects the content of the future SASB standards. The SASB Conceptual Framework has undergone several revisions and sets out the basic concepts, principles, definitions, and objectives that guide SASB in its approach to setting standards for sustainability accounting. Public comments on the proposed conceptual framework were received from August 28–December 31, 2020, and SASB staff in the October 2021 board meeting presented a status update on important issues of materiality and opportunities to improve the content of the proposed conceptual framework.

The SASB, on October 1, 2021, had a board meeting to discuss several of its current sustainability initiatives and projects, including its conceptual framework with a main focus on the materiality concept and core tenets.[60] The sustainability topics discussed in the meeting were aimed at conducting more consultations and research to better understand the implications of current and future standards; systemic risk in asset management to refine the disclosure topic and related accounting metrics; alternative products in food and beverages; marine transportation; and human capital and related standards of workplace culture, diversity, inclusion, and equity. Business organizations should report both financial ESP and non-financial ESG sustainability performance information that has the greatest impact on short- and long-term strategic sustainability planning, decisions, and operations. The materiality of reporting sustainability information should reflect the organization's overall purpose, mission, vision, strategies, stakeholder welfare, societal impacts, and environmental issues. Materiality is defined in financial reporting as any information that may influence investor decisions. The materiality concept is relatively well-defined in financial reporting of financial ESP but has yet to be defined for non-financial ESG dimensions of sustainability performance. Materiality is determined by professional judgment, and its qualitative and quantitative measures for both financial ESP and non-financial ESG sustainability performance require proper professional judgment. The materiality concept applies to sustainability reporting covering a wide range of economic, governance, social, ethical, and environmental performance measures and should be reported by corporations. Companies should focus on important and material issues to their stakeholders when reporting both financial ESP and non-financial ESG sustainability performance. The Committee on Capital Markets Regulations urges the SEC to establish rules and interpretations to raise the threshold of materiality required to make a misstatement important to the level that is subject to litigation.[61] A more reasonable and comprehensive materiality standard should be established for financial ESP and non-financial ESG sustainability performance.

The materiality concept is a fundamental principle in ESG sustainability reporting that focuses on the significance or relevance of specific ESG factors of planning, performance, risk, and disclosure to a company's overall performance and its stakeholders. ESG reporting involves disclosing material information about a company's ESG planning and practices, and materiality assists companies in prioritizing and focusing on the most relevant sustainability issues. Several sustainability reporting frameworks and standards, including the GRI and the SASB, promote the importance of materiality in ESG reporting and provide guidelines to ensure consistency and comparability in ESG reporting across companies and industries. The materiality concept should be applied to all four sustainability factors: planning, performance, risk, and disclosure. During sustainability planning, companies should conduct materiality assessments to identify and prioritize important and relevant ESG issues that are most significant to their business and stakeholders by considering the potential impact of each ESG planning on financial performance and stakeholder relationships. The materiality concept should also be used to assess and manage important ESG risks and focus on important ESG sustainability performance and reporting. Materiality enables companies to focus on material ESG information by avoiding information overload and focusing on disclosing important and relevant sustainability information to their investors, customers, employees, and other stakeholders. Materiality also assists in aligning sustainability efforts of planning, performance, risk, and disclosure with business strategy, contributes to building trust with stakeholders, and fosters transparency and reputation.

III.2.4 International Sustainability Standards Board (ISSB)

The International Financial Reporting Standards (IFRS) Foundation's consultation on establishing a global non-financial ESG reporting framework has highlighted the need for global sustainability reporting standards and received strong support from investors, the corporate sector, accounting professionals, policymakers, regulators, and central banks.[62] These sustainability disclosure initiatives, whether mandatory or voluntary, are intended to reflect the financial, social, and environmental impacts of a company's business operation and, thus, provide relevant and reliable financial and non-financial information for all stakeholders, including investors. There are debates among policymakers and scholars that international accounting standard-setters, such as the Financial Accounting Standards Board (FASB) and International Accounting Standards Board (IASB), should issue accounting standards for proper disclosure of ESG sustainability information. In April 2021, IRFS put out an exposure draft proposing targeted amendments to the Foundation's Constitution to create IFRS sustainability standards. In this exposure draft, the proposals include expanding the Foundation's efforts to create a new board to set sustainability standards, creating the International Sustainability Standards Board (ISSB) under IFRS governance, and amending the Foundation's governance structure. The exposure draft also included several pieces about the IFRS Foundation, including its objectives, governance, trustees, and further information about the International Accounting Standards Board (IASB), the Monitoring Board, and the Interpretations Committee.[63]

The International Sustainability Standards Board (ISSB) is a sustainability standard-setting body created by the International Financial Reporting

Standards (IFRS) Foundation in November 2021. The ISSB's mission is to establish sustainability-related financial reporting standards to satisfy investors' information demands and needs for sustainability reporting.[64] The primary mission of the ISSB is to establish global sustainability-related disclosure standards that provide investors and other capital market participants with material and relevant sustainability information about companies' factors of planning, performance, risk, and disclosure to enable them to make informed decisions. The ISSB is established to function on four key principles: comprehensive global baseline, consolidation, and building on existing initiatives (e.g., GRI, SASB), informed by the ISSB reporting expert advice and global footprint.[65] In March 2022, the ISSB issued two exposure drafts of proposed general sustainability-related disclosure requirements (IFRS S1) and climate-related disclosure requirements (IFRS S2).

IFRS S1 proposes overall standards for disclosing sustainability-related financial information to provide stakeholders, including investors, with a complete set of sustainability-related financial disclosures.[66] IFRS S2 proposal establishes the requirements for identifying, measuring, and disclosing climate-related risks and opportunities.[67] These two proposals are driven by the recommendations of the Task Force on Climate-Related Financial Disclosures (TCFD) and industry-based disclosure requirements of SASB Standards. In June 2023, the ISSB issued its inaugural global sustainability disclosure standards of IFRS S1 and IFRS S2 to establish a common language for disclosing the effect of climate-related risks and opportunities on a company's prospects.[68] IFRS S1 provides a set of disclosure requirements intended to assist companies in communicating with their investors about sustainability-related risks and opportunities. IFRS S2 establishes specific, climate-related disclosures and is intended to be used with IFRS S1.

III.2.5 United Nations Global Compact

The sustainability report released by the United Nations Global Compact (UNGC) in 2015 addresses the state of corporate sustainability today and presents the actions companies worldwide take in integrating sustainability into their strategies, operations, and culture. The report encourages companies to engage their suppliers in establishing more sustainable practices and integrating sustainability into their supply chain processes.[69] This establishment takes significantly more resources of various kinds to create efficient and effective sustainable practices in the supply chain process. Supply chains are a hurdle for sustainability reporting for large and growing companies. This is more likely due to the fact that many companies lack the implementing measures and reporting metrics to remediate their supply chain rather than the actual supply chain itself.[70] Global Compact participants rank supply chain practices as the largest challenge firms face regarding improving their sustainability performance.[71] Many problems extend from the size of the supply chain, distance from suppliers, and operating with low standards. Progress can be made when organizations set a tone at the top to prioritize sustainability within the supply chain.

The report finds that companies are increasingly focusing on business sustainability and making progress in setting expectations for their suppliers to integrate sustainability into their strategies and practices. Many large companies show significantly more effort in their commitment to action towards sustainability standards and, therefore, are also leading motivators. Other sustainability reporting benefits include improved reputation, increased employee loyalty, and higher customer satisfaction. However, several sustainability challenges could threaten the business value if they are not addressed properly, but these challenges can also be turned into business opportunities.

According to the most recent update on global sustainability by the UNGC, over 12,000 organizations in over 160 countries are currently members of the Global Compact, with the majority coming from Europe and Latin America. The new Guide presents the performance of member organizations worldwide with respect to the ten principles of the UNGC that are related to human rights, labor, environment, and anti-corruption. The Guide indicates that investors continue to demand companies to act upon and report sustainability, while companies have found that it is beneficial to integrate corporate responsibility into their business operations. These new initiatives help to improve corporations' reputations and demonstrate that these corporations are active participants in the Global Compact, which in turn enhances stakeholder relations, improves commitment by the CEO, promotes internal information sharing, and provides information for investors.[72]

III.2.6 Principles of Responsible Investment

In 2005 the United Nations Secretary-General Kofi Annan invited a group of large institutional investors to join a process to develop the Principles of Responsible Investment (PRI), launched in April 2006, and the number of signatories has grown significantly from 100 to over 3,000.[73] The PRI addresses the long-term interests of its signatories and financial markets and economies as related to the ESG sustainability factors of performance, risk, and disclosure and their integration into investment decisions. The PRI partners with the UN Environment Program Finance Initiative and the UN Global Compact have committed to adopt and implement its six aspirational principles relevant to ESG, including:[74]

- Integrating ESG factors into investment analysis and decision-making processes.
- Incorporating ESG factors into asset ownership policies and practices.
- Obtaining disclosures on ESG issues by investee companies.
- Advancing acceptance and implementation of the principles within the investment industry.
- Promoting the effectiveness in implementing the principles.
- Reporting on ESG activities and progress towards implementing the principles.

III.2.7 United Nations Sustainable Development Goals

Back in 2015 the UN General Assembly adopted 17 SDGs as part of its 2030 Agenda for Sustainable Development.[75] The 17 Sustainable Development Goals (SDGs) build on the United Nations Millennium Development Goals of 2000–2015 and involve new areas, such as climate change, economic inequality, innovation, sustainable production and consumption, and peace and justice.[76]. These SDGs are relevant to the three dimensions of sustainability development: economic, social, and environmental development. Thus, they can be linked to ESP and ESG sustainability performance. The 17 SDGs address broad global goals, including no poverty (Goal 1), zero hunger (Goal 2), quality education (Goal 4), gender equity (Goal 5), responsible consumption and production (Goal 12); climate action (Goal 13); life on land (Goal 15); peace and justice (Goal 16); and partnerships for the goals (Goal 17). The SDGs are accompanied by a total of 169 associated targets and 232 approved indicators that are intended to be achieved by 2030. The SDGs are considered a framework for prioritizing business sustainability strategies and related reporting and are being integrated into investment strategies.

III.2.8 Value Reporting Foundation

In late 2020, the Sustainability Accounting Standards Board (SASB) and the International Integrated Reporting Council (IIRC) merged into one organization, the Value Reporting Foundation. This merger encourages integrated collaboration on topics surrounding sustainability and the improvement of enterprise value.[77] As previously stated, the Global Reporting Initiative (GRI) and Sustainability Accounting Standards Board (SASB) joined together to create the *Practical Guide to Sustainability Reporting Using GRI and SASB Standards*. This Practical Guide helps recognize the similarities and differences between the standards in terms of materiality, disclosures, audiences, and set standards.[78]

III.2.9 International Corporate Governance Network (ICGN)

The International Corporate Governance Network (ICGN) is a coalition of investors that establishes investor-led global governance principles and global stewardship principles.[79] The ICGN is led by global institutional investors who manage more than $59 trillion in assets to establish corporate governance and stewardship principles to enable long-term and sustainable value creation that contributes to sustainable economies, a healthy environment, and social prosperity worldwide. The ICGN's global governance and stewardship principles are relevant to business sustainability and are intended to promote both financial ESP and non-financial ESG sustainability performance.

III.3 Emerging Sustainability Developments and Initiatives

Several sustainability developments and initiatives have emerged in the past three decades that shape and influence sustainability factors of planning, performance, risk, and disclosure. These sustainability developments and initiatives are highlighted below and discussed throughout the book. Business sustainability is advancing worldwide with many developments and initiatives aimed at addressing both ESP and ESG opportunities and challenges. Below are some key trends, developments, and initiatives in sustainability:

1. Institutional investors insist on better sustainability by focusing on evidence of financial materiality and the link between financial and ESG performance.
2. Regulators worldwide are moving toward mandating ESG disclosures from both companies and investors.
3. There has been a move toward renewable energy sources, such as solar and wind power, to reduce reliance on fossil fuels and combat climate change.
4. Companies are making progress in achieving their ESG goals.
5. Circular business models minimize negative environmental impact by reducing waste by promoting the recycling, reuse, and repurposing of materials.
6. Continuous commitments by regulators and businesses globally to carbon neutrality and net-zero emissions reduce greenhouse gas emissions and offset the remaining emissions through afforestation or carbon capture initiatives.
7. Sustainability is integrating into corporate culture, business environment, and managerial strategies through a focus on corporate social responsibility (CSR), ethical business practices, social impacts, community engagement, and environmental stewardship and impacts.
8. SASB publishes its codified ESG standards for 80 industries in the United States, focusing on ESG materiality.
9. Standard-setters focus on complementary frameworks and better alignment among professional sustainability-promoting organizations (GRI, IIRC, SASB, ISSB).
10. Legislators are now expressing interest in better disclosure of ESG issues.
11. Eco-friendly technologies and solutions have been developed, including electric vehicles, smart cities that optimize resource use, and sustainable agriculture practices.
12. The impact-first concept focuses on sustainable investments, green bonds, and sustainable finance options to fund socially responsible and environmentally friendly projects.
13. The United Nations Global Sustainable Development Goals (17 SDGs) address global sustainability challenges, including social issues, poverty, inequality, environmental degradation, and climate change.
14. Global companies take steps towards better sustainability disclosure as concerns about climate change and cyber security greatly increase.
15. Sustainable agriculture policies and procedures include sustainable farming practices, precision farming, and organic agriculture, minimizing the environmental impact of food production.

16. Policies and practices address the plastic pollution crisis, reduce single-use plastics, and promote plastic recycling.
17. The Sustainability Accounting Standards Board (SASB) and the International Integrated Reporting Council (IIRC) have emerged to create the Value Reporting Foundation (VRF) that promotes the relevance of sustainability disclosures to investors and focuses on producing material and useful sustainability information by business organizations in all industries.
18. The Global Reporting Initiative (GRI) and the SASB have joined in issuing a *Practical Guide to Sustainability Reporting* from market participants' perspectives.
19. The Financial Accounting Standards Board (FASB), the International Accounting Standards Board (IASB), the International Financial Reporting Standards, and the International Sustainability Standards Board are working on accounting standards for sustainability to enable effective and relevant corporate reporting.
20. The American Institute of Certified Public Accountants (AICPA), the Public Company Accounting Oversight Board (PCAOB), and the International Accounting and Auditing Standards Board (IAASB) are working on the development of assurance standards for sustainability reports.
21. Regulators worldwide, including the Securities and Exchange Commission, require more robust and relevant disclosures of sustainability-related disclosure issues, including climate change and human capital.

These sustainability developments and initiatives, among others, are relevant to all sustainability factors of planning, performance, risk, and disclosure presented in this chapter and reflect a move toward more sustainable practices in various sectors. Regulators, businesses, and investors play vital roles in driving these sustainability initiatives and developments to foster a more sustainable future.

IV. CONCLUSION

Sustainability is taking centre stage in global business as businesses attempt to survive, maintain their sustainability, and care for the safety, health, and well-being of their employees, customers, suppliers, and other stakeholders. Global investors demand financial ESP and non-financial ESG sustainability performance information; regulators require disclosing such information, and business organizations produce sustainability reports. Business sustainability has advanced from focusing on CSR to integrating ESG sustainability performance into organizations' environment, strategic plan, business culture, and practices for achieving long-term and multidimensional sustainability performance. This chapter introduces the business sustainability factors of planning, performance, risk, and disclosure. Sustainability performance consists of financial economic sustainability performance (ESP) to create value for shareholders while achieving non-financial environmental, social, and governance (ESG) sustainability performance in protecting the interests of other stakeholders. The collaboration of investors, businesses, and regulators promotes business sustainability. This chapter also offers guidance to organizations to properly integrate all dimensions of sustainability into their business models, strategic plans, and practices.

The sustainability disclosure initiatives discussed in this chapter, whether mandatory or voluntary, are intended to reflect the financial, social, and environmental impacts of a company's business operation and, thus, provide relevant and reliable financial ESP and non-financial ESG sustainability performance information for all stakeholders, including investors. This chapter presents a synopsis of sustainability factors of planning, performance, risk, and disclosure, as well as the sources and drivers of business sustainability. There are debates among policymakers, regulators, and scholars that international accounting standard-setters, such as the Financial Accounting Standards Board (FASB) and International Accounting Standards Board (IASB), should issue standards for properly disclosing financial ESP and non-financial ESG sustainability information.

V. TAKEAWAYS

- Business sustainability has advanced from greenwashing and branding to a business imperative, integrating into the business environment, corporate culture, and strategic plan.
- There is a growing demand by investors for relevant and reliable non-financial ESG information for making investment decisions.
- Business organizations should build awareness of growing sustainability opportunities, challenges, and risks.
- Business organizations should integrate financial ESP and non-financial ESG dimensions of sustainability performance into their strategic plans, business processes, and supply chains.
- Business organizations should tell their successful sustainability performance stories and best practices of sustainability performance through sustainability reporting.
- Business organizations should identify non-financial metrics on non-financial dimensions of sustainability performance (governance, social, and environmental) and link non-financial sustainability performance metrics to the sustainable financial success of the business.
- Business organizations should use holistic and integrated internal and external reports to effectively communicate their business sustainability strategic decisions, actions, and performance to both internal and external users of sustainability reports.

- Business organizations should integrate business sustainability factors of planning, performance, risk, and disclosure into their strategic planning, business environment, and corporate culture.

Notes

1 This definition of business sustainability is adapted from Rezaee, Z. and T. Fogarty. 2019. *Business Sustainability, Corporate Governance, and Organizational Ethics*. John Wiley and Sons, Inc. New Jersey, United States.
2 Value Reporting Foundation. 2021. About The Value Reporting. September 7, 2021. https://www.valuereportingfoundation.org/about/
3 International Sustainability Standards Board (ISSB). 2021. Available at https://www.ifrs.org/groups/international-sustainability-standards-board/
4 Securities and Exchange Commission (SEC). 2022. SEC Proposes Rules to Enhance and Standardize Climate-Related Disclosures for Investors. Available at https://www.sec.gov/news/press-release/2022–46
5 European Union (EU). 2023. Corporate Sustainability Reporting Directive (CSRD). https://finance.ec.europa.eu/capital-markets-union-and-financial-markets/company-reporting-and-auditing/company-reporting/corporate-sustainability-reporting_en
6 Much of discussion in this section comes from Rezaee, Z. 2020. *Business Sustainability Tactors of Performance, Risk, and Disclosure*. Business Expert Press. New York, NY 10017, USA.
7 Brockett, A. and Z. Rezaee. 2012. *Corporate Sustainability: Integrating Performance and Reporting*. Wiley & Sons, New York.
8 United Nations (UN). 2013, February. *How Investors are Addressing Environmental, Social and Governance Factors in Fundamental Equity Valuation*. United Nations-supported Principles for Responsible Investment (PRI). Available at: http://www.unpri.org/viewer/?file=wp-content/uploads/Integrated_Analysis_2013.pdf
9 Organisation of Economic Co-operation and Development (OECD). 2003. Guidelines for Multinational Enterprises. Available at www.oecd.org.
10 Shingler, Thomas. November 5, 2021. Callan Survey Finds Nearly 50% of Respondents Incorporate ESG, Highest Level Ever. Callan Institute. https://www.callan.com/blog-archive/2021-esg-survey/
11 Callan Institute. 2018. Survey. ESG Hitting its Stride in U.S. July 2018. Available at https://www.callan.com/esg-survey-2018/
12 Rezaee, Z. 2015. *Business Sustainability: Performance, Compliance, Accountability and Integrated Reporting*. Greenleaf Publishing Limited, Sheffield, UK.
13 SEC Regulations and Firms. March 2020. Stern School of Business. Available at: http://dx.doi.org/10.2139/ssrn.3625115
14 Securities and Exchange Commission (SEC). 2016. Business and Financial Disclosure Required by Regulation S-K. Release No. 33–10064; 34–77599; File No. S7-06-16, Available at https://www.sec.gov/rules/concept/2016/33–10064.pdf
15 US Securities and Exchange Commission. Sample Letter to Companies Regarding Climate Change Disclosure. https://www.sec.gov/corpfin/sample-letter-climate-change-disclosures

16 Securities and Exchange Commission (SEC). March 2021. SEC Announces Enforcement Task Force Focused on Climate and ESG Issues. Available at https://www.sec.gov/news/press-release/2021–42
17 Securities and Exchange Commission (SEC). March 21, 2022. SEC Proposes Rules to Enhance and Standardize Climate-Related Disclosures for Investors. Available at https://www.sec.gov/news/press-release/2022–46
18 Securities and Exchange Commission (SEC). March 6, 2024. The Enhancement and Standardization of Climate-Related Disclosures for Investors. 17 CFR 210, 229, 230, 232, 239, and 249, [Release Nos. 33–11275; 34–99678; File No. S7–10–22]. Available at https://www.sec.gov/files/rules/final/2024/33–11275.pdf
19 Securities and Exchange Commission (SEC). August 26, 2020. SEC Adopts Rule Amendments to Modernize Disclosures of Business, Legal Proceedings, and Risk Factors Under Regulation S-K. Available at https://www.sec.gov/news/press-release/2020–192
20 Financial Accounting Foundation. July 31, 2023. Proposed Accounting Standards Update, FASB In Focus. Available at https://www.fasb.org/page/PageContent?pageId=/news-media/fasbinfocus/fif-income-statement-reporting-comprehensive-income-expense-disaggregation-disclosures-subtopic-220–40-disaggregation-of-income-statement-expenses.html&bcpath=tff
21 Nasdaq. 2023. Nasdaq's Board Diversity Rule: What Companies Should Know, as of February 28, 2023. Available at https://www.skadden.com/-/media/Files/Publications/2021/08/SEC-Approves-Nasdaq-Board-Diversity-Listing/Nasdaqs-Board-Diversity-Rule.pdf
22 The Securities and Exchange Commission. June 11, 2021. SEC Announces Annual Regulatory Agenda. For Immediate Release 2021–99. Washington, D.C. Available at https://www.sec.gov/news/press-release/2021–99
23 Accountable Capitalism Act. 2018. Available at https://www.warren.senate.gov/newsroom/press-releases/warren-introduces-accountable-capitalism-act/
24 The White House. May 20, 2021. Executive Order on Climate-Related Financial Risk. Availableathttps://www.whitehouse.gov/briefing-room/presidential-actions/2021/05/20/executive-order-on-climate-related-financial-risk/
25 US Securities and Exchange Commission. Sample Letter to Companies Regarding Climate Change Disclosure. SEC.gov | Sample Letter to Companies Regarding Climate Change Disclosures. Available at https://www.sec.gov/corpfin/sample-letter-climate-change-disclosures
26 Herren Lee, Allison. March 15, 2021. Public Input Welcomed on Climate Change Disclosures. Statement from the U.S. Securities and Exchange Commission. SEC.gov | Public Input Welcomed on Climate Change Disclosures. Available at https://www.sec.gov/news/public-statement/lee-climate-change-disclosures
27 European Union (EU) Directive 2014/95/EU. "Directive 2014/95/EU of the European Parliament and of the Council Amending Directive 2013/34/EU as Regards Disclosure of Non-financial and Diversity Information by Certain Large Undertakings and Groups." Available at https://eur-lex.europa.eu/legal content/EN/TXT/PDF/?uri=CELEX:32014L0095&from=EN
28 The European Parliament and the Council of the European Union (EDR). December 12, 2019. Regulations on Sustainability-related Disclosures in the Financial Services Sector. *Official Journal of the European Union*, 2019. Available at https://eur-lex.europa.eu/eli/reg/2019/2088/oj

29 United Nations. Department of Economic and Social Affairs Sustainable Development. 2030 Agenda. Available at https://sdgs.un.org/goals

30 EDR. 2019

31 United Kingdom's Financial Conduct Authority (UK/FCA). March 2020. Proposals to Enhance Climate-related Disclosures by Listed Issuers and Clarification of Existing Disclosure Obligations, Consultation Paper. Available at https://www.wlrk.com/docs/FCA_-_Consultation_Paper.pdf

32 Ellerman, John, Kesner, Mike, and Ringle, Lane. March 16, 2021. "Inclusion of ESG Metrics in Incentive Plans: Evolution or Revolution?" Available at https://www.paygovernance.com/viewpoints/inclusion-of-esg-metrics-in-incentive-plans-evolution-or-revolution

33 The European Parliament and the Council of the European Union (EDR). December 12, 2019. Regulations on sustainability-related disclosures in the financial services sector. *Official Journal of the European Union*, 2019. Available at https://eur-lex.europa.eu/eli/reg/2019/2088/oj

34 United Kingdom's Financial Conduct Authority (UK/FCA). March 2020. *Proposals to Enhance Climate-Related Disclosures by Listed Issuers and Clarification of Existing Disclosure Obligations.* ConsultationPaper. Available at https://www.wlrk.com/docs/FCA_-_Consultation_Paper.pdf

35 European Commission (EC). January 5, 2023. The Corporate Sustainability Reporting Directive (CSRD). Available at https://finance.ec.europa.eu/capital-markets-union-and-financial-markets/company-reporting-and-auditing/company-reporting/corporate-sustainability-reporting_en

36 Much of the discussion in this section come from Rezaee, Z., J. Tsui, P. Cheng and St Zhou. 2019. *Business Sustainability in Asia: Compliance, Performance, and Integrated Reporting and Assurance*, John Wiley.

37 United Nations Global Compact (UN Global Compact). 2013. *Global Corporate Sustainability Report.* Available at https://www.unglobalcompact.org/docs/about_the_gc/Global_Corporate_Sustainability_Report2013.pdf

38 Hong Kong Stock Exchange (HKEX). 2015. Appendix 27 Environmental, Social, and Governance Reporting Guide. Available at https://www.hkex.com.hk/-/media/hkex-market/listing/rules-and-guidance/listing-rules-contingency/main-board-listing-rules/appendices/appendix_27

39 UN Sustainable Development Goals report (UNSDGs). 2015. "Indicators and a Monitoring Framework for the Sustainable Development Goals Launching a Data Revolution for the SDGs", available at http://unsdsn.org/wp-content/uploads/2015/03/150320-SDSN-Indicator-Report.pdf (accessed August 10, 2017).

40 Wang, X., Cao, F., and Ye, K. 2016. "Mandatory Corporate Social Responsibility (CSR) Reporting and Financial Reporting Quality: Evidence from a Quasi-Natural Experiment." *Journal of Business Ethics*, 1–22.

41 Vermander, B. 2014. *Corporate Social Responsibility in China: A Vision, an Assessment and a Blueprint.* World Scientific Publishing Co. Pte. Ltd, Singapore.

42 Hong Kong Stock Exchange (HKEX). 2018. "Exchange Publishes its Latest Review of Listed Issuers' Corporate Governance Practices and Updates its Guidance Material on ESG Reporting." www.hkex.com.hk/News/News-Release/2018/181116news?sc_lang=en

43 Organisation of Economic Co-operation and Development (OECD). 2023. *OECD Guidelines for Multinational Enterprises on Responsible Business Conduct.* Available at: www.oecd.org. https://mneguidelines.oecd.org/targeted-update-of-the-oecd-guidelines-for-multinational-enterprises.htm

44 OECD (2023), G20/OECD Principles of Corporate Governance 2023, OECD Publishing, Paris, https://doi.org/10.1787/ed750b30-en.

45 OECD. 2011 edition. *OECD Guidelines for Multinational Enterprises on Responsible Business Conduct.* Available at https://www.oecd.org/daf/inv/mne/oecdguidelinesformultinationalenterprises.htm

46 Global Reporting Initiative (GRI). 2013. *Sustainability Reporting Guidelines.* Available at https://www.globalreporting.org/resourcelibrary/GRIG4-Part1-Reporting-Principles-and-Standard-Disclosures.pdf (accessed March 29, 2016).

47 Ibid.

48 Ibid.

49 Ibid.

50 Global Sustainability Standards Board. 2020. GRI. Available at https://www.globalreporting.org/standards/gssb-and-standard-setting/

51 Global Sustainability Standards Board. 2020. Due Process Development. GRI. Available at https://www.globalreporting.org/standards/gssb-and-standard-setting/due-process-development/

52 Global Reporting Initiative (GRI). October 2021. Universal Standards: Setting a New Global Benchmark for Sustainability Reporting. Available at https://www.globalreporting.org/standards/standards-development/universal-standards/

53 Global Reporting Initiative (GRI). October 2022. Universal Standards: GRI Standards. Available at https://www.globalreporting.org/how-to-use-the-gri-standards/gri-standards-english-language/

54 International Integrated Reporting Committee (IIRC). 2013. IIRC Consultative Draft. Section 3.12, page 19. http://www.theiirc.org/consultationdraft2013/

55 Ibid.

56 Integrated Reporting (IR). May 2020. International Framework Revision Consultation Draft and Companion Document. Available at: https://integratedreporting.org/resource-type/technical/

57 The Sustainability Accounting Standards Board (SASB). Available at https://www.sasb.org/contact/

58 Sustainability Accounting Standards Board (SASB). October 2013. Conceptual Framework of Sustainability Accounting Standard Board. Available at http://www.sasb.org/wp-content/uploads/2013/10/SASB-Conceptual-Framework.pdf

59 Sustainability Accounting Standards Board (FBASB). February 2017. SASB Conceptual Framework. Available at https://www.sasb.org/wp-content/uploads/2020/02/SASB_Conceptual-Framework_WATERMARK.pdf

60 Ibid.

61 The Committee on Capital Markets Regulation. November 30, 2006. Interim rRport of the Committee on Capital Market Regulation. Available at: www.capmktsreg.org/research.html

62 The International Financial Reporting Standards (IFRS). September 2020. Consultation Paper on Sustainability Reporting. https://cdn.ifrs.org/-/media/project/sustainability-reporting/consultation-paper-on-sustainability-reporting.pdf

63 IFRS (April 2021). IFRS Foundation Exposure Draft: Proposed Targeted Amendments to the IFRS Foundation Constitution to Accommodate an International Sustainability Standards Board to Set IFRS Sustainability Standards. https://www.ifrs.org/content/dam/ifrs/project/sustainability-reporting/ed-2021–5-proposed-constitution-amendments-to-accommodate-sustainability-board.pdf

64 International Sustainability Standards Board (ISSB). 2022. About International Sustainability Standards Board. Available at https://www.ifrs.org/groups/international-sustainability-standards-board/
65 ESG Enterprise. 2022. What is International Sustainability Standards Board? Available athttps://www.esgenterprise.com/esg-reporting/what-is-international-sustainability-standards-board-issb-accounting-reporting/
66 International Sustainability Standards Board (ISSB). March 2022. IFRS Sustainability: Exposure Draft IFRS S1 General Requirements for Disclosure of Sustainability-related Financial Information. Available at https://www.ifrs.org/content/dam/ifrs/project/general-sustainability-related-disclosures/exposure-draft-ifrs-s1-general-requirements-for-disclosure-of-sustainability-related-financial-information.pdf.
67 International Sustainability Standards Board (ISSB). March 2022. IFRS Sustainability: Exposure Draft: FRS S2 Climate-related Disclosures. Available at https://www.ifrs.org/content/dam/ifrs/project/climate-related-disclosures/issb-exposure-draft-2022-2-climate-related-disclosures.pdf.
68 The International Sustainability Standards Board (ISSB). June 25, 2023. ISSB Issues Inaugural Global Sustainability Disclosure Standards. Available at https://www.ifrs.org/news-and-events/news/2023/06/issb-issues-ifrs-s1-ifrs-s2/
69 United Nations Global Compact (UNGC). 2015. *Guide to Corporate Sustainability.* Available at https://www.unglobalcompact.org/docs/publications/UN_Global_Compact_Guide_to_Corporate_Sustainability.pdf (accessed March 29, 2016).
70 TriplePundit. October 2013. UN Global Compact Releases Sustainability Research Findings. Available at: https://www.triplepundit.com/story/2013/un-global-compact-releases-sustainability-research-findings/48701
71 United Nations Global Compact. 2020. *Guide to Corporate Sustainability: Shaping a Sustainable Future.* Available at: https://d306pr3pise04h.cloudfront.net/docs/publications%2FUN_Global_Compact_Guide_to_Corporate_Sustainability.pdf
72 Ibid.
73 Principles for Responsible Investment (PRI). Available at https://www.unpri.org/pri/about-the-pri
74 Ibid.
75 United Nations Development Program. June 16, 2020. "UNDP Launches Standards for Bond Issuers and Private Equity Funds Seeking SDG Impact." Available at https://www.undp.org/content/undp/en/home/news-centre/news/2020/UNDP_launches_standards_for_bond_issuers_and_private_equity_funds_seeking_SDG_impact.html
76 UN Sustainable Development Goals (UNSDG). 2015. "Indicators and a Monitoring Framework for the Sustainable Development Goals Launching a Data Revolution for the SDGs." Available at http://unsdsn.org/wp-content/uploads/2015/03/150320-SDSN-Indicator-Report.pdf (accessed August 10, 2017).
77 Value Reporting Foundation Integrated Reporting Framework. 2020. IIRC and SASB Announce Intent to Merge in Major Step Towards Simplifying the Corporate Reporting System. https://integratedreporting.org/news/iirc-and-sasb-announce-intent-to-merge-in-major-step-towards-simplifying-the-corporate-reporting-system/ (accessed September 8, 2021).
78 Ibid.
79 International Corporate Governance Network (ICGN). 2021. About. Available at https://www.icgn.org/about

Chapter 2

Business Sustainability Models

Shareholder Primacy and Stakeholder Primacy

I. INTRODUCTION

The amount of environmental, social, and governance (ESG) funds available to US investors has increased substantially in 2019 to $20.6 billion, about four times more than the funds invested in ESG in 2021.[1] The Global ESG assets through sustainability investment by socially responsible investors are expected to exceed $53 trillion by 2025.[2] The World Economic Forum (WEF, 2020) states that a business organization is more than an economic unit generating wealth for shareholders and should attempt to have social and environmental impacts.[3] Business organizations are expected to fulfill human, environmental, and societal aspirations as part of the broader social system of achieving the desired return for shareholders while having social and environmental impacts.[4] Thus, the purpose of business organizations has transformed from profit maximization and shareholder wealth creation to the generation of shared value for all stakeholders. The ever-increasing erosion of public trust, social trust, and investor confidence in the sustainability of large businesses, the widening concern about social responsibility and environmental matters, social unrest, overconsumption of natural resources, the global government bailout of big businesses, and the perception that government cannot solve all problems of businesses underscores the importance of keen focus on business sustainability.

DOI: 10.4324/9781003437949-2

There have been two distinct models of shareholder primacy and stakeholder primacy with their own attributes and purposes.[5] The shareholder primacy model focuses on shareholder value creation and thus makes the board of directors' fiduciary responsibility only to shareholders in protecting their interests with the main mission of creating value primarily for shareholders. This shareholder primacy model, also known as the US capitalism system, is criticized for focusing on generating short-term profits for shareholders while compromising long-term sustainability performance that creates shared value for all stakeholders and promotes innovation, growth, and social and environmental impacts. Corporations can create the right balance between generating wealth-maximization for shareholders under the shareholder primacy model and achieving welfare-maximization for all stakeholders under the stakeholder primacy model.

The Business Roundtable (BRT), in 2019, announced the adoption of a new Statement on the Purpose of a Corporation, signed by 181 high-powered chief executive officers (CEOs), which recommends the move away from the shareholder primacy concept toward the stakeholder primacy concept that promotes sustainability of creating shared value for all stakeholders.[6] Corporate profit-with-purpose and stakeholder considerations have gained worldwide recognition in the business community in generating shared value for all stakeholders. Stakeholder primacy encourages companies to place stakeholders at the heart of their purpose. The shift in corporate purpose from shareholder primacy to stakeholder primacy is reinforced by the US Business Roundtable's Statement on the Purpose of a Corporation. This focus, combined with public pressure for public companies to engage on social, environmental, and political topics (e.g., human capital, diversity, climate change, immigration, gun control, gender pay equity), encourages corporate America to advance toward business sustainability and public companies worldwide to move toward the stakeholder primacy model. This chapter presents shareholder primacy and stakeholder primacy models and corporate governance under both models.

II. SHAREHOLDER PRIMACY MODEL AND SHAREHOLDER GOVERNANCE

II.1 Shareholder Primacy Model

The shareholder primacy model is a corporate governance concept that asserts that the primary purpose of a business entity is to maximize shareholder value. This model suggests the protection of the interests of shareholders should be the top priority for corporate decision-making, and thus, corporate directors and executives should focus on generating profits and increasing the corporate value that ultimately benefits the shareholders. Under the shareholder primacy model, the primary purpose of a corporation is to generate returns for shareholders; thus, corporate activities are managed toward creating shareholder value. This shareholder primacy model, also known as the US corporate governance model, makes the board of directors' judiciary responsible only to shareholders in protecting their interests. This corporate governance model has been criticized for focusing on generating short-term profits for shareholders while compromising long-term sustainability performance that creates shared value for all stakeholders and promotes innovation, growth, and social and environmental impacts.[7]

Shareholder primacy is an owner-centric form of corporate governance that focuses on maximization of shareholder wealth before considering the interests of other stakeholders, such as employees, customers, society, community, consumers, and the environment. Corporations as legal entities are incorporated under state law with many privileges, enabling them to raise public capital, operate within the framework of applicable laws and rules, and create wealth for their owners. Under the agency's view of the relationship between owners and management, a main concern is that directors and executives might use their discretion to advance their interests at the expense of shareholders. Sufficient corporate governance measures should be developed and implemented to minimize the potential conflicts of interest and a fundamental tension between the need to grant directors and executives adequate discretion to fulfill their duties while preventing possible opportunistic behavior. The primacy model assumes that shareholders own the corporation and it should be run for their sole benefit. This model has been the dominant organizing framework for corporate governance since the 1980s in the United States.

It could be argued that the prioritization of shareholder wealth maximization has contributed to wealth inequity and populism in the United States to the extent that capitalism's nature, extent, and value are being questioned. Policymakers and regulators worldwide also promote the move toward a more balanced-purpose model for public companies. For example, Senator Elizabeth Warren introduced the Accountable Capitalism Act in 2018, which, if enacted, would require public companies in the United States with more than $1 billion in revenues to obtain a federal charter stating the company's "purpose of creating a general public benefit," defined as, "a material positive impact on society resulting from the business and operations" of the company.[8] Among the requirements is the mandate that at least 40% of the directors of public companies in the United States be elected by employees and that directors consider the interests of all corporate stakeholders, including customers, suppliers, employees, investors, and the communities in which the corporation operates. Some Democratic congresspersons elected in 2019 advocate social responsibility for corporations. The congresspersons' initiatives reflect the larger debate regarding the role of corporations in society that calls into question the fiduciary model of shareholder primacy and advocates a move towards stakeholder primacy.

The capitalist system in the United States has traditionally contributed to the nation's economic growth and prosperity. However, like any other system, it has its own challenges, as many may believe the capitalist system has not benefited society.[9] With the recent focus on environmental and social issues worldwide, many business organizations and their boards of directors are paying attention to the growing interest in and demand by socially responsible investors and regulators to focus on the sustainability factors of planning, performance, risk, and disclosure and integrating them into their business and strategic decision-making. Profit-oriented business organizations and their boards of directors address these sustainability factors in many of their corporate decisions, including financial economic sustainability performance and non-financial environmental, ethical, social, and governance sustainability performance, their relationships with current or potential employees, customers, suppliers, their ability to attract capital and investor interest and to recruit, develop and retain a talented and motivated workforce. Under the shareholder primacy model, corporate social responsibility (CSR) and non-financial ESG activities are often seen as secondary to the primary goal of creating shareholder value, and thus, ESG activities come at the expense of shareholder returns. Business organizations should prepare for new sustainability strategic planning to respond effectively to the request from stakeholders for improvement in non-financial ESG activities and performance, as well as the demand by shareholders for improving financial economic sustainability performance in terms of total shareholder return (TSR). The US capital markets driven by the shareholder primacy and capitalism model have been perceived as promoting shareholder wealth maximization without creating an inclusive and equitable economy for all Americans. Many corporate leaders, including boards of directors and management, have stronger incentives to give substantial weight to the interests of shareholders with minimal or no incentive to advance stakeholders' interests beyond that which would benefit the shareholder.

In summary, the shareholder primacy model suggests that the primary responsibility of a corporation is to maximize shareholder value with minimal efforts to protect the interests of other stakeholders, including employees, customers, suppliers, and the broader community. Some of the important aspects and attributes of the shareholder primacy model: (1) business organizations should focus on strategies actions and decisions that maximize shareholder value by generating the highest possible returns for shareholders through maximizing profits, increasing share prices, and paying dividends; (2) the primary fiduciary duties of the board of directors and executives are to shareholders; (3) the focus on maximizing shareholder wealth can indirectly contribute to overall economic growth and societal well-being that benefit other stakeholders; (4) advancing shareholder interests can contribute to efficient capital allocation by investing in projects that generate the highest return on investment; (5) prevent conflicts of interest by aligning the interests of management with those of shareholders; and (6) mere focus on maximizing shareholder value can lead to negative consequences of short-termism, neglect of interest of other stakeholders, and potential for unethical behavior.

II.2 Shareholder Governance

The shareholder aspect of corporate governance is based on the premise that shareholders provide capital to the corporation, which exists for their benefit. It supports the agency theory that corporate directors and executives' fiduciary duties are to shareholders who have a residual claim on the company's assets and cash flows. Shareholders (principals) provide capital to the company, which is run by management (agents). The principal–agent problem exists because corporations are separate entities from their owners – management needs physical capital (investment funds), and investors need skilled human capital (management) to run the company. According to the principal–agent theory, also called the shareholder model of corporate governance, the primary objective of the company is to maximize shareholder wealth and, thus, the role of corporate governance is to ensure the enhancement of shareholder wealth and to align the interests of management with those of the shareholders. The principal–agent problem arises from two factors: the separation of ownership and control and, most importantly, incomplete contracts or costly enforceable contracts between the agents and principals, known as agency costs. Shareholder governance consists of the mechanisms, measures, and processes through which shareholders can exercise their voting rights of electing the board of directors to represent them, participate in decision-making, make investment decisions, and hold corporate directors and management accountable for protecting their interests.

The corporate governance structure should consist of mechanisms (internal and external) designed to effectively align the behavior of management (agents) and its interests with the desires of the principals (shareholders). The agency problem exists when the interests of management and shareholders are not in accord and when there are difficulties in verifying management activities. Agency costs also arise when there is an "information asymmetry" between management and shareholders and when the company's board of directors fails to fulfill its fiduciary duties of effectively carrying out its assigned oversight role. The agency problem can never be perfectly solved in the real world, and agency costs cannot be eliminated. If complete contracts were feasible and efficiently enforceable, there would be no agency costs, in the sense that investors would have known exactly what management was doing with their funds, and management would know investors' expectations. However, complete contracts are neither feasible nor enforceable, resulting in the occurrence of "residual contract rights" of making decisions based on rights not specified in the contract or on unforeseen circumstances. The residual contract rights may cause asymmetric information problems as management possesses information not disclosed or available to investors, which may result in management entrenchment.

Under the shareholder aspect, corporate governance is designed to reduce the agency costs and align the interests of management with those of investors through (1) providing incentives and opportunities for management to carry out its function effectively and maximize shareholder wealth by providing executive compensation plans, ownerships, or stock options; (2) strengthening shareholder rights to monitor, control, and discipline management through enforceable contracts or legal protection; (3) promoting shareholder democracy; (4) improving the vigilance of the board's oversight function; (5) holding directors accountable and liable for the fulfillment of their fiduciary duties; and (6) improving the effectiveness of both internal corporate governance mechanisms (board of directors, internal controls) and external corporate governance mechanisms (external audit, monitoring, and regulatory functions). Shareholders as owners of public companies should be attentive and protect their investment by attending shareholders' annual meetings (in person and/or virtually) to vote on corporate governance issues as reflected in management and shareholders' resolutions. Shareholders play a crucial role in corporate governance through their voting rights and engagements in meetings and discussions with the board of directors and management. These engagements enable shareholders to submit their governance proposals at the annual meetings.

Shareholders play an important role in corporate governance by electing directors who appoint management to make day-to-day business decisions for public companies. In addition, shareholders vote on many important issues that can create value for them. Generally, at annual shareholder meetings, shareholders vote for or against candidates for director positions, obtain detailed information regarding executive compensation plans, put forth proposals for consideration by other shareholders, and attend special shareholder meetings to vote on important corporate structure matters (mergers and acquisitions). Shareholders can vote at the meetings in person or "by proxy," including online, by mail, or by phone. Shareholders play an important role in corporate governance by exercising their voting rights and engaging in meetings and discussions with the board and management. This engagement becomes increasingly crucial when shareholders submit their proposals at the companies' annual meetings.

Agency/shareholder theory focuses on risk sharing and agency problems between shareholders and management by suggesting that the interests of principals (owners) and their agents (executives) are often not aligned. Thus, in the context of agency theory, corporate governance's role is to align management's interests with those of shareholders. Moral hazards can occur in the presence of information asymmetry where the agent (management) acting on behalf of the principal (shareholders) knows more about its actions and/or intentions than the principal does due to a lack of effective corporate governance in properly monitoring management. The implications of agency/shareholder theory for corporate governance are that management incentives and activities often focus on short-term earnings targets and self-serving maximization of executive compensation rather than improving long-term performance in creating shareholder value. Thus, corporate governance measures should be in place to ensure management focuses on creating stakeholder value.

Directors have fiduciary duties of care and loyalty that they must uphold. These duties require the directors to use informed, deliberate decision-making and act disinterestedly and independently when making decisions. They are required to use good faith and judgment to act in the best interest of the company and the shareholders they represent. Directors should be well-advised and properly informed, using all material information. They must be comfortable with all processes, keep confidential information confidential, weigh risks and rewards and compare them to alternatives, and respond appropriately to all issues. Finally, they must act in good faith and decide what they believe is in the company's best interest. A big responsibility that directors must deal with is effective oversight over the company and its risk management. Protocols to monitor and avoid risk and comply with laws and regulations must be implemented to avoid a breach of fiduciary duties. A good board process creates an appropriate framework for any situation while recording how situations were handled and serving as evidence for the director's completion of the fiduciary duties. This is all very important because if the director is sent to court, the burden is now on the plaintiff to provide evidence of gross negligence regarding a director's fiduciary duties due to the business judgment rule. This rule, reliance on company records, indemnification, expense advancement, exculpation of certain personal liabilities, and directors' and officers' (D&O) liability insurance, helps directors satisfy their fiduciary duties and protect them from possible accusations of breach.

A growing debate in corporate governance is whether corporate gatekeepers, including directors and top management teams, should consider only the interests and wealth of shareholders or should also consider the interests and welfare of all stakeholders such as employees, customers, suppliers, the environment, and local communities when making business decisions. While the corporate governance and agency theory suggests the primary fiduciary duty of corporate gatekeepers is to shareholders, stakeholder governance and stakeholder theory advocate corporate gatekeepers' responsibility to all stakeholders in creating shared value for them. Stakeholder governance has made significant progress in recent years as an alternative to shareholder governance to place more emphasis on impact investing and achieving a desirable rate of returns on investment for shareholders while generating social and environmental impacts.

In summary, effective shareholder governance is crucial for maintaining a balance of power between shareholders, directors, and management within corporations, ensuring that the interests of shareholders are aligned with the long-term sustainability of the company, and promoting overall corporate responsibility and accountability. Some of the aspects and attributes of effective shareholder governance are: (1) shareholders possess certain rights, including voting on electing directors and key issues and receiving information about the company's financial performance that enable them to participate in corporate governance; (2) shareholders participation in annual general meetings (AGMs): to discuss important matters, voice concerns and express their views on corporate decisions, vote on resolutions, and receive updates from the management regarding the strategic plans; (3) shareholders can vote to elect directors to represent their interests and oversee the company's management; and (4) shareholders have the right to propose resolutions that are put to the vote during AGMs that can influence corporate policies and practices and address ESG sustainability issues.

III. STAKEHOLDER PRIMACY MODEL AND STAKEHOLDER GOVERNANCE

The goal of companies has evolved from profit maximization to shareholder wealth enhancement to the creation of shared value for all stakeholders. However, corporations are now facing pressures from social activists and stakeholders to pay attention to the interests of customers, suppliers, employees, society, and the environment, among others, to create shared value for all stakeholders. In August 2019, the Business Roundtable issued a statement, signed by the CEOs of 187 major public companies, in which they committed to "lead their companies to the benefit of all stakeholders" and to "deliver value" not just to shareholders but also to employees, customers, suppliers, and communities.[10] The World Economic Forum (WEF) highly recommends companies move from the traditional model of "shareholder capitalism" to the model of "stakeholder capitalism."[11] WEF supports the stakeholder governance concept in the context of the stakeholder primacy model. As part of its COVID Action Platform, it has developed the stakeholder governance principles to protect the interests of shareholders, employees, customers, suppliers, governments, and society.[12]

III.1 Stakeholder Primacy Model

The stakeholder primacy model, better known as the European corporate governance model, makes the board of directors fiduciarily responsible for protecting all stakeholders' interests, including shareholders, creditors, employees, customers, suppliers, society, and the environment. The stakeholder primacy model considers the interests of all stakeholders, including shareholders, in this era of sustainability-oriented investors, directors, and executives' commitments to sustainability, a major challenge in determining the determinants and consequences of business sustainability. The major determinants of business sustainability are determined by the shareholder primacy and stakeholder primacy model and the firm's size, leverage, maturity, complexity, merger and acquisition activity, restructuring charges, operation in a more litigious industry, corporate governance measures, and internal control effectiveness. The four business sustainability factors of planning, performance, disclosure, risk are intended to generate positive consequences of financial and market performance, earnings quality, and financial reporting conservatism. The stakeholder primacy model focuses on the impact investing concept of generating desired financial returns on shareholders' investments while protecting other stakeholders' interests and achieving social and environmental impacts. Under the stakeholder primacy model, while shareholders have the right to protect their investments, they also benefit in the long term, where their company is sustainable in creating shared value for all stakeholders. Stakeholder welfare creation rather than shareholder wealth creation is promoted under stakeholder capitalism.

In recent years, there has been a rise in stakeholder engagement, which has grown with the increasing pressure for companies to respect all stakeholders including shareholders. The digital age has created a new way of work, shifting the service economy to more automated, resulting in the need for more skilled, talented, and experienced workers. Employees, customers, suppliers, and even the local and global communities are now considered major stakeholders central to a company's long-term success and sustainability. Stakeholders are individuals or groups who affect the company's strategic decisions, operations, and performance and are also affected by its decisions or activities. Traditionally, shareholders have been the primary users of the company's financial reports, which reflect the company's financial condition and the results of operations. While shareholders are still the primary recipients of the company's reports on economic performance, stakeholders are now becoming more engaged and interested in the company's multiple bottom lines (MBL) performance on various economic, governance, ethical, social, and environmental issues. Shareholders' initiatives, proposals, and resolutions on environmental and social issues are being considered by the board of directors and incorporated into the corporate governance structure.

The stakeholder primacy model is gaining support after the 2007–2009 global financial crisis and the move toward business sustainability. This model requires (1) identification of all stakeholders who affect and are affected by the organization's business and affairs, including investors, creditors, customers, employees, suppliers, society, and the environment; (2) determination of rights, authorities, responsibilities, and accountability of each stakeholder; (3) development of a systematic process to ensure proper accountability for the stewardship of the organization's resources and capitals; and (4) establishment of a fair system of rewards based on the risk taken by stakeholders. Under the stakeholder theory of corporate governance, the primary objective is to achieve sustainable financial and non-financial performance by creating shared value for all stakeholders. Some of the aspects and attributes of the stakeholder primacy model are: (1) balancing interests of all stakeholders by recognizing that business organizations create shared value for all stakeholders including shareholders and their impact extends beyond shareholders to encompass employees, customers, suppliers and the wider community; (2) engagement of a diverse set of stakeholders in decision-making processes to ensure that decisions involve all concerned stakeholders, reflect a broader range of perspectives, and consider the potential impacts on a variety of stakeholders; (3) focus on the long-term sustainability of a company and its stakeholders by improving by relationships with employees, investors, customers, suppliers, communities, society, and the environment; (4) compliance with the principles of corporate social responsibility by taking take actions on voluntary basis beyond what is required by law to benefit society; (5) promotion of responsible business practices that go beyond mere compliance with laws, rules, regulations, and standards; (6) recognition of the importance of considering societal and environmental concerns and impacts by adopting adopt sustainable and environmentally friendly and socially responsible practices; (7) using globally accepted sustainability reporting guidelines and frameworks (GRI, SASB, ISSB) to disclose the companies' ESP and ESG sustainability performance; and (8) adherence to stakeholder governance measures presented in the next section.

Several initiatives have been undertaken in moving away from shareholder primacy and toward stakeholder primacy under this new corporate governance model, including:[13]

1. The board's fiduciary duty is extended to all stakeholders, and the board of directors should be accountable to all stakeholders, not just shareowners.
2. Corporate purpose statements should specifically state that corporations benefit society positively by creating shared value for all stakeholders.
3. Multiple stakeholders, including employees, should be represented on corporate boards.
4. Large corporations should be required to be organized under federal charters to facilitate governance reform accountability that requires responsibility to all stakeholders.
5. Legislative acts and regulatory mandates.

III.2 Stakeholder Governance

Stakeholder governance consists of governance measures, mechanisms, practices, and processes used to protect the interests of all stakeholders by managing the company's relationships and interactions with various stakeholders. Unlike the shareholder governance model presented in the previous section, which focuses primarily on shareholders, stakeholder governance addresses the interests of a broader range of stakeholders, including shareholders, employees, customers, suppliers, society, communities, and the environment. Stakeholder governance is a holistic and sustainable approach to corporate governance that recognizes that a company's success is linked to the well-being of various stakeholders. Stakeholder governance effectiveness has been the main focus of business organizations and their stakeholders, including shareholders, employees, suppliers, customers, and communities. Stakeholder governance recognizes the importance of business survival and continuity in the short term and sustainable value creation for all shareholders in the long term as a corporate strategy. The stakeholder model of corporate governance focuses on the broader view of the company with purpose and profit at the nexus of contracts among all corporate governance participants with the common goal of creating shared value for all stakeholders.

The stakeholder model concentrates on the maximization of wealth for all stakeholders, including (1) contractual participants such as shareholders, creditors, suppliers, customers, and employees; and (2) social constituents including the local community; society and global partners; local, state, and federal governments; and environmental matters. Under stakeholder governance, public companies must be socially responsible, be good citizens, and be responsible agents of using the nation's physical and human capital, managed in the public interest to leave a better environment for the next generations. Thus, the performance of public companies is measured in terms of key financial indicators (earnings, market share, stock price), social indicators (employment, customer satisfaction, fair trading with suppliers), ethical indicators (proper business culture, business code of conduct), and environmental indicators (antipollution, preservation of natural resources). Public companies' performance is measured based on financial, social, and environmental impacts.

Stakeholders have a reciprocal relationship and interaction with a firm in that they contribute to its value creation, and the firm's performance affects their well-being. Stakeholder theory applies to all managerial processes in that the synergy and integration among all elements of the business model and its processes are essential in achieving overall sustainable performance objectives. From the stakeholder's perspective, an organization is part of a network of groups that work together to achieve the network/system goals. However, management may take actions to improve sustainability performance that benefit stakeholders (shareholders) who have the power to influence its compensation. The application of stakeholder theory to corporate governance and, thus, management processes suggests that a company should be viewed as a nexus of all stakeholders. Corporate stakeholders are shareholders, creditors, customers, suppliers, employees, government, competitors, the environment, and society. Under stakeholder theory, management's role is to improve sustainable performance and create shared value for all stakeholders. The stakeholder governance paradigm requires a new set of guiding principles driven by shared value concepts, new governance functions redefining the fiduciary duties of directors and executives to all stakeholders, and a new set of corporate governance measures to ensure its effectiveness.

The board should also provide oversight, insight, and foresight function on the achievement of both financial economic sustainability performance (ESP) and non-financial environmental, social, and governance (ESG) sustainability performance driven by financial, human, social, manufacturing capitals as well as innovation, culture, corporate governance, and ESG initiatives.[14] The board's role under the stakeholder primacy, as opposed to the shareholder primacy model, oversees the managerial function of focusing on long-term sustainability performance, effectively communicating sustainability performance information to all stakeholders. The board should be informed of and understand the stakeholders' objectives and rationales for focusing on sustainability factors of performance, risk and disclosure, managerial, strategic planning, sustainable operational performance, and executive compensation in promoting long-term corporate value. The board should also provide oversight, insight, and foresight function on achieving financial ESP and non-financial ESG performance driven by financial, human, social, and manufacturing capitals, as well as innovation, culture, corporate governance, and ESG initiatives.[15] The financial and non-financial key performance indicators (KPIs) should be identified, measured, and disclosed through metrics reflecting the corporate value, long-term investment, and innovation on ESG initiatives. In general, the four sustainability oversight functions of the board of directors are:[16]

1. Refocusing on the long-term – companies and their investors, boards of directors, and executives should focus on long-term sustainable goals and achievements rather than short-term gains, as the short-term focus may discourage them from investing in research, technology, innovation, and ESG initiatives.

2. Identifying, measuring, and disclosing key drivers of long-term value – the four major drivers of long-term value are:

    - Talent – employees can significantly influence a company's ability to generate long-term value by implementing its strategy, improving operational effectiveness, and developing new ideas for success and growth. The three areas that the talent can affect regarding sustainability of long-term performance and related metrics and disclosures are: human capital development, management, engagement, and turnover; organizational culture and related employee views and data; employee health programs, participation, and impact on productivity.
    - Innovation and consumer trends – companies should ensure that their innovation is meeting the evolving demands of customers and other stakeholders and continuously interact with them to assess their innovation and develop related metrics to measure and disclose their success in addressing overall innovation strategy performance and metrics; consumer trust scores and consumer health impacts.
    - Society and the environment – the concept of impact investing, focusing on both financial returns and social and environmental impacts of business organizations, is gaining momentum with investors. Companies should identify and measure their impacts on society and the environment by linking their strategic goals to the United Nations' Sustainable Development Goals (SDGs).
    - Corporate governance – there has been much progress in corporate governance and its measures in the past two decades. However, corporate governance is a process (journey) that needs continuous improvements. Areas of improvement in corporate governance are the robust and continuous evaluation of the board's effectiveness, composition, diversity, and dynamics; board oversight function in creating value and protecting value; and corporate governance reporting in properly disclosing its success and long-term performance.

3. Developing company-specific sustainability metrics – sustainability metrics on financial ESP and non-financial EGS should be tailored to the company's mission, purpose, culture, strategy, objectives, and operating activities

    Identifying sustainability issues that drive value – the Sustainability Accounting Standards Board (SASB) released its new standards in November 2018, which are intended to enable business organizations in different industries to identify, measure, report, and manage their sustainability factors of performance, risk, and disclosure. These standards can be tailored to a particular company's operations and can have long-term financial impacts. The SASB identifies 28 sustainability factors and issues broadly organized into the four groups as previously discussed[17]

The stakeholder governance concept focusing on stakeholders has recently been debated among policymakers, regulators, investors, the business community, and the accounting profession, with both discussion of the positive impacts of benefiting all stakeholders and the imposition of additional costs on shareholders and society.[18] However, the World Economic Forum (WEF) advocates the stakeholder governance concept promoted by stakeholder capitalism and has established the principles to protect all stakeholders' interests, including shareholders, employees, customers, suppliers, governments, and society.[19] The International Business Council (IBC) of the World Economic Forum (WEF), in collaboration with the big four accounting firms, has released its final recommendations for a set of globally accepted, standardized, and industry-oriented environmental, social, and governance (ESG) sustainability performance metrics and disclosures.[20] These recommendations are intended to provide guiding principles for focusing on the ESG sustainability factors of performance, risk, and disclosures on governance, people, planet, and prosperity.

Stakeholder governance principles guide corporate gatekeepers and participants, from the board of directors to executives, investors, legal counsel, financial advisors, and auditors, to discharge their responsibility effectively and fulfill their accountability. Stakeholder governance guiding principles are advancing and intended to provide a basic framework and foundation for effective governance in protecting the interests of all stakeholders, and as such, they apply to all types and sizes of organizations. The primary oversight function of the board of directors under stakeholder governance is to protect multi-stakeholders' interests by appointing competent, accountable, ethical, and responsible executives to manage the business for the benefit of all stakeholders. Regulators worldwide should promulgate proactive, cost-efficient, effective, and scalable rules and regulations to protect the interests of all stakeholders. Internal and external governance mechanisms should be established to achieve the organization's purposes, mission, vision, values, and goals. Internal mechanisms consist of a vigilant board of directors overseeing the organization's purpose, mission, objectives, and strategies; and executives' commitments to implement proper strategies to minimize the negative impacts and maximize positive impacts of the organization's activities, operations, and performance. External mechanisms established by policymakers, regulators, and standard setters can play an important role in stakeholder governance in establishing applicable laws, regulations, rules, and standards intended to benefit all stakeholders and protect their interests.

The new stakeholder governance paradigm recognizes the importance of short-term and long-term sustainable value creation for all stakeholders by viewing governance as coordination and collaboration among all corporate governance participants, from shareholders to boards of directors, executives, and other stakeholders to achieve financial ESP and non-financial ESG sustainability performance in creating shared value for all stakeholders. The emerging new stakeholder governance enables global business organizations to better realize their responsibility for the safety, health, and well-being of shareholders, employees, customers, and suppliers. It also redefines its business purpose of achieving financial ESP and non-financial

ESG sustainability performance. The new stakeholder governance paradigm requires a new coherent set of guiding principles provided by the WEF and driven by a shared value concept, new governance functions redefining the fiduciary duties of directors and executives to all stakeholders, and a new set of internal and external governance mechanisms.

Stakeholder governance defines governance participants' roles and responsibilities, including the board of directors, executives, auditors, and investors, and has been the main focus of business organizations and their stakeholders. The new paradigm for corporate governance recognizes the importance of short-term performance, including business survival and continuity, and long-term performance in creating shared value for all stakeholders. The new paradigm views corporate governance as coordination and collaboration among all corporate governance participants, from shareholders to boards of directors, executives, and other stakeholders, to achieve financial and non-financial sustainability performance in creating shared value for all stakeholders. It provides a road map for all corporate governance participants, including shareholders, to be attentive in monitoring their investments; boards of directors in providing effective and engaged oversight; executives in diligently implementing short-, medium-, and long-term sustainable business strategies; and other corporate gatekeepers (auditors, legal counsel, financial analysts) in protecting interests of all stakeholders.

Stakeholder governance represents a broader trend in corporate governance practices and discussion by emphasizing a more inclusive and sustainable approach to corporate governance. Some of the important aspects and attributes of stakeholder governance are: (1) identification of all stakeholders that have a stake in the company and take risk including shareholders, creditors, employees, customers, suppliers, society and the environment; (2) active involvement and engagement of all concerned stakeholders by seeking input, feedback, and collaboration from them to ensure more comprehensive and diverse perspectives of decision-makings and actions; (3) improving transparent and open communication with stakeholders by providing clear and accessible information about the company's strategic planning, activities, and impacts; (4) focusing on the social and environmental responsibilities of the company by taking initiatives that contribute positively to society and the environment; (5) understanding that the success of a company is intertwined with the well-being of its stakeholders by focusing on sustainable business practices; (6) implementation of governance mechanisms for ongoing engagement with all stakeholders through regular meetings, surveys, feedback channels, and other means to ensure proper communication and responsiveness to stakeholder concerns; and (7) focusing on addressing stakeholder expectations by being adaptable and responsive to evolving circumstances.

IV. CONCLUSION

Public companies have significantly grown, and their purpose has evolved in the past several decades from profit maximization to creating shared value for all stakeholders.

During and in the aftermath of the 2020 COVID-19 pandemic, business organizations became better off by focusing on the stakeholder primacy model of creating shared value for all stakeholders. The mission of profit-with-purpose for business organizations demands a focus on sustainability strategies that have become integral components of the business environment and corporate culture. This emerging trend of moving away from shareholder primacy toward stakeholder primacy and index funding has led to a debate on the implications of common ownership and the main mission of business organizations.

Under the stakeholder primacy model, there is spread ownership, and the main mission is to create shared value for all stakeholders. Policymakers, regulators, and society have questioned the fiduciary model of shareholder primacy and advocate moving toward stakeholder primacy. The shareholder primacy model has served investors well in creating value and maximizing their wealth. However, it is criticized for focusing on serving only one group of stakeholders and generating short-term profits at the expense of long-term sustainability, performance innovation, and growth. This model often ignores the social and environmental impacts of corporations. The focus on shareholder wealth creation may not benefit other stakeholders, such as employees, customers, creditors, suppliers, government, society, and the environment. Business organizations are given rights to operate and generate profits for their shareholders, but with these rights come public interests and societal responsibilities of having social and environmental impacts.

The shareholder aspect of corporate governance implies that shareholders, by virtue of their ownership investment in the company, are entitled to direct and monitor the company's business and affairs. Shareholders influence corporate governance by exercising their right to elect directors, who appoint management to run the company. Directors and officers, as agents of the company, act as trustees on behalf of shareholders, and their primary responsibilities and fiduciary duties are to shareholders. While directors' and officers' legal fiduciary duties are only extended to shareholders who invested in the company, they may have many nonfiduciary duties to other stakeholders, who may have various interests and claims to the company's assets and welfare. Shareholders' rights, including the right to elect, the right to put propositions before the annual shareholder meetings, and the right to reliable and accurate financial information, are legally enforceable, and offending directors and officers can be brought to justice through the courts. Corporate purpose is now changing as there is more support for stakeholder governance and the stakeholder primacy model in creating shared value for all stakeholders and maximizing stakeholder welfare than just creating shareholder value and maximizing shareholder wealth.

There has been a move toward the stakeholder capitalism and primacy model to ensure the long-term sustainability of business corporations in generating desired financial returns for their shareholders while protecting the interests of all stakeholders. Stakeholders such as employees, creditors, customers, suppliers, social responsibility activists, and communities, who are affected by and can affect the company's success, do not have the right to engage with the company regarding its mission, purpose, strategic plans, performance, and accomplishments. Nonetheless, stakeholders' interests are protected under the contract and tort laws and the stakeholder capitalism and primacy model. Stakeholder capitalism and stakeholder governance are intended to benefit all stakeholders. The stakeholder governance paradigm, including guiding principles, functions, and measures, should assist governance participants from the board of directors to management, accountants, auditors, legal counsel, and stakeholders to address and act in protecting the interests of all stakeholders. Stakeholder governance is driven by the primacy concept, which focuses on creating and protecting shared value for all stakeholders. Business organizations worldwide should modify corporate governance to protect all stakeholders' interests. Business organizations should understand the move towards stakeholder governance with a focus on sustainability factors of performance, risk, and disclosure and integration of these factors into corporate culture and business environment, as well as managerial policies, decisions, and processes to protect the interests of their stakeholders. Modifications in corporate governance structure under the stakeholder primacy model, including principles, functions, and measures presented in this chapter, can be used by policymakers, regulators, standard-setting bodies, and businesses to evaluate the efficiency and effectiveness of new laws, rules, regulations, standards, and their practices in creating shared value for all stakeholders.

V. TAKEAWAYS

- Promote a profit-with-purpose mission to create shared value for all stakeholders.
- Consider moving away from the shareholder primacy model and moving toward the stakeholder primacy model.
- Achieve impact investing to generate desired financial returns for shareholders while achieving social and environmental impacts.
- Establish measures of both financial ESP performance and non-financial ESG sustainability performance.
- Communicate the achievement of both financial ESP performance and non-financial ESG sustainability performance to all stakeholders.

Notes

1 Lacurci, G. January 14, 2020. "Money Moving into Environmental Funds Shatters Previous Record." *CNBC*. Available at https://www.cnbc.com/2020/01/14/esg-funds-see-record-inflows-in-2019.html

2 Bloomberg. February 23, 2021. "Bloomberg Professional Services: ESG Assets May Hit $53 Trillion by 2025, a Third of Global AUM." Bloomberg Intelligence. Available at https://www.bloomberg.com/professional/blog/esg-assets-may-hit-53-trillion-by-2025-a-third-of-global-aum/

3 World Economic Forum. September 7, 2021. About: Our Mission. https://www.weforum.org/about/world-economic-forum
4 Ibid.
5 Much of the discussion in this chapter comes from Rezaee, Z. July 2021. *Corporate Sustainability: Shareholder Primacy Versus Stakeholder Primacy.* Business Expert Press.
6 Business Roundtable (BRT). August 19, 2019. Statement on the Purpose of a Corporation. Available at https://opportunity.businessroundtable.org/wp-content/uploads/2019/09/BRT-Statement-on-the-Purpose-of-a-Corporation-with-Signatures-1.pdf
7 Rezaee, Z. and T. Fogarty. 2019. *Business Sustainability, Corporate Governance and Organizational Ethics.* John Wiley and Sons, Inc., Hoboken, New Jersey, United States.
8 Warren, E. August 15, 2018. Warren Introduces Accountable Capitalism Act. Available at https://www.warren.senate.gov/newsroom/press-releases/warren-introduces-accountable-capitalism-act.
9 Rezaee, Z. July 2021. *Corporate Sustainability: Shareholder Primacy Versus Stakeholder Primacy.* Business Expert Press.
10 Business Roundtable. August 19, 2019. *Business Roundtable Redefines the Purpose of a Corporation to Promote "An Economy That Serves All Americans."* https://www.business-roundtable.org/business-roundtable-redefines-the-purpose-of-a-corporation-to-promote-an-economy-that-serves-all-americans.
11 World Economic Forum (WEF). December 2, 2019. "Davos Manifesto 2020: The Universal Purpose of a Company in the Fourth Industrial Revolution." https://www.weforum.org/agenda/2019/12/davos-manifesto-2020-the-universal-purpose-of-a-company-in-the-fourth-industrial-revolution/
12 World Economic Forum (WEF). April 24, 2020. "World Economic Forum Pledges to Stand By Stakeholders in the COVID-19 Era." Available at https://www.weforum.org/agenda/2020/03/world-economic-forum-launches-covid-action-platform/
13 Palladino, L. and Karlsson, K. October 2018. *Towards "Accountable Capitalism": Remaking Corporate Law Through Stakeholder Governance* . http://rooseveltinstitute.org/wp-content/uploads/2018/10/Towards-%E2%80%98Accountable-Capitalism%E2%80%99-issue-brief.pdf
14 Klemash, S., J. C. Smith and R. Doyle. June 13, 2019. "Stakeholder Capitalism for Long-Term Value Creation." Harvard Law School on Corporate Governance and Financial Regulation. Available at https://corpgov.law.harvard.edu/2019/06/13/stakeholder-capitalism-for-long-term-value-creation/
15 Klemash, S., J. C. Smith and R. Doyle. June 13, 2019. "Stakeholder Capitalism for Long-Term Value Creation. Harvard Law School on Corporate Governance and Financial Regulation." Available at https://corpgov.law.harvard.edu/2019/06/13/stakeholder-capitalism-for-long-term-value-creation/
16 Ibid.
17 Sustainability Accounting Standards Board (SASB). November 2018. Current Standards. Available at https://www.sasb.org/standards-overview/download-current-standards/
18 Rezaee, Z. and N. Rezaee. 2020. "Stakeholder Governance Paradigm in Response to the COVID-19 Pandemic." *Journal of Corporate Governance Research* Vol. 4, No. 1, November.
19 Ibid.
20 World Economic Forum (WEF). September 2020. *Measuring Stakeholder Capitalism Towards Common Metrics and Consistent Reporting of Sustainable Value Creation.* White Paper. Available at https://www.wlrk.com/docs/sWEF_IBC_Measuring_Stakeholder_Capitalism_Report_2020.pdf

Chapter 3

Profit-With-Purpose Sustainability and Shared Value Concept

I. INTRODUCTION

Business organizations have been encouraged and often required to refocus their objectives, goals, and strategies on the profit-with-purpose mission of creating shared value for all stakeholders. In the current business environment, the goal of profit maximization and, thus, shareholder value creation may no longer be desirable and sustainable for business organizations. Thus, public companies should pay attention to the impacts of their operations on society, communities, and the environment. The corporation's purpose has evolved in recent decades from profit maximization to shareholder-wealth maximization to creating shared value for all stakeholders. The latter purpose can be achieved when corporations focus on the profit-with-purpose mission of generating desired financial returns for their shareholders, achieving social and environmental impacts and protecting the interests of other stakeholders, including customers, employees, suppliers, communities, society, and the environment.

The global economy, prosperity, stakeholder expectations, business environment, and corporate culture have changed in the post-COVID-19 pandemic era, and thus, business organizations are adopting new missions and purposes. Purpose determines why the organization exists, its mission, who the stakeholders are, its objectives and strategies for achieving the objectives, and their matrices in measuring success. The main objective function for any business organization has been and continues to be

DOI: 10.4324/9781003437949-3

the achievement of sustainable performance in creating shared value for all stakeholders, including shareholders, customers, suppliers, employees, creditors, government, society, and the environment. Changes in business organizations' purpose, mission, objectives, and strategies after the COVID-19 pandemic are needed to achieve sustainable financial economic sustainability performance (ESP) and non-financial environmental, social, and governance (ESG) sustainability performance.

The effective design, implementation, and achievement of the profit-with-purpose mission enables business organizations to create shared value for all stakeholders. The shared value creation concept means that the interests of all stakeholders should be protected, and thus, corporate resources and activities should be managed to create shared value for all stakeholders.[1] The board of directors should promote the shared value concept in fulfilling their responsibility to protect the interests of all stakeholders. Management, as the steward of business resources, should promote the shared value concept, has the primary role of improving performance and managing related risks, maximizing utilization of all capital from strategic to operational, financial, reputational, manufactured, human, social, and environmental to create shared value for all stakeholders. The other corporate gatekeepers should consider sustainability in enabling opportunities to create shared value by focusing on the continuous improvements of short-term and mid-term performance and sustainable long-term growth. This chapter examines the business sustainability mission of profit-with-purpose in creating shared value for all stakeholders, including obtaining the desired rate of returns for shareholders while achieving social and environmental impacts. This chapter also examines the importance and relevance of the profit-with-purpose concept in promoting business sustainability and creating shared value for all stakeholders.

II. PROFIT-WITH-PURPOSE MISSION

The concept of profit-with-purpose represents a business strategy used by business entities that combine financial success and viability with a commitment to social and environmental impacts by aligning their business strategies with broader societal goals, environmental impacts, and ethical practices. The concept suggests that the corporate mission should go beyond simply maximizing profits for shareholders and be extended to creating shared value for various stakeholders, including investors, employees, customers, suppliers, communities, society, and the environment. This concept suggests that while the main objective function for any business organization is to earn profit for its owners, it should also have a purpose specified in the article of incorporation (e.g., serving the community, promoting diversity, and having social and environmental impacts). The global move toward adopting benefit corporations, profit-with-purpose companies, and focus on sustainability performance, reporting, and assurance is inevitable as sustainability initiatives are integrated into the business environment, corporate culture, strategies, supply chain, decisions, actions, and performance. The COVID-19 pandemic has caused substantial economic, societal, and business challenges, which demand that business organizations reevaluate their priorities and purpose. The board of directors should review and reevaluate the statement of the purpose from the traditional shareholder primacy model to the emerging stakeholder primacy model. Under the stakeholder primacy model, the board is responsible for protecting the interests of all stakeholders, including shareholders, employees, customers, suppliers, communities, society, and the environment. The stakeholder primacy model promotes the nexus between corporate financial performance and societal well-being and increases the public perception and awareness of corporate social responsibility and business sustainability. It defines the new purpose of securing employees, customers, and suppliers' safety, health, and well-being, making a profit for shareholders, and moving toward the "profit-with-purpose" concept discussed in the next section.

Business organizations are being criticized for directing a keen focus on profit maximization for their shareholders with minimal or no attention to the impacts of their operations on society, communities, and the environment. As business sustainability is gaining more attention and being integrated into the business environment and corporate culture, there has been a shift from creating shareholder value to developing "sustainable shared value creation" to protect the interests of all stakeholders with a broader focus on the profit-with-purpose mission. Under the shared value creation concept, the board of directors' fiduciary duties are to protect the interests of all stakeholders and oversee management activities of focusing on the continuous performance improvement of business operations in generating long-term value while maximizing the positive impacts of operations on society, communities, and the environment by measuring sustainable performance in terms of both ESP and ESG sustainability performance. Thus, corporate objectives have advanced from profit maximization to increasing shareholder wealth and creating shared value for all stakeholders. Companies implementing a profit-with-purpose mission often integrate social and environmental considerations into their strategic planning and decision-making processes to positively impact society and the environment while being financially successful.

This profit-with-purpose mission represents a growing acceptance that businesses can significantly address environmental and societal challenges. Every company should have its unique purpose determined in its charter of incorporation to maximize its positive impacts on all stakeholders, including communities, society, and the environment, and to minimize the negative impacts on multi-stakeholders. In case of a nonexistent and/or inadequate "statement of purpose," the board of directors, in collaboration with management, should develop the statement of purpose and obtain approval by majority shareholders. The statement of purpose should include the mission, which reflects the organization's determination to stay with its purpose and its short-, medium-, and long-term achievement. Companies are now adopting the corporate mission of profit with the purpose of creating shared value for all stakeholders by shifting their goals to create shareholder value while fulfilling their social, environmental, and governance responsibilities. The statement of purpose should also define objectives, which have substantially evolved to survival in the short term, continuity in the medium term, and sustainability in the long term. The board of directors pays more attention to the well-being, safety, and health of their employees, customers, and suppliers. In collaboration with management, the board of directors should also design strategies to achieve new objectives by designing business continuity plans, deliberate decisions, and crisis management. This chapter introduces the concept of profit-with-purpose for creating shared value for all stakeholders.

There has been much debate over the Business Roundtable's updated Statement on the Purpose of a Corporation, published in August 2019 and signed by more than 180 CEOs.[2] The Statement suggests a move away from shareholder primacy as a guiding principle and outlines a move toward stakeholder primacy with a modern corporate responsibility standard that commits to all stakeholders. The shareholder primacy model suggests that corporations exist principally to serve shareholders, and the interests of other stakeholders are not considered. Thus, society and all stakeholders deserve an economy that allows people to succeed through hard work, dedication, commitment, and creativity and to lead a life of meaning, fairness, and dignity. Stakeholder capitalism focusing on the free-market system promotes hard work and quality performance, creating good jobs, a strong and sustainable economy, innovation, economic opportunity, a healthy environment, and social justice for all. Businesses play a vital economic role by creating jobs, fostering innovation, and providing essential goods and services. Businesses make and sell consumer products, create jobs, manufacture equipment and vehicles, grow and produce food, support the national defense, generate, and deliver energy, provide health care, and offer financial and other services that underpin economic growth and prosperity for the nation.

On February 23, 2022, the European Union Commission launched its Corporate Sustainability Due Diligence Directive proposal. However, there were a few issues related to this Directive that the Commission is working to address including the ongoing debate about the definition of stakeholders versus shareholders. This allows companies to fall into a primacy model that puts too much emphasis and energy on maximizing value for one group and not the other, leading to inequalities in power dynamics. An example of this would be maximizing shareholder wealth and not factoring in the interests of other stakeholders. Another issue was not changing company law to incorporate sustainability in business decision-making and the possibility of "box-ticking" instead of thoroughly evaluating sustainability principles.[3]

A survey shows increasing enthusiasm for defining corporate purpose and that it is in investors' interests to hold companies accountable for the defined purpose rather than viewing it as an unnecessary distraction.[4] Furthermore, the survey indicates that (1) the majority of investors (93%) agree that it is important for a company to define its purpose, especially to set a long-term business strategy that creates value and strengthens corporate culture and that this was the responsibility of the board; (2) about 75% of the respondents suggest that companies should disclose and implement sustainability information through their key performance indicators (KPIs); and (3) more than 59% agree that these KPIs may be included in new executive pay programs.[5] French legislation on the corporate purpose of "Pacte Statute" on the Development and Transformation of Businesses states that each French company must now be managed "in furtherance of its corporate interest" and "while taking into consideration the social and environmental issues arising from its activity."[6]

II.1 Sustainability Trends Toward Profit-with-Purpose

The World Economic Forum (WEF) advocates the stakeholder governance concept with a focus on "profit-with-purpose" that has been promoted by the stakeholders to protect the interests of all stakeholders, including shareholders, employees, customers, suppliers, governments, and society.[7] The International Business Council (IBC) of the World Economic Forum, in collaboration with the big four accounting firms, has released its final recommendations for a set of (ESG) sustainability performance metrics and disclosures that can be globally accepted and implemented.[8] These recommendations provide guiding principles and metrics for focusing on the ESG sustainability factors of performance, risk, and disclosures relevant to governance, people, planet, and prosperity.

The IBC/WEF framework defines a set of "Stakeholder Capitalism Metrics" pertaining to ESG sustainability factors of performance, risk, and disclosure that affect public companies' governance, people, planet, and prosperity. These metrics also determine a company's compliance with and contributions to achieving the Sustainable Development Goals (SDGs) that the United Nations has promoted. These recommendations and related metrics reflect the insights of many regulators, standard-setters, and professional organizations promoting business sustainability and its ESG components. The recommendations encourage companies to report on their core ESG metrics using a "disclose or explain" approach by focusing on a "materiality test" of reporting ESG information that is material, important, and relevant to achieving profit-with-purpose in creating long-term shared value for all stakeholders.

Profit-with-purpose strategies consist of a range of approaches that businesses can adopt to accomplish financial success while having some social and environmental impacts. Business organizations can adopt metrics relevant to (1) governance issues, including corporate purpose; shared value, quality of governing body; composition, competencies, and diversity of the board of directors and board committees; stakeholder engagement and participation; and ethical behavior and practices of all corporate governance; (2) people: core values including dignity and equality (diversity, inclusion, and fair compensation); skills for the future (training hours and expenses); health and safety and well-being; (3) planet concerns including climate change and climate-related financial disclosures; freshwater availability; nature loss;

and (4) prosperity issues including earnings quality and quantity; employment and wealth generation, innovation and growth through offering the best products and services.

Business sustainability requires business organizations to expand their mission to generate profit, create shareholder value, and ensure shared value for all stakeholders. The concept of shared value challenges how we think about profits, the planet, people, philanthropy, sustainability, and development. Sustainable shared value creation enables business organizations to integrate financial ESP with non-financial ESG into business culture and corporate environment. Shared value creation for all stakeholders can be achieved when business organizations advance their competitiveness in improving the quality and quantity of earnings and, thus, financial returns for shareholders while contributing to the well-being of employees, customers, suppliers, society, the environment, and the communities in which they operate.[9] Shared value creation with the profit-with-purpose mission for business organizations requires: (1) producing products and services that are not detrimental to society and the environment, increase shareholder wealth, and meet customers and societal needs; (2) improving productivity in the supply chain by investing in training and resources to create high-quality products and enhance ESP and ESG sustainability performance; (3) developing key performance indicators to effectively measure and report revenue, costs, and value of the organizations; and (4) periodically accessing the selected KPIs and related matrices.

Purpose determines why the organization exists, its mission, who the stakeholders are, and its objectives and strategies for achieving the objectives. The main objective function of any business organization has been and continues to be creating shared value for all stakeholders, including shareholders, creditors, customers, suppliers, employees, government, society, and the environment. Changes in business organizations' purpose, mission, objectives, and strategies need to be assessed and modified by focusing on achieving sustainable financial-economic and non-financial ESG sustainability performance.

Traditionally, business organizations and their boards of directors and executives have focused mainly on the bottom line of maximizing profit for investors under the shareholder primacy model. In recent years, public companies have moved toward the mission of profit-with-purpose in creating shared value for all stakeholders. The Business Roundtable (BRT), in August 2019, released a new Statement on the Purpose of a Corporation that promotes the move toward ESG sustainability of creating shared value creation for all stakeholders.[10] The concept of purpose suggests that business organizations should determine their mission of creating shared value for all stakeholders, including employees, customers, suppliers, society, and the environment, as a fundamental reason for their existence.

The statement of purpose should include the mission, which reflects the organization's determination to stay with its purpose and its short-, medium-, and long-term achievement. Companies are now adopting the corporate mission of profit with the purpose of creating shared value for all stakeholders by shifting their goals to create shareholder value while fulfilling their social, environmental, and governance responsibilities. The statement of purpose should also define objectives, which have sustainably changed in the post-COVID-19 pandemic to survival in the short term, continuity in the medium term, and sustainability in the long term. The board of directors pays more attention to the well-being, safety, and health of their employees, customers, and suppliers. In collaboration with management, the board of directors should also design strategies to achieve new objectives by designing business continuity plans, deliberate decisions, and crisis management.

Improving the quality of ESG disclosures requires a close look at the transparency of the financial information and the perceptions of the short- and long-term strategies related to addressing these material risks and opportunities. Deloitte suggests that companies must navigate societal and environmental trends to begin integrating ESG into their business while preparing transparent and high-quality ESG disclosures. The key steps for ESG integration and disclosure strategy include governance and organizational structure, benchmarking and roadmap development, materiality assessment, integration into strategy, data and process management, target setting and alignment with business goals, internal audit and external assurance, and disclosure preparation.[11] The public and investors are demanding enhancements to sustainability disclosure and ESG accountability. To answer the call to transparency, companies should develop a robust governance structure, further integrate internal audits and boards of directors, and obtain external assurance to improve the related disclosure of information and ultimately reduce risks related to omitted or misleading disclosures.

Claudia Saran, the Vice Chair of Culture at KPMG US, states that CEOs should intensely focus on work culture, values, and purpose during this time of high pressure. According to the KPMG survey, the biggest group of CEOs (25%) believed that connecting their brand with a compelling corporate purpose was their organization's most important reputational factor.[12] Other companies, such as PricewaterhouseCoopers, find that their significant progress on upskilling their employees will lead to progress on building their employee engagement, resulting in improved efficiency, lower employee turnover, and higher employee job satisfaction, which, in effect, means a stronger workforce.[13] This upskilling has been proven to breed confidence in the company's sustainability. CEOs of more advanced upskilling organizations were optimistic about economic growth, with 34% expecting improvement versus 15% from the previous survey. These CEOs also have more confidence in their revenue growth, with 38% being "very confident" versus 20% from the previous survey.

Further, an EY survey found that culture and trust have become the top critical factors in shaping the future of corporate reports. According to the EY Financial Accounting Advisory Services (FAAS) global corporate reporting survey, the majority of finance leaders (79%) say that they have the data volumes today to give stakeholders the insight they want into company culture; however, only 37% report quantifiable key performance indicators (KPIs) in this area.[14] Some say corporate reporting may need a "culture shock," highlighting the need for more transparency and actionable insights for investors and shareholders. The EY report advises businesses to put a robust approach to culture reporting in place, invest in a talent mix to drive change and build trust, and install ethical algorithms into AI that can provide the insights the investors increasingly require.[15]

Business organizations should adopt long-term sustainable strategies of focusing on the profit-with-purpose mission of creating shared value for all stakeholders. The board of directors should review management's vision and decision for long-term sustainable strategic planning and the direction in areas of operational, investment, and financing activities, including investments in technology, manufacturing plans, research and development, and workforce training and other initiatives to ensure safety, health, and well-being of employees, suppliers, and customers in the aftermath of the COVID-19 pandemic. Business purpose should be integrated into long-term strategic planning and provide benchmarks against which performance is evaluated, and decisions are made. Business organizations should communicate their mission of profit-with-purpose through the means of:

1. The revised article of incorporation with profit-with-purpose statement.
2. A letter to shareholders by the chair of the board of directors that clearly states the purpose statement and strategic sustainability planning.
3. Management discussion and analysis (MD&A) report showing management commitment to achieving profit-with-purpose through strategic sustainability planning.
4. Corporate website under the general heading of business sustainability.
5. Corporate public filings such as Form 10K, 10Q, and proxy statements.

BlackRock Investment Stewardship suggests the following topics to be addressed in the statement of strategy, purpose, and culture:[16]

1. The evolution of the company's strategic framework and the drivers of such (e.g., changing customer needs, resources/input constraints, industry dynamics, and global megatrends).
2. The definition of a "long-term" strategic plan and whether that time frame is most appropriate.
3. The board's engagement in strategy, purpose, and culture and its oversight function of overseeing and approving management's implementation of the agreed plans and policies.
4. The strategic milestones against which shareholders should assess long-term strategic performance.
5. Employee engagement in shaping strategy, purpose, and culture and the feedback in improving its implementation.
6. Assessment of the compatibility of the company's culture, purpose, and strategy by the board of directors and management.

7. Alignment of the short-term dynamics in the business with the long-term strategy.
8. Short-term pressures on the company and how management and the board deal with them for a long-term focus.

Over the past five years, support for ESG shareholder resolutions has increased from 27% to 46% across 50 large fund families. Of these groups, 15 fund groups expanded their support in 2019 by more than 20% over their previous four-year averages. In 2015, only 12 of these fund groups supported the ESG-shareholder proposals and resolutions. These numbers include 11 fund groups that supported more than 75% of ESG proposals 2019.[17] Five of the ten largest fund families, including Vanguard, BlackRock, American Funds, T. Rowe Price, and DFA Funds offered by Dimensional Fund Advisors, voted against more than 88% of ESG-related shareholder resolutions.[18] The effects of these large fund groups voting against ESG-related shareholder resolutions and improvements have kept many initiatives from achieving support and becoming a reality.

II.2 Best Practices of Sustainability-Driven Profit-with-Purpose

The effective achievement of both ESP and ESG sustainability performance necessitates properly establishing and implementing the concept of profit-with-purpose. Companies that have defined their statement of purpose have more incentives to disclose ESP and ESG sustainability performance information by issuing sustainability reports. The recent 2020 KPMG survey covers key global trends in sustainability reporting as relevant to reporting on the risks of biodiversity loss, reporting on climate-related risk and carbon reduction, and reporting on the UN Sustainable Development Goals (SDGs). The 2020 KPMG survey specifically suggests that:[19]

1. Many countries have seen dramatic shifts in the number of companies reporting on sustainability, driven not only by new laws and regulations but also by a growing understanding in the finance sector of ESG issues' power to impact financial performance and corporate value.
2. Sustainability reporting is now so nearly universally adopted that the small minority of companies not yet reporting will find themselves seriously out of step with global norms.
3. This survey also makes it increasingly apparent that risk is the new lens through which to consider sustainability or ESG. Changing attitudes to climate change have been the key drivers behind this trend.
4. Attitudes towards the financial risks of climate change in the financial and corporate sectors have changed beyond recognition. Climate change is only the first of a series of sustainability or ESG issues that will be perceived as financial risks and opportunities.

5. Social issues such as child labor, forced labor, working conditions, diversity and equality, fair pay, and more will soon take on the same financial relevance. The survey suggests reporting on biodiversity should be a key priority for any business, particularly those operating in high-risk sectors.
6. The business leaders should focus on biodiversity and understand how their company contributes to biodiversity loss and the related risks.
7. The number of 100 sustainability reporting rates in the Americas has increased by seven percentage points since 2017 to an impressive 90 percent of companies reporting.
8. Sustainability reporting in Asia Pacific has grown by six percentage points since 2017 to 84 percent.
9. The rate of sustainability reporting in Europe is at the same level in 2020 as in 2017 (77 percent).
10. In the Middle East and Africa, sustainability reporting increased by seven percentage points, with South Africa (96 percent) and Nigeria (85 percent) remaining strong.

Business companies should follow the guidelines of the "Statement of Purpose" released by the Business Roundtable (BRT) and assess whether they have adequately adopted a clear corporate purpose that focuses on their long-term strategic goals, implemented ESG policies and practices that advance those goals, have communicated those goals and objectives effectively and have held their board of directors and executives responsible for achieving the stated purposes. The updated BRT Statement on the Purpose of a Corporation declares that companies should not only serve their shareholders but also deliver value to their customers, invest in employees, deal fairly with suppliers, and support the communities in which they operate.[20] Stakeholders, including shareholders, should demand a clear statement of purpose and raise their concerns directly with the Company's directors and officers. The European Union is updating the EU Non-financial Reporting Directive and is considering developing non-financial reporting standards. The World Economic Forum has released its paper on common metrics and consistent reporting for sustainable value creation, defining 21 core metrics.

The five major non-financial reporting organizations (GRI, SASB, IIRC, CDSB, and CDP) have published a "Statement of Intent," committing to work together towards comprehensive corporate reporting. Following GRI Global Sustainability Standards relevant to performance indicators, corporations should: (1) develop goals around ESG performance, sourcing raw materials and inputs for production, health or social impacts, employee safety, training, diversity, safety, health, and well-being of employees; (2) emphasize customers and suppliers by generating product innovations that lead to positive environmental compliance with ethical principles and human rights standards; and (3) take community initiatives in health and well-being, education, employment, and economic empowerment. The GRI has three new topic standards on tax, occupational health and safety, and water and effluents.

The tax standard promotes transparency on tax contributions by enabling companies to report tax payments country-by-county alongside their management approach to tax. The second new topic addresses occupational health and safety management, which includes a central focus on the safety and well-being of employees, especially during the challenges of the COVID-19 pandemic. Finally, the third new topic considers how water is managed, including impacts on local communities and gives a full picture of water usage from withdrawal to consumption and discharge.[21]

The International Financial Reporting Standards (IFRS) Foundation's consultation on establishing a global non-financial reporting framework has already received strong support from other organizations.[22] The IFRS, in consultation with a cross-section of stakeholders involved in development sustainability reporting, including global policymakers, regulators, standard-setters, investors, businesses, auditing firms, and other service providers, is promoting business sustainability and sustainability reporting. The IFRS, while realizing that sustainability is gaining considerable attention and sustainability reporting continues to be important and relevant, acknowledges there are differences in the scope and nature of sustainability reports, and thus, it calls for improvements in standardization, comparability, and consistency in sustainability reporting. The IFRS concludes that a set of globally accepted, consistent, and comparable accounting and assurance standards is needed to foster public trust and investor confidence in sustainability performance information. This move toward reliable, relevant, and transparent sustainability performance information enables business organizations to focus on achieving their profit-with-purpose mission. Indeed, the following best practices of ESP and ESG sustainability with a keen focus on the concept of profit-with-purpose are gaining considerable attention and acceptance:

- **Purpose statement**: Develop a concise and clear corporate purpose statement with a keen focus on the profit-with-purpose mission and ensure that the statement of purpose is broadly communicated and understood across the organization. There is a renewed interest in the company's purpose in society and responsibility to all stakeholders, including producing the goods and services that meet basic needs, promote innovation, and are not detrimental to society and the environment.
- **Sustainability strategy**: Establish a sustainability strategy of achieving both financial ESP and non-financial ESG sustainability performance and shifting emphasis from shareholder primacy to stakeholder primacy to protect the interests of a broader set of stakeholders.
- **Priorities:** Identify ESP and ESG priorities for the business as a roadmap for achieving organizational goals and objectives. Accelerate interest in non-financial ESG performance and matters by addressing social issues, including racial diversity, inclusion and gender equality, and social justice.
- **Commitment and responsibility:** Set the tone at the top demonstrating commitment from the board of directors and executives to achieving the mission of profit-with-purpose.

- **Accountability:** Hold the board of directors, executives, and employees accountable for working toward achieving the profit-with-purpose mission. Promote the development of business models and accountability processes that address concerns about business continuity.
- **Governance:** Establish proper and effective governance measures for directors and executives to ensure the achievement of goals and objectives, focusing on the value of human capital and related improvements in the workplace.
- **Stakeholders:** Establish effective two-way communication channels with all stakeholders, including shareholders, customers, suppliers, employees, and others.
- **Measure both ESP and ESG performance:** Establish key performance indicators (KPIs) for properly measuring, recognizing, and reporting sustainability performance information.
- **Communications:** Provide a uniform, consistent ESP and ESG narrative, and tell your sustainability stories and messaging across all communication channels with all stakeholders.
- **Sustainability rating and ranking:** Ensure that sustainability ranking and rating organizations include your sustainability matrices in their indexes.

III. SUSTAINABLE SHARED VALUE CREATION

There has been a shift in recent decades from creating shareholder value to developing "sustainable shared value creation" to protect the interests of all stakeholders.[23] Shared value is defined as "policies and practices that enhance a company's competitiveness while advancing the economic and social conditions in the communities in which it operates."[24] Under the shared value creation concept, the board of directors' fiduciary responsibility is extended to all stakeholders in protecting their interests. Management focuses on the continuous performance improvement of business operations in generating long-term value for shareholders while maximizing the positive impacts of operations on society and the environment. Operational performance is measured in terms of both financial ESP and non-financial ESG sustainability performance. Thus, corporate objectives have advanced from profit maximization to increasing shareholder wealth and creating shared value for all stakeholders.

Management should manage multidimensional aspects of sustainability performance, which could be viewed as complementary or conflicting as the interests of shareholders may not be congruent with those of other stakeholders. Thus, management approaches to sustainability can vary among organizations in creating the right balance between apparent conflicts of interest among stakeholders. Investors and public companies now focus on financial ESP and long-term market performance indicators such as long-term stock prices, return on investment, return on assets, earnings growth, and research and development. Recently, KPMG uploaded their *Market Insights Survey* to demonstrate efforts toward value creation in private equity firms. Several insights were discovered in this survey. Only a few private equity firms have reached their potential in terms of their investment value. Value creation continues to impact businesses and their decision-making. Improved analytics help drive deal processes. The top metrics/levers for value creation involve innovation and people ("buy and build" and "people and talent investment"). Private equity firms utilize external advising at earlier stages to maximize investment value. Over 70% of ESG factors get evaluated at the start of evaluating deals and during the due diligence and investment decision-making process. [25]

Academic research suggests that ESP is crucial in creating shareholder value by finding that firms with better ESP exhibit better financial and market performance and lower cost of equity, and that link between ESP and cost of equity is more pronounced in the presence of ESG.[26] However, the 2020 global COVID-19 pandemic crisis has caused a significant decline in CEO confidence in global growth within their companies, around one-third (32%), whereas only 17% are less confident in the future of their company altogether. The crisis has accelerated digital growth for most of the responses, as 75% say that thepandemic has accelerated the creation of a seamless digital customer experience, with over 1 in 5 (22%) of those saying progress "has sharply accelerated, putting us years in advance of where we expected to be."[27] As companies plan for their strategic shift for long-term growth, many business leaders are now recognizing a shortage in talent which is affecting workforce productivity. Talent risk was rated at 2% in 2019 but shot up to 21% in July/August of 2020, which makes it the highest risk to most businesses, according to their CEOs.[28]

In shared value creation, stakeholders are classified as internal stakeholders, shareholders, and employees with direct interest (stake) and bear risks associated with business activities and other external stakeholders. Other stakeholders, including creditors, customers, and suppliers, have reciprocal relationships and interactions with a firm because they contribute to firm value creation (stake), and their well-being is affected by the firm's activities (risk). Stakeholder interests in a firm are equity capital, human capital, social capital, compliance capital, and reputational capital, as presented in Chapter 6. Stakeholders' sustainability-related risks are strategic, financial, operational, compliance, and reputational risks, as presented in Chapter 7. Agency theory in defining the relationship between the agent (management) and principals (shareholders) has traditionally been the dominant theory of corporate finance, management, and governance research in creating shareholder value.[29] While agency theory has been used to explain the principal–agent relationship and interest divergence for individualistic utility maximization and motivation, this theory may be irrelevant and undesirable under the emerging complex organization structure oriented toward stakeholders and the corporate strategy of shared value creation. Under stakeholder and stewardship theories, management, considering interests (stakes) and risks to shareholders (its main and direct stakeholders), may engage in non-financial ESG sustainability performance activities to protect non-shareholding stakeholders' interests and ensure firm legitimacy and reputation.[30]

Shared value creation can be promoted within the wealth-maximization framework and implemented in the context of welfare maximization in pursuing the goal of profit-with-purpose for corporations that protect the interests of all stakeholders. Corporations can balance wealth and wealth maximization for shareholders under the shareholder primacy concept while achieving welfare maximization for all stakeholders (e.g., safety, health, and well-being of employees, suppliers, and customers) under the stakeholder primacy concept. The concept of impact investing, focusing on the importance and relevance of corporate investment strategies in creating the desired returns on investment for shareholders and providing positive social and environmental impacts, is gaining acceptance. Business organizations must attain sustainable financial performance and have positive and measurable effects on the environment and society. Positive effects on the environment, communities, and society can be achieved when corporations invest in ESG activities, which may require allocating scarce resources that could otherwise be used to maximize firms' financial and economic performance. The board of directors and executives are important in promoting business sustainability performance, assessing and managing continuity and sustainability risk, and properly disclosing sustainability information in an integrated sustainability report.

III.1 Move Toward a Shared Value Creation Concept

There has been a global move toward shared value creation for all stakeholders in the past two decades, either under the mandatory ESG initiatives in Europe and Asia or the voluntary ESG initiatives in the United States. For example, large European companies have been required to disclose their ESG activities that reflect information on shared value creation for all stakeholders since the 2017 annual report. In August 2019, the Business Roundtable (BRT) announced adopting a new Statement on the Purpose of a Corporation, signed by 181 high-profile chief executive officers (CEOs), promoting sustainability by creating shared value for all stakeholders.[31] Many business organizations have voluntarily considered the BRT Statement in the past year in creating shared value for their stakeholders. The BRT Statement emphasizes the significance of shareholders in business development, the need for companies to maintain values for shareholders in the long run, and the need to protect the interests of other stakeholders such as customers, employees, and communities.

A major concern is whether BRT CEOs want to change stakeholder governance to avoid accountability. There are also concerns regarding political and social objectives in the BRT Statement and whether business organizations should consider societal goals higher than shareholders. Nonetheless, the BRT statement does not prioritize societal objectives over shareholders. The BRT statement just acknowledges the importance of meeting the expectations of a wider range of stakeholders to maintain the company's "long-term success." Thus, the BRT Statement does not require CEOs to consider a major change in the way they operate their business and take care of their shareholders. Indeed, the Statement suggests public companies pay attention to all stakeholders, including shareholders, to create and maintain sustainable performance and maximize shared value for all stakeholders. The BRT Statement suggests moving away from the shareholder primacy concept toward the stakeholder primacy concept that promotes sustainability and creates shared value for all stakeholders.[32] Corporate purpose and stakeholder considerations have gained recognition in the business community worldwide. Stakeholder primacy challenges companies to put stakeholders at the heart of their purpose. There has been a shift in corporate purpose from shareholder primacy to stakeholder primacy, reinforced by the US Business Roundtable's Statement on the Purpose of a Corporation. This focus is combined with public pressure for CEOs to engage on social and political topics (e.g., human capital, diversity, immigration, gun control, gender pay equity).

The interests and values of shareholders play a crucial role in value creation. On November 2, 2021, the Securities and Exchange Commission put out a bulletin concerning the processes for proposals for shareholder consideration in Rule 14a-8 and the exceptions to the rule. One exception was Rule 14a-8(i)(7), also known as the "ordinary business" exception, which excludes proposals relating to a business's ordinary operations to keep that at the discretion of management and the board of directors. Another exception is Rule 14a-8(i)(5), also known as the "economic relevance" exception, which excludes proposals that affect operations that account for less than 5% of the company's total assets and/or net income or gross revenue. Another rule concerning 14a-8 was Rule 14-a8(d), which requires proposals and supporting statements to be 500 or fewer words.[33]

Bain and Company outlined information in their 2021 Global Private Equity Report about the growing importance of ESG initiatives in private equity firms. ESG is paramount to improving shareholder value and reducing risk. According to the report, Europe is leading the world in valuing global standards in sustainability. It found 80% of European funds were committed to Principles for Responsible Investment, Net-Zero Asset Owner Alliance, or Task Force on Climate-related Financial Disclosures. In the last few years, the highest EcoVadis scores for Europe and the US centered around the ESG categories of environment, labor/human rights, and ethics. The report took data from various stakeholders, including customers, employees, partners, creditors, and regulators. The report also outlines methods companies can take in order to have successful ESG initiative execution. This includes a clear and focused direction of where companies want to go, complete integration from top to bottom, and continuous building upon results.[34]

Several examples of the new purpose mission for high-profile companies are BP, International Paper, Microsoft, and FedEx, among others. For example, in its 2019 annual report, BP defines its corporate mission as "Energy with Purpose," "Our purpose is reimagining energy for people and our planet," and "We want to help the world reach net zero and improve people's lives." In its 2019 annual report, the Swedish private equity firm EQT defines its statement of purpose as "To future-proof companies and make a positive impact, To be the most reputable investor and owner" with the mission of "With the best talent and network around the world, EQT uses a thematic investment strategy and distinctive value creation approach to future-proof companies, creating superior returns to EQT's investors and making a positive impact with everything we do." Corporations are moving toward purpose strategies that drive value for all stakeholders. With these emerging "profit-with-purpose" missions, the finance function led by the CFO is an integrated strategic unit, leading operating and finance activities and performance, to achieve specific financial and performance reporting objectives that can be measured, held accountable, and rewarded. Aforementioned evidence suggests the following attributes of shared value creation:

1. Set the tone at the top by the board of directors in promoting stakeholder primacy and shared value creation models by signing the statement of purpose pledging to operate their business in the interests of all stakeholders, including shareholders, employees, suppliers, customers, and communities. This can be achieved by having a sustainability-centric board, a director interested in ESG sustainability, and/or a sustainability board committee.
2. Extract commitment by senior executives, including the CEO and CFO, to sustainability and stakeholder primacy with a shared value focus. This can be achieved by either linking executive compensation to sustainability achievement and/or creating the executive position of the Chief Sustainability Officer.
3. Opt-in as a benefit corporation with a specified purpose statement in the corporate charter of incorporation.

Several companies have been transparent with their considerations of ESG and its relation to their business operations. BlackRock has recently published its efforts to create sustainable value for its consumers and shareholders in its *Investment Stewardship Report.*[35] They want to give their client good returns on their investment by engaging with other companies on value creation, voting to further clients' interests, and being open and honest in their activities. When engaging with other companies to create value for customers and stakeholders, their priorities are good quality leadership, purposeful strategy, incentives, movements toward a low-carbon economy, and social impacts.[36] PwC outlined in its December 2021 issue of year-end reporting from the Governance Insights Center the impact that sustainability has on financial statements. Audit committees must analyze the impacts of companies' strategies to decrease carbon emissions and other sustainability efforts. PwC outlined various risks with climate direct management planning, which affect financial conditions reflected in financial statements.[37]

III.2 The Role of the Board of Directors in Shared Value Creation

The board's role in shared value creation under stakeholder primacy/capitalism as opposed to shareholder primacy/capitalism is to oversee the managerial function of achieving the long-term ESP and ESG sustainability performance and effectively communicating sustainability performance information to all stakeholders. The board should be vigilant and understand the stakeholders'; objectives and rationales for focusing on sustainability factors of performance, risk and disclosure, managerial, strategic planning, sustainable operational performance, and executive compensation in promoting long-term corporate value. The board should also provide oversight, insight, and foresight function on the achievement of both financial ESP and non-financial environmental, social, governance, (ESG) sustainability performance driven by financial, human, social, environmental, and manufacturing capitals as well as innovation, culture, corporate governance. The board of directors and senior executives, especially the CFO, play an important role in promoting business sustainability performance, assessing and managing sustainability risk, and properly disclosing sustainability information in an integrated sustainability report.

The primary oversight function of the board of directors remains in protecting the interests of multi-stakeholders during this challenging time and appointing competent, responsible, accountable, and ethical executives, including CEOs, CFOs, and other C-suite executives, to manage the business for the benefit of all stakeholders. It is expected that boards of directors engage more proactively in the oversight of strategic priorities in dealing with global economic and political uncertainties and challenges caused by the COVID-19 pandemic and the potential risk of substantial interruptions in business operations and supply chains. The fiduciary duties of the board of directors are expected to be extended to multi-stakeholders, including shareholders, creditors, customers, suppliers, employees, government, society, and the environment with the move toward a profit-with-purpose mission. The expanded fiduciary duty to all stakeholders requires the board of directors to establish proactive, strategic profit-with-purpose missions, goals, and objectives to ensure business continuity and sustainability in creating long-term shared value and oversee managerial decisions and actions in effectively implementing these strategic goals.

The board of directors should set an appropriate tone of reserving and promoting the corporate culture of competency, integrity, and transparency. Revising and reinforcing the corporate purpose of protecting the interests of all stakeholders becomes more relevant and important to the board of directors. The board of directors should review and revisit executive compensation by creating the right balance between managerial efforts and compensation on surviving the COVID-19 pandemic and ensuring the safety, health, and well-being of employees, customers, suppliers, supply-chain partners, communities, shareholders, and other stakeholders. There should be a move away from the traditional fiduciary loyalty model of the board of directors to shareholders under the shareholder capitalism and shareholder primacy and a move toward the board fiduciary due to all stakeholders under the stakeholder capitalism and stakeholder primacy model. There is an alternative to changing corporate law on the fiduciary duties of the board of directors as it relates to board composition, adding the corporate purpose statement, and allowing non-shareholder stakeholders to be represented on the board.

III.3 Management Role Under Shared Value Concept

Management, as the steward of business resources, has the primary role of improving sustainability performance and managing related risks, maximizing utilization of all capital from strategic to financial, reputational, manufactured, human, social, and environmental to create shared value for all stakeholders. Second, business organizations' main goal and objective function is to maximize firm value. The goal of firm value maximization can be achieved through continuous improvements of both financial ESP and non-financial ESG sustainability performance. The ESP and ESG sustainability performance dimensions are interrelated and complement/complete each other, and thus, they should be integrated into supply chain management. Third, the focus of business sustainability should be on creating long-term and sustainable shared value for all stakeholders, including investors, creditors, suppliers, customers, employees, the environment, and society. Finally, companies should effectively and transparently communicate their business sustainability with all stakeholders by periodically releasing their sustainability reports.

Management should know what "the purpose" is. Every company should have its unique purpose determined in its charter of incorporation to maximize its positive impacts on all stakeholders, including society and the environment, and to minimize the negative impacts on multi-stakeholders. In case of the nonexistence of and/or inadequate statement of purpose, management should work with the other executives in the C-suite under the oversight function of the board of directors and approval by majority shareholders to establish an appropriate stakeholder-inclusive statement of purpose. Management should work effectively with other executives under the oversight function of the board of directors to implement and achieve the adopted statement of purpose. Finally, the CFO should collaborate with the CEO in preparing and certifying the integrated sustainability reports in disclosing the achievement of the adopted statement of purpose. This integrated sustainability report can disclose the achievement of both financial returns and social and environmental impacts. This integrated report enables shareholders and other stakeholders to learn about and assess the company's success in achieving its adopted purpose. This assessment can positively impact investor risk-premium and their willingness to invest in the company's stock. This is the only path forward toward stakeholder capitalism rather than societal socialism to achieve long-term, durable, and sustainable growth and performance. It is obvious that the challenge is not whether a statement of purpose is desirable and achievable, but the hurdle is whether high-profile corporate executives, including CEOs, CFOs, and institutional investors, collaborate to make it happen. Policymakers, investor activists, regulators, and rating agencies continuously monitor management, demanding real action on financial ESP and non-financial ESG sustainability performance goals and achievements. The time has passed for using sustainability as a greenwashing and branding tool for companies and their management for writing climate, sustainability, and diversity reports without firm commitments to pursue the mission of profit-with-purpose in creating shared value for all stakeholders. Management should be held accountable for failure to achieve ESP and ESG sustainability.

The board of directors should set an appropriate tone at the top, promoting the concept of profit-with-purpose, and overseeing managerial commitments, decisions, and actions in achieving financial ESP and non-financial ESG sustainability performance. Management should establish the following policies and procedures to obtain the profit-with-purpose mission:

- Develop a statement of purpose that is commonly acceptable by all stakeholders and is fair, transparent, and attainable.
- Design and implement the profit-with-purpose mission to achieve the adopted statement of purpose goal.
- Focus on achieving both financial ESP and non-financial ESG sustainability performance.
- Hold individuals throughout the organization accountable for contributing toward achieving the profit-with-purpose mission.
- Design sustainability metrics and effectively measure key performance indicators relevant to financial ESP and non-financial ESG sustainability performance.
- Prepare and disclose integrated sustainability reports presenting both financial ESP and non-financial ESG sustainability performance.
- Communicate the statement of purpose, the profit-with-purpose mission, and both financial ESP and non-financial ESG sustainability performance with all stakeholders.
- Tell the sustainability stories and both financial ESP and non-financial ESG accomplishments. Provide a consistent ESG narrative and messaging across all communications channels.

III.4 COVID-19 Pandemic Effects on the Shared Value Concept

The COVID-19 pandemic has been an exogenous shock in the global economy and capital market, substantially impacting individuals, organizations, and society. The pandemic has changed people's everyday lives, and new realities of economic shutdowns, business closures, social distancing, and individual lockdowns have created unique challenges for firms. Many countries have begun to reopen their economies and businesses by adopting a new normal. Daily activities and business practices have significantly adjusted to the "new normal" with new social distancing, remote working, virtual meetings, business office designs, business continuity, and transformation. The pandemic has had significant implications for people and organizations worldwide and has affected the sustainability of many business organizations. In the post-COVID-19 era, business organizations are now focusing on the shared value concept as they are more concerned about the safety, health, and well-being of their employees, customers, and suppliers relevant to human capital and business sustainability.

The COVID-19 pandemic has affected business sustainability and human capital and can impact shared value in several ways. First, the idea of remote work and the flexible work schedule has been in place for some time. It became a new normal during the COVID-19 pandemic, creating adaptive behaviors and new norms. Second, firms need to invest in human capital as technology in corporate governance has accelerated in the post-COVID-19 era, enabling remote work and virtual meetings. Finally, despite the devastating effects of the COVID-19 pandemic on human lives, the economy, and business operations, people and business organizations worldwide have demonstrated their resilience and determination to transform these challenges into opportunities by adopting a new normal that affects human capital and business sustainability. It is expected that firms pay more attention to their financial ESP as well as non-financial ESG sustainability performance, including human capital.

The COVID-19 pandemic has encouraged business organizations and their boards of directors and executives to take the following actions to create shared value for all stakeholders:

- Establish a renewed focus on and interest in the company's purpose in society in producing goods and services that meet the basic needs of customers in the aftermath of the COVID-19 pandemic.
- Ensure focus is on the safety, health, and well-being of their employees, customers, and suppliers.
- Shift emphasis from shareholder primacy to stakeholder primacy of protecting the interests of all stakeholders, including shareholders, creditors, employees, customers, suppliers, communities, society, and the environment.
- Focus on achieving financial economic sustainability performance to generate the desired rate of returns for shareholders while generating ESG sustainability performance in protecting the interests of all stakeholders.
- Pay attention to the value of human capital and related improvements in the nature of work and the workplace, addressing social issues, including issues of racial and gender equality and social justice.

IV. CONCLUSION

Business organizations worldwide now recognize the importance of shared value creation and sustainability performance and the link between financial ESP and non-financial ESG sustainability performance with the profit-with-purpose mission. Justifications for business sustainability are moral obligation, social responsibility, maintaining a good reputation, ensuring sustainability, environmental consciousness, licensing to operate, and creating shared value for all stakeholders. In creating shared value for all stakeholders, corporations identify potential social, environmental, governance, and ethical issues and integrate them into their strategic planning and supply chain management. There are many factors why a company should integrate sustainability performance into its supply chain management, including the pressure of the labor movement, the development of moral values and social standards, the development of business education, and the change in public opinion about the role of business, environmental matters, governance, and ethical scandals. Companies that are, or aspire to be, leaders in sustainability are challenged by raising public expectations, increasing innovation, continuous quality improvement, effective governance measures, high standards of ethics and integrity, and heightened social and environmental problems. The emerging mission of profit-with-purpose corporations suggests that public companies have the dual mission of profit-making function of creating shareholder value while protecting the interests of other stakeholders through their social benefit function. It appears there is a move away from pure shareholder primacy to stakeholder primacy of profit-with-purpose corporations. It appears that European and Asian companies are moving closer to the concept of stakeholder primacy with the profit-with-purpose mission than their counterparts in North America.

Globalization has provided incentives and opportunities for business organizations, stakeholders, and executives to influence their business sustainability initiatives and strategies and integrate them into their supply chain management. Corporations can choose from various sustainability initiatives and performances regarding the scope, extent, and type of sustainability strategies that focus on different issues, functions, areas, and supply chain management. The four integrated strategies of stewardship theory implication, continuous performance improvements, sustainable shared value creation, and sustainability performance reporting and assurance, can enable business organizations to achieve long-term success. Organizations of all types and sizes can integrate the suggested sustainability framework consisting of the stewardship theory implementation, continuous improvements of both ESP and ESG sustainability performance, shared value creation, and sustainability disclosures into their corporate culture business model to effectively achieve their missions and goals of creating shared value for all stakeholders.

V. TAKEAWAYS

- The main objective of business organizations has evolved from profit maximization to increasing shareholder wealth. This objective has changed in recent years, considering the recent developments in corporate governance and business sustainability, to create shared value for all stakeholders.
- To effectively achieve this new objective, corporations are expanding their performance to both financial/quantitative economic sustainability performance (ESP) and non-financial/qualitative environmental, social, and governance (ESG) sustainability performance.

- Companies are now adopting the corporate mission of profit with the purpose of creating shared value for all stakeholders by shifting their goals to create shareholder value while fulfilling their social, environmental, and governance responsibilities.
- Public companies must clearly define their purpose of creating shared value for all stakeholders.
- In collaboration with C-suite officers, the board of directors should publish a statement of purpose to create shared value for all stakeholders, which shareholders approve.
- Incorporate the profit-with-purpose concept into the article of incorporation.
- Accept the mission of profit-with-purpose in creating shared value for all stakeholders.
- Establish the right balance between making a profit for shareholders and generating social and environmental impacts.
- Focus on ensuring employees, customers, and suppliers' safety, health, and well-being in the aftermath of the 2020 COVID-19 pandemic.

Notes

1 Much of the discussion in this chapter comes from Rezaee, Z. July 2021. *Business Sustainability: Profit-With- Purpose Focus*. Business Expert Press.

2 Business Roundtable (BRT). August 19, 2019. Statement on the Purpose of a Corporation. Available at https://opportunity.businessroundtable.org/wp-content/uploads/2019/09/BRT-Statement-on-the-Purpose-of-a-Corporation-with-Signatures-1.pdf

3 Sjafiell, Beate and Mahonen, Jukka. April 12, 2022. "Corporate Purpose and the EU Corporate Sustainability Due Diligence Proposal." The ECGI Blog.

4 Dubois, Edouard and Saribas, Ali. 2020. "Making Corporate Purpose Tangible – A Survey of Investors." Harvard Law School Forum on Corporate Governance. Available at https://corpgov.law.harvard.edu/2020/06/19/making-corporate-purpose-tangible-a-survey-of-investors/

5 Ibid.

6 Benoit, Robe, Delaunay, and Dunn. June 8, 2019. "French Legislation on Corporate Purpose." Harvard Law School Forum on Corporate Governance. Available at https://corpgov.law.harvard.edu/2019/06/08/french-legislation-on-corporate-purpose/

7 Ibid.

8 World Economic Forum (WEF). September 2020. *Measuring Stakeholder Capitalism Towards Common Metrics and Consistent Reporting of Sustainable Value Creation*. White Paper. Available at https://www.wlrk.com/docs/WEF_IBC_Measuring_Stakeholder_Capitalism_Report_2020.pdf

9 Porter, M. E. and Kramer, M. R. 2011. "Creating Shared Value," *Harvard Business Review* January–February, 62–77.

10 Business Roundtable (BRT). August 19, 2019. Statement on the Purpose of a Corporation. Available at https://opportunity.businessroundtable.org/wp-content/uploads/2019/09/BRT-Statement-on-the-Purpose-of-a-Corporation-with-Signatures-1.pdf

11 Inna Vodovoz, Christine Robinson, and Kristen Sullivan. September 22, 2020. "DeloittESGnow – Enhancing Trust in ESG Disclosures." *Heads Up* Vol. 27, No. 20. Available at https://dart.deloitte.com/USDART/home/publications/deloitte/heads-up/2020/deloittESGnow-enhancing-trust-in-esg

12 KPMG. 2020. Culture and Purpose. "How Honorably Companies Navigate their Businesses Through the Pandemic." Available at https://home.kpmg/us/en/home/insights/2020/09/culture-purpose.html

13 PwC. 2020. Talent Trends. "Upskilling: Building Confidence in an Uncertain World." Available at https://www.pwc.com/gx/en/ceo-survey/2020/trends/pwc-talent-trends-2020.pdf

14 EY. 2019. EY Survey Finds Culture and Trust have Become Critical Priorities that Will Shape Future Corporate Reports. Available at https://www.ey.com/en_gl/news/2019/12/ey-survey-finds-culture-and-trust-have-become-critical-priorities-that-will-shape-future-corporate-reports

15 Ibid.

16 BlackRock. 2018. *Investment Stewardship's Approach to Engagement on Long-term Strategy, Purpose, and Culture*. Available at https://www.blackrock.com/corporate/literature/publication/blk-annual-stewardship-report-2018.pdf.

17 Cook, Jackie and Jon Hale. March 23, 2020. *2019 ESG Proxy Voting Trends by 50 U.S. Fund Families*. Available at https://corpgov.law.harvard.edu/2020/03/23/2019-esg-proxy-voting-trends-by-50-u-s-fund-families/

18 Ibid.

19 KPMG. 2020. *The Time Has Come: The KPMG Survey of Sustainability Reporting 2020*. Available at https://assets.kpmg/content/dam/kpmg/xx/pdf/2020/11/the-time-has-come.pdf

20 Business Roundtable. 2020. "One Year Later: Purpose of a Corporation." Available at https://purpose.businessroundtable.org/

21 GRI. January 13, 2021. "Three GRI Standards Come into Effect for Sustainability Reports in 2021." Available at https://www.globalreporting.org/about-gri/news-center/2021-01-13-three-gri-standards-come-into-effect-for-sustainability-reports-in-2021/

22 The International Financial Reporting Standards (IFRS) Foundation. September 2020. *Consultation Paper on Sustainability Reporting*. Available at https://cdn.ifrs.org/-/media/project/sustainability-reporting/consultation-paper-on-sustainability-reporting.pdf

23 Porter, M. E. and Kramer, M. R. 2011. "Creating Shared Value," *Harvard Business Review* January–February, 62–77.

24 Ibid.

25 KPMG. 2022. *Delivering on the Promise of Value Creation. 2022 Market Insights Survey*. https://assets.kpmg/content/dam/kpmg/xx/pdf/2022/03/delivering-on-the-promise-of-value-creation.pdf

26 Ng, A.C. and Rezaee, Z. 2015. Business Sustainability Performance and Cost of Equity Capital. *Journal of Corporate Finance* Vol. 34, 128–149.

27 KPMG. 2020. "Long-term Growth Amid Talent and Digital Issues." Available at https://home.kpmg/xx/en/home/insights/2020/09/ceo-are-building-a-path-to-long-term-growth-for-their-businesses.html

28 Ibid.

29 Rezaee, Z and T. Fogarty. 2019. *Business Sustainability, Corporate Governance, Organizational Ethics*. John Wiley and Sons, Inc. New Jersey, United States.

30 Ibid.
31 Business Roundtable (BRT). August 19, 2019. Statement on the Purpose of a Corporation. Available at https://opportunity.businessroundtable.org/wp-content/uploads/2019/09/BRTStatement-on-the-Purpose-of-a-Corporation-with-Signatures-1.pdf
32 Ibid.
33 US Securities and Exchange Commission. 3 November 2021. Shareholder Proposals: Staff Legal Bulletin No. 14L (CF). Division of Corporation Finance Securities and Exchange Commission. Available at https://www.sec.gov/corpfin/staff-legal-bulletin-14l-shareholder-proposals?
34 Seeman, Axel, Hardcastle, Dale, Diers, Deike, and Han, Jacqueline. 1 March 1, 2021. *The Expanding Case for ESG in Private Equity. Global Private Equity Report.* Bain and Company. https://www.bain.com/insights/esg-investing-global-private-equity-report-2021/
35 BlackRock. 2021. *Pursuing Long-term Value for our Clients. BlackRock Investment Stewardship: A Look into the 2020–2021 Proxy Voting Year.* Available at https://www.blackrock.com/corporate/insights/investment-stewardship
36 BlackRock. February 2024. *BlackRock Investment Stewardship: Engagement Priorities.* Available at https://www.blackrock.com/corporate/literature/publication/blk-stewardship-priorities-final.pdf
37 PwC. December 2021. *Approaching the 2021 Year-End Financial Reporting Season: Your Guide to Year-End Reporting Developments.* Governance Insights Charter.

Chapter 4

Business Sustainability Strategic Plans

I. INTRODUCTION

The role of business corporations in our society has evolved from profit maximization to increasing shareholder wealth and, in recent years, to creating shared value for all stakeholders. Firm performance is measured in terms of financial economic sustainability performance (ESP) and related financial metrics and by the mechanisms in which business success and sustainability are determined in terms of non-financial environmental, social, and governance (ESG) sustainability performance as discussed in Chapter 1. Business sustainability encourages management to establish synergy and congruence between short-term planning to make a profit and long-term planning to ensure continuity of operation and integrate sustainability into the business environment, corporate culture, and strategic plans to generate earnings and social and environmental impacts. Business sustainability factors of planning, performance, risk, and disclosure were introduced in Chapter 1, which considers activities that generate financial ESP and non-financial ESG sustainability performance to maximize firm value and create shared value for all stakeholders. This chapter attempts to build a bridge between short-term and long-term planning by focusing on internal sustainability information systems and external sustainability initiatives and requirements, as these two functions are interrelated and interdependent. This chapter provides insights into managerial initiatives for advancing business sustainability from greenwashing and business branding to creating opportunities for revenue generation with social and environmental impacts affecting cost management, supply chain, business growth, products and services innovation, and shared value

DOI: 10.4324/9781003437949-4

creation for all stakeholders. Integrated short-term and long-term planning for business sustainability suggests that a firm must extend its focus beyond maximizing short-term shareholder profit by considering the impact of its operations on the long-term interests of all stakeholders, including shareholders, creditors, customers, employees, the community, society, and the environment.

II. STRATEGIC SUSTAINABILITY PLANNING

Business sustainability requires adopting strategies and practices that contribute to short-, medium-, and long-term financial ESP and non-financial ESG sustainability performance, focusing on economic viability. Business organizations are criticized for focusing on short-term profit maximization for their investors with minimal attention to the long-term strategic sustainable planning of generating sustainable financial and non-financial performance. Sustainability is a process that should be integrated into the business environment and corporate culture to create sustainable shared value, to protect the interests of all stakeholders with a keen focus on the strategic planning of developing a profit-with-purpose mission. Under the strategic shared value creation concept, management focuses on the continuous performance improvement of business operations in creating long-term value while maximizing the positive impacts of operations on society, communities, and the environment by measuring sustainable performance in terms of both ESP and ESG sustainability performance. Thus, corporate objectives have advanced from profit maximization to increasing shareholder wealth and strategic sustainability of creating shared value for all stakeholders.

Sustainability strategic planning has short-term and long-term implications. When companies have a short-term mindset, they are primarily focused on maximizing profits and increasing shareholder wealth. The ideas managers work through are how to keep sales costs down or keep sales up. This can often come at the expense of choosing environmentally friendly products or manufacturing processes. This can also come at the expense of more ethical business practices. If managers can bypass those factors to cut costs and generate more sales, it is more likely to happen if they are incorporating a short-term vision. This short-term vision will allow businesses to continue their operations for the foreseeable future and generate profits in a way that will allow employees to be adequately compensated and shareholders to continue receiving dividends. Taken together, short-term practices maximizing short-term reported performance are detrimental to long-term investment, research and development, training, and other sustainable, value-enhancing corporate activities. Thus, the focus on short-term considerations has an adverse impact on long-term and sustainable shareholder value creation and reduces the expected value of future returns and, thus, the current share price. Stocks can be priced lower than their potential value by overemphasizing short-term considerations, encouraging asset managers to trade more frequently, and forcing long-term investors to become short-changed.

Consequences of short-term considerations (short-termism) are a divergence of resources from contributing to economic growth and ineffective misallocation of resources in several ways, including: (1) sacrificing, delaying, or decreasing discretionary spending on long-term investments or projects to achieve short-term financial targets that meet financial market expectations; (2) gearing management's time and efforts toward meeting expectations of short-term results rather than focusing on activities that add sustainable value to the company; (3) encouraging earnings management by either deferring costs or shifting revenues; (4) tying excessive executive compensation to the achievement of short-term financial targets at the expense of sustainable economic value creation; (5) higher risk premiums resultant from frequent trading by speculators who target short-term movement in stock prices; (6) incurring expenses by mutual funds because of overactive trading caused by focus on short-term considerations; and (7) delaying investment in sustainability initiatives. This short-termism undermines the sustainable economic performance of many companies by encouraging management to emphasize short-term financial performance with little or no focus on the sustainability of economic performance and its impacts on people, planet, and society measured in terms of ESG sustainability performance. Sustainability reporting, on the other hand, reduces pressures on management from the market to meet short-term targets and thus has the potential to affect earnings management.

Long-term sustainability planning takes on so many more factors, outside of just profits and shareholder wealth maximization, to create a shared value for all stakeholders. If companies want long-term success, they will need to factor in environmental consciousness, ethics, social impacts, diversity and inclusion, and customer satisfaction and reputation. They will need to ensure that their products and services are environmentally friendly and minimize negative impacts on society and the environment. Furthermore, companies should accept their ESG obligations and make it a practice to be active in their communities through neighborhood cleanups and volunteering with non-profit organizations that assist in communities' environmental and educational development. Fostering a workplace that pushes these actions can help sustain a company long-term through a symbiotic relationship and reputation enhancements. Companies that help protect the environment through eco-friendly business practices and involvement in community outreach projects can help communities progress and improve the environment for the next generations. This, in turn, will create a sense of trust in their respective communities, and the chances of them conducting business with these companies will increase.

Regarding long-term sustainability planning within a company, managers should continuously foster an ethical work environment, a culture of diversity, inclusion, and equity, and have whistleblower protections in place. In addition, the company's board of directors should seek feedback and ideas at all levels by establishing a two-way communication mechanism. Employee involvement throughout the company leads to more opportunities involving business improvement and exemplifies the importance a company places on its employees. This gives potential employees and stockholders greater confidence in a company's management performance. Several high-profile companies are taking sustainability initiatives and telling their good sustainability stories, for example reducing waste and excess plastic in their supply chain. Pepsi and Coca-Cola have made water replenishment part of their sustainability story. BMW, Toyota, and Tesla have focused on energy efficiency and reducing pollution that's normally associated with the use of automobiles.[1]

Strategic sustainability planning enables business organizations to focus on the profit-with-purpose mission of maximizing their positive impacts on all stakeholders, including shareholders, employees, communities, customers, society, and the environment, and to minimize the negative impacts on multi-stakeholders. In case of nonexistence of and/or inadequate statement of purpose and strategic sustainability planning, the board of directors, in collaboration with management, should develop the statement of purpose and strategic sustainability planning. The statement of purpose should include the mission, which reflects the organization's strategic sustainability planning in achieving short-, medium-, and long-term sustainable performance. Companies are now adopting the corporate mission of profit with purpose and strategic sustainability planning to create shared value for all stakeholders by shifting their goals to create shareholder value while fulfilling their social, environmental, and governance responsibilities. The statement of purpose, along with strategic sustainability planning, should define objectives for survival in the short term, continuity of business in the medium term, and strategic sustainability planning in the long term. In collaboration with management, the board of directors should also design strategic sustainability planning to achieve new objectives by designing business continuity plans, long-term strategic plans, and crisis management strategies.

II.1 Sustainability Planning

Sustainability planning consists of (1) evaluation and assessment of business activities and priorities; (2) establishment of goals and objectives; (3) stakeholder engagement and communication; (4) implementation and monitoring; and (5) reevaluation, reassessment, and adaptation, as highlighted in Chapter 1.

II.1.1 Evaluation and Assessment

Business organizations should evaluate and assess their activities, set priorities, and define strategies to determine their economic, environmental, and social impacts. The appetite for investment in firms focused on ESG sustainability has increased significantly in the last decade. There are currently several sustainability investment strategies: "Impact First," "Finance First," "Impact Investing," and "Anti-ESG." "Impact First" refers to an investment strategy that prioritizes the social, environmental, or ethical consequences and benefits of a decision or investment above financial considerations. In this approach, the primary goal is to make a positive impact on society or the environment, and financial returns are seen as secondary or even as a means to further the impact goals. It measures success based on non-financial metrics, such as social impact, sustainability, or ethical performance. "Finance First" is an investment strategy that prioritizes financial returns as the primary and often only consideration in decision-making. The primary goal for business organizations is to maximize profitability and financial gain, and other factors, such as social or environmental impact, are seen as secondary. It measures success primarily through financial metrics, such as return on investment (ROI) profit margins and shareholder wealth creation. It may consider social or environmental factors only to the extent that they directly affect financial performance. Anti-ESG is an investment strategy that does not consider ESG factors.

II.1.2 Establishment of Goals and Objectives

To ensure sustainable performance, business organizations should establish specific, attainable, relevant, measurable short-term and long-term goals aligning with sustainability priorities. There can be multiple goals of balancing profit, people, planet, and prosperity. The Business Roundtable (BRT), on August 19, 2019, announced the adoption of a new Statement on the Purpose of a Corporation that promotes the move toward sustainability of creating shared value for all stakeholders. The Business Roundtable (BRT) is a not-for-profit organization composed of chief executive officers of leading companies throughout the United States with the main purpose of promoting a better national economy and increasing opportunities for prospective businesspeople through policymaking to make businesses benefit the entire society.[2] According to polling data from the BRT from 2021, 65% of respondents believe that big corporations successfully promote an economy that all Americans can benefit from through hard work and creativity and which can lead to a meaningful and dignified life. More than 50% said that large corporations positively impact shareholders, customers, local communities, and the workforce. Over 37% said that US companies prioritize stakeholders the same as their shareholders, environment, workers, communities, and customers. Over 40% believe the country needs a better form of capitalism to achieve a greater society for future generations and to help the average American.

II.1.3 Stakeholder Engagement and Communication

Business organizations should engage diverse stakeholders, including local communities, employees, customers, and environmental groups, and collect their input to better understand their sustainability opportunities, preferences, concerns, and expectations. Sustainability goals and progress should be effectively and timely communicated to all stakeholders as transparency builds trust and support.

II.1.4 Implementation and Monitoring

Sustainability strategic plans should be implemented and monitored continuously to ensure the effective achievement of sustainability goals. Business organizations should monitor the implementation of (1) measures to reduce energy and water consumption through energy-efficient technologies, renewable energy sources, and water-saving practices; (2) processes for minimizing waste generation and promoting recycling and reuse; (3) considering the entire life cycle of products and services; (4) engagement in initiatives that contribute positively to local communities, such as job creation, education, and healthcare; and (5) ensure that sustainability plans and operations promote diversity, equity, and inclusion both within the organization and in the broader community.

II.1.5 Regulatory Compliance

Many sustainability local, national, and international regulations apply to organizations of all types and sizes. Compliance with applicable sustainability laws, rules, regulations, standards, and best practices ensures the achievement of sustainability goals and missions.

II.1.6 Reassessment and Adaptation

Business organizations should reevaluate and reassess their success and progress toward achieving their sustainability purposes by identifying key performance indicators (KPIs) for all five economic, environmental, ethical, social, and governance dimensions of sustainability performance. These KPIs should be regularly monitored to track progress toward sustainability goals. This continuous monitoring and assessment assists in identifying areas for improvement and adapting plans based on changing circumstances.

II.1.7 Innovation and Adaptability

Technological innovation enables businesses to apply cutting-edge technologies and embrace innovative technologies that can improve sustainability performance. Adaptability provides flexibility and responsiveness to changing economic, environmental, and social conditions.

II.1.8 Education and Training

Provide continuous education to ensure employees are educated about sustainability strategies and practices and empowered to contribute to sustainability goals. Inform and educate all key stakeholders and the broader community about sustainable practices and their role in promoting sustainability by telling your good sustainability stories.

II.2 Sustainability Strategic Plans in Action

Business companies should follow the guidelines of the Statement on the Purpose of a Corporation released by the Business Roundtable (BRT) and assess whether they have adequately adopted a clear corporate purpose that focuses on their long-term strategic goals, implemented ESG policies and practices that advance those goals, communicated those goals and objectives effectively, and held their board of directors and executives responsible for achieving the stated purposes.[3] The updated BRT Statement on the Purpose of a Corporation declares that companies should not only serve their shareholders but also deliver value to their customers, invest in employees, deal fairly with suppliers, and support the communities in which they operate.[4] This statement of purpose is the first step in the right direction of focusing on strategic sustainability planning. However, critics argue that CEOs should not have released the statement without the full support and approval of their boards of directors as representative of shareholders.[5] The argument is that if these elite CEOs believed that this updated statement would have truly affected the company's well-being, they would not have signed without the board's approval. These CEOs believe they are meeting shareholders' expectations by providing shared value to the stakeholders. The Business Roundtable clarified their statement's wording with a strong defense in support of the free-market system and a commitment to generate "long-term value for shareholders, who provide the capital that allows companies to invest, grow and innovate." For companies to be successful in the long term while also returning value to shareholders, they must also consider the interests of all stakeholders, such as customers, employees, and even the communities in which they operate.[6] This shift in mindset has progressed as the call for more responsible capitalism has increased in popularity.

The World Economic Forum (WEF) advocates the stakeholder governance concept with a focus on "profit-with-purpose" and strategic sustainability planning that promotes managing and running an organization to protect the interests of all stakeholders, including shareholders, employees, customers, suppliers, governments, and society.[7] The International Business Council (IBC) of the World Economic Forum (WEF), in collaboration with the big four accounting firms, has released its final recommendations for a set of ESG sustainability performance metrics and disclosures that can be globally accepted and implemented.[8] These recommendations are designed to provide guiding principles and metrics for focusing on the ESG sustainability factors of performance, risk, and disclosures relevant to governance, people, planet, and prosperity.

The recommendation metrics put forth by the WEF are divided into four pillars, as previously stated: principles of governance, planet, people, and prosperity. The principles of governance pillar coordinates business strategies and practices to create positive societal impact through agency, accountability, and stewardship. The pillar of the planet focuses on actions taken by companies to coordinate their supply chain to be environmentally conscious and impact society and customers positively.

Over the past decade, active ownership and engagement strategies have gained traction due to the influence of soft and hard law initiatives and investor demand for positive change. The launch of the the Principles for Responsible Investment was swiftly followed by the global economic crisis, both highlighting the importance of long-term sustainability and the risks associated with climate change and social inequalities. Soft law initiatives, such as the PRI and local stewardship codes, have further fueled investor engagement. Regulations in the European Union have made engagement disclosure mandatory. Investor engagement has expanded to focus on concrete actions aligned with the UN Sustainable Development Goals. Engagement practices vary across regions, with climate change consistently a top priority globally. Other ESG topics like governance, diversity, equality, human rights, and labor rights are also significant. Overall, engagement is becoming an integral part of responsible investment and investor stewardship worldwide.[9]

The principles of governance pillar encompasses governing purpose, quality of governing body, stakeholder engagement, ethical behavior, and risk and opportunity oversight. Governance aims to develop, manage, and follow through on a mission. The quality of the governing body relates to the composition of governance bodies and how they focus on strategic milestones and compensation. Stakeholder engagement goes into the material issues that could affect stakeholders' interests. Ethical behavior seeks to avoid corrupt business, encourage honesty and integrity, and influence public policy. Risk and opportunity oversight incorporates risk factors and opportunities for environmental, economic, and social progress.[10]

The pillar of people focuses on embracing values such as human rights, inclusion, and diversity. Companies ultimately want to place value on their employees and customers to sustain stakeholder value. The themes brought up with people were dignity and equality, health and well-being, and skills for the future. Dignity and equality relate to diversity, inclusion, anti-discrimination, reduced pay disparity, and reduced risk for unfair labor practices. Health and well-being relate to safety and proper care for workers. Skills for the future relate to employee training in an organization.[11]

The pillar of prosperity incorporates economic growth and innovation to combat poverty and economic inequality. The themes within prosperity are employment and wealth generation, innovation of better products and services, and community and social vitality. Employment and wealth generation deals with employment rates, investments in infrastructure, and the economic effects. Innovation is measured through social value, Vitality index, and research and development costs. Community and social vitality deal with taxes and social investments.[12]

The planet pillar is concerned with climate change, nature loss, freshwater availability, pollution, solid waste, and resource availability. Climate change action involves responding to greenhouse gas emissions and implementing the recommendations of the Task Force on Climate-related Financial Disclosures. Nature loss is concerned with sensitivity to land use and ecosystems. Freshwater availability addresses the consumption and withdrawal of water in stressed areas. Pollution covers the types of pollutants in the air and water and their impact on the environment. Solid waste deals with minimal use and eventual waste of plastics and other solids, as well as its associated impacts. Resource availability is related to reporting the right circularity metrics for the company.[13]

Strategic sustainability planning requires companies to define their purpose, which determines why the organization exists, what its mission is, who the stakeholders are, and what its objectives and strategies for achieving the objectives are. The main objective function of any business organization has transformed from making a profit to creating shared value for all stakeholders, including shareholders, employees, creditors, customers, suppliers, government, society, and the environment. Changes in the purpose, mission, objectives, and strategies for business organizations in the aftermath of the COVID-19 crisis need to be assessed and modified by focusing on the achievement of sustainable financial-economic performance (ESP) and non-financial environmental, social, and governance (ESG) sustainability performance.

Every company should have its unique purpose determined in its charter of incorporation to maximize its positive impacts on all stakeholders, including communities, society, and the environment, and to minimize the negative impacts on multi-stakeholders. In case of nonexistence of and/or inadequate statement of purpose, the board of directors, in collaboration with management, should develop the statement of purpose and obtain approval from majority shareholders. The purpose of profit maximization and shareholder wealth creation has changed to create shared value for all stakeholders. To effectively achieve this new purpose, corporations are expanding their performance to financial/quantitative economic sustainability and non-financial/qualitative environmental, social, and governance (ESG) sustainability performance. The statement of purpose should include the mission, which reflects the organization's determined purpose for existence, including the values and aims of the organization as defined in the strategic sustainability planning. The mission statement defines goals and intended objectives of achieving performance in the short, medium, and long term and an ongoing commitment to its stakeholders. Companies are now adopting the corporate mission of profit to create shared value for all stakeholders by shifting their goals to create shareholder value while fulfilling their social, environmental, and governance responsibilities. The statement of purpose should also define objectives, which have sustainably changed in the post-COVID-19 pandemic to survival in the short term, continuity in the medium term, and sustainability in the long term. The board of directors pays more attention to the well-being, safety, and health of their employees, customers, and suppliers. In collaboration with management, the board of directors should also design strategies to achieve new objectives by designing business continuity plans, deliberate decisions, and crisis management.

Professional organizations (GRI, SASB, IIRC, CDSB, and CDP) that promote business sustainability initiatives have published a Statement of Intent, committing to work together towards comprehensive corporate reporting. Following GRI Global Sustainability Standards relevant to performance indicators, corporations should discuss goals around ESG performance; the sourcing of raw materials and inputs for production; health or social impacts; employee safety, training, and diversity; safety, health and well-being of employees, customers, and suppliers; product innovations that lead to positive environmental impact; compliance with ethical principles and human rights standards; and community initiatives in the areas of health and well-being, education, employment, and economic empowerment. The GRI has three new topic standards on tax, occupational health and safety, and water and effluents. The Standard promotes transparency on tax contributions by enabling companies to report tax payments country-by-county alongside their management approach to tax. This is meant to respond to the information needs requested by outlets, such as investors, civil society, and labor organizations.

Further, the updated Standard addresses occupational health and safety management, which includes a central focus on the safety and well-being of employees, especially during the challenges of the COVID-19 pandemic. This occupational health and safety management includes reduced harm and better health in the workplace. Finally, the Standard now considers how water is managed, including impacts on local communities, and gives a full picture of water usage from withdrawal to consumption and discharge. The water and effluents standards ultimately seek to provide a holistic picture of the impacts on water-related resources.[14]

Several high profile companies have now incorporated the new Standard into their company mission statements, including BP, International Paper, Microsoft, FedEx, Walmart, and Deloitte. Here are a few more examples of companies and their purpose missions:

1. Patagonia: In its mission statement, Patagonia, an outdoor clothing and gear company, states, "Build the best product, cause no unnecessary harm, use business to inspire and implement solutions to the environmental crisis." They emphasize their commitment to sustainability and minimizing their impact on the planet.[15]
2. Tesla: Tesla's mission is to "accelerate the world's transition to sustainable energy." The company focuses on developing and producing electric vehicles and renewable energy solutions to combat climate change and reduce dependence on fossil fuels.[16]
3. Unilever: Unilever, a multinational consumer goods company, aims to "make sustainable living commonplace." Its mission involves improving the health and well-being of people, reducing environmental impact, and enhancing livelihoods through products and operations.[17]
4. Danone: Danone's mission is to "bring health through food to as many people as possible." The company emphasizes the importance of nutrition, sustainability, and social responsibility in its business practices.[18]

5. Google: Google's mission statement is to "organize the world's information and make it universally accessible and useful." While not explicitly focused on sustainability, Google has committed to operating its data centers with renewable energy and achieving carbon neutrality.[19]

For example, in its 2019 annual report, BP defines its corporate mission as "Energy with Purpose." "Our purpose is reimagining energy for people and our planet," and "We want to help the world reach net zero and improve people's lives." In its 2019 annual report, the Swedish private equity firm EQT defines its statement of purpose as to "future-proof companies and make a positive impact, to be the most reputable investor and owner" with the mission of "With the best talent and network around the world, EQT uses a thematic investment strategy and distinctive value creation approach to future-proof companies, creating superior returns to EQT's investors and making a positive impact with everything we do." Walmart recently updated its ESG reporting in terms of its engagement in public policy. The corporation makes it clear that it wants to build its business around key strategies and progress. The strategies and progress include governance and transparency, advocating for public policy, engagement in the political process, and working through business organizations. They have outlined that their public policy practices include health and safety, climate change, and racial equity. The business organizations that they side with include the Business Roundtable, Consumer Goods Forum, Americas Business Dialogue, and the International Chamber of Commerce.[20]

Deloitte has made its principles of diversity, inclusion, and integrity explicit in its vision, values, and strategy page. Its core principles include integrity, outstanding value to markets and clients, commitment to each other, and strength from cultural diversity.[21] Deloitte recently conducted a global survey outlining the interests and desires of millennials and Gen Z. They reported key findings surrounding health and employment, mental health, societal impact, and systemic racism.[22] Corporations are moving toward purpose strategies that drive value for all stakeholders. With these emerging "profit-with-purpose" missions, boards of directors and executives have integrated strategic sustainability planning into the business environment and corporate culture, as well as operating and finance activities and performance. Proper strategic sustainability planning requires the board of directors and executives to:

1. Set the right tone at the top in promoting stakeholder primacy by signing the statement of purpose pledging to operate their business in the interests of all stakeholders (e.g., shareholders, employees, suppliers, customers, and communities).
2. Ensure senior executives commit to sustainability and stakeholder primacy and strategic sustainability planning implementation. The evidence of this commitment includes executive compensation linked to sustainability achievement and the position of the chief sustainability officer.

Sustainability information on long-term financial ESP and non-financial ESG performance increases the quality and quantity of the firm's performance and related disclosures and, thus, more focus on long-term and sustainable performance and fewer incentives for short-term performance that could be detrimental to long-term sustainability. Sustainability-disclosing firms are expected to provide fewer incentives and opportunities for short-termism and, thus, more focus on long-term strategic sustainability planning. Investor interest in sustainable and long-term investments, products, and services has grown, and policymakers and regulators have begun to focus more on business sustainability. The demand for sustainability policies and initiatives is growing rapidly and is required globally. Several strategic sustainability plans need to be developed before effectively implementing them and their integration into the business environment. First, a well-regulated sustainable finance ecosystem is needed to support broader and global sustainability-related policy initiatives, particularly the massive amount of capital needed to address global climate change. Second, there should be robust standards to mitigate the risk of sustainability greenwashing and "branding" and to allow investors to make informed choices about the actual sustainability characteristics of their investments. [23] Third, the big three asset management firms of BlackRock, Vanguard, and State Street have a fiduciary responsibility to their investing clients to engage with public companies' boards of directors and management to achieve financial returns on investment and non-financial ESG sustainability factors of performance, risk, and disclosure.

Based on their investment preferences and short-term and long-term investment goals, investors determine their investment strategies to achieve their goals based on risk appetite. An investment strategy guides an investor's decisions based on investment goals, strategic sustainability planning, future needs for capital, risk tolerance, and expected rate of returns on invested capital. Some investors prefer annual dividends on their investments, while others have more long-term goals of capital appreciation, and some may prefer dividends and capital gain. Investment strategies determine how investors choose their investment portfolio with socially responsible investment and how they manage such portfolios. Experienced and engaged investors typically prefer to choose and manage their investment portfolio and thus often follow the strategy of buying low and selling high, whereas less-engaged investors usually follow the market movements and invest in funds that track the market index with a long-term view. Some investors are risk-averse, and some are risk-takers; thus, the investment risk appetite and tolerance determine the investment strategy. In assessing and managing investment risk, investors should understand that the higher the risk, the higher the potential returns on investment, and therefore, they should take the risk that they can afford to lose.

In recent years, both retail and institutional investors have shown more interest in sustainable investing than in socially responsible companies. Sustainable investing is an investment strategy that considers both financial ESP and non-financial ESG sustainability factors of performance and risk and disclosure to achieve a desired rate of returns on investment while considering an investment's social and environmental impacts. The 2020 US SIF Foundation's *Report on US Sustainable and Impact Investing Trends*, found one out of every three dollars under professional investment management in the United States amounting to $17.1 trillion by the end of 2019 was managed according to sustainable investing strategies, which was a 42% increase from the $12.0 trillion invested in the two years prior.[24] There are several incentives and reasons for sustainable investing, such as focusing on non-financial ESG sustainability performance, more socially responsible investors, personal and social values and goals, and more attention to social and environmental matters. Sustainable and socially responsible investors, while they continue to seek strong financial ESP, show a preference for investments that generate ESG sustainability performance, including community development loan funds, clean tech portfolios, and socially responsible investment portfolios. Sustainable and socially responsible investors often choose investment strategies by investing in sustainable companies whose stocks outperform less ESG-sustainable companies. They may also prefer investing in companies that serve poor and underserved communities worldwide.

Recently, investors have been interested in socially responsible investing (SRI), which focuses on environmental and social concerns alongside financial gains. SRI funds have experienced substantial asset growth as they strive to promote positive conduct. However, despite their efforts to choose companies with better environmental and social behavior, SRI funds have limited influence on improving the behavior of the companies in their portfolios. Even though they support shareholder proposals on these issues, their investments do not result in significant transformations. This highlights the need for alternative strategies or stronger regulatory oversight to drive corporate conduct change effectively.[25]

The following issues should be addressed in promoting sustainable investing strategies, encouraging socially and environmentally responsible business practices, and investing in capital that generates social and environmental impacts across the economy worldwide:

- Investor's sentiment should be on a long-term sustainable strategy to achieve sustainable performance rather than obtaining short-term gains.
- Management should focus on the profit-with-purpose mission of achieving both financial ESP and non-financial ESG sustainability performance.
- Shareholders, their representatives, and the board of directors should oversee management sustainability performance achievements of generating both ESP and ESG sustainability performance.
- Focus on strategic business sustainability and continuity plans, perform scenario analyses to reveal potential disruption risks, and design strategies to minimize their negative impacts.
- Investors should invest in stocks of companies that are sustainable and considered socially and environmentally responsible.

III.3 Components of Sustainability Strategic Plans

The components of a sustainability plan can vary based on the nature of the business, its mission, and industry and regional factors. Thus, business organizations should tailor their strategies to their business environment and corporate culture to align with their unique circumstances and goals. Several main components of strategic plans for business sustainability are presented in this section.

III.3.1 Economic Sustainability and Viability

The primary objective of business entities is to make money for their owners. This objective function can be achieved by (1) establishing a short-term, medium-term, and long-term financially sound business model that generates value for investors through the achievement of ESP; (2) diversifying revenue streams by improving business opportunities and optimizing business risks to enhance financial stability and resilience; and (3) fostering technology and innovation to stay competitive in the market and ensure economic growth and development. Business organizations should adopt a future-oriented approach that considers long-term objectives and possibilities that underscore the need to focus on talent and culture, risk management, digital transformation, ESG priorities, and organizational resilience. Investors increasingly demand businesses establish sustainable strategic plans to ensure economic prosperity and financial viability. Thus, the board of directors should actively ensure that the company's purpose aligns with its strategy and values and communicate its significance to management and investors.

III.3.2 Corporate Governance Effectiveness

Business entities should establish effective corporate governance to achieve financial ESP and economic prosperity. Effective corporate governance requires measures and mechanisms for determining the roles and responsibilities of all corporate governance participants, from investors to the board of directors, management, accountants, auditors, regulators, legal counsel, and financial advisors. Sustainable investment strategies enable institutional investors to integrate both financial ESP and non-financial ESG sustainability performance into their investment processes. These strategies are gaining attention from institutional investors, as evidenced by the growth of the Principles for Responsible Investment (PRI) network and investor signatories to PRI principles and guidelines. The Principles for Responsible Investment is an independent network that seeks to understand the implications of how investments affect environmental, social, and governance factors and to support its network of international investor signatories. There are six principles: incorporating ESG issues into investment analysis and decision-making, being active owners and incorporating ESG issues into ownership, seeking appropriate disclosure on ESG issues, promoting acceptance and implementation of the principles, working together to enhance the effectiveness of Principles implementation, and reporting on the activities and progress towards implementation. A scholarly paper examines the financial performance of companies worldwide that apply and comply with PRI compared to those that do not and finds: (1) institutions that joined the PRI exhibited significantly better financial ESP and non-financial ESG performance, particularly in social and governance dimensions of sustainability and less in the environmental components; (2) PRI signatories change their behavior after committing to the Principles and show that institutional investors generally improve their sustainable ESG portfolio; (3) social and environmental norms are relatively stronger in Europe mainly because responsible investing has been more broadly practiced; (3) a portfolio's ESG sustainability performance is negatively associated with portfolio risk; and (4) there is no link between the commitment of some US-domiciled PRI signatories and their ESG portfolio integration intensity, whereas as link is strong in Europe where European PRI signatories are more ESG sustainable than non-PRI signatories.

Corporate boards have undergone changes due to factors like activist investors and a focus on shareholder interests. Directors now collaborate with executives to enhance decision-making and place trust in their CEOs. The relationship between the board and executives is complex, involving the participation of other executives in board discussions. Directors emphasized the importance of a positive board environment that fosters constructive conflict. Diversity on the board is valued for its benefits, encompassing various backgrounds and perspectives. Executive sessions, with or without the CEO, play a vital role in confidential discussions. The managerial implications include building trust, involving executives in board meetings, promoting diversity, and recognizing the significance of executive sessions. Corporate boards encounter changing obstacles influenced by factors such as the pandemic, ESG concerns, and stakeholder governance. They aim to operate a legal, ethical, profitable, and sustainable business involving all vital stakeholders. Boards need to adapt their operations, establish the company's purpose, incorporate ESG into strategies, and provide sustainable value. They should effectively manage crises, supervise risk and ESG effects, engage with shareholders, and assess performance. Corporations should prioritize directors' expertise, specialized committees, equitable compensation, data sharing, and fostering teamwork. In essence, boards must strike a balance between stakeholder interests to foster long-term growth. Board diversity plays a crucial role in making informed decisions and managing risks by gathering insights from different perspectives, including middle management and external stakeholders.

III.3.3 Environmental Stewardship and Performance

Environmental stewardship and performance are becoming an important and integral part of sustainable strategic planning as regulators, businesses, investors, and societies worldwide are becoming more concerned about climate change, global warming, and the exhaustion of natural resources. Environmental strategies such as implementing eco-friendly practices to reduce negative environmental impacts, adopting energy-efficient technologies and renewable energy sources, minimizing waste generation, and promoting recycling are crucial in achieving effective environmental performance and leaving a better environment for the next generations. In order to establish sustainable strategies with a clear net-zero vision, it is imperative to account for climate change. Companies can adopt the return-driven strategy framework and utilize management tools like strategic risk assessment, strategic valuation, and strategic lifecycle analysis to develop and execute environmental sustainability strategies. Accurate measurement and valuation of emissions play a crucial role in effectively measuring environmental performance.

III.3.4 Social Commitment and Responsibility

In recent years, the "corporate purpose" concept has gained attention as it encompasses a corporation's commitment to stakeholder governance, environmental sustainability, and social responsibility. The stakeholder corporate governance models should balance profit and societal well-being. Social commitment emphasizes the importance of anticipating, fulfilling, and communicating social responsibilities to maintain social performance. Socially responsible business practices are corporate giving to and support for communities and ensuring fair labor practices, customer satisfaction, and employee well-being and safety.

III.3.5 Supply Chain Sustainability

Integrating ESG issues into corporate strategies and linking management incentives to ESG performance are integral components of sustainable supply chain management. Boards are crucial in overseeing ESG risks and opportunities, necessitating systematic identification and assessment of ESG factors and integrating them into the supply chain management system. The importance of periodically reevaluating the oversight structure of the supply chain system is crucial in measuring, monitoring, and tracking key ESG metrics, setting goals, and considering ESG metrics for incentives. Supply chain sustainability should address ways to evaluate and improve the sustainability of the supply chain, collaboration with suppliers to ensure responsible sourcing, reduction of the carbon footprint related to the supply chain, and improvement and intergradation of the supply chain system to overall strategic planning.

III.3.6 Stakeholder Engagement

Stakeholder engagement and participation in strategic planning is essential to ensure that their interests are being addressed. A broad range of stakeholders, from shareholders to creditors, employees, suppliers, customers, society, communities, and the environment, should be heard and have a voice in setting strategic planning. This includes building strong relationships with stakeholders, encouraging their participation in strategic planning processes, and periodic communication with them regarding sustainability initiatives and progress.

III.3.7 Regulatory Compliance

The effective design and implementation of strategic plans requires compliance with all applicable laws, rules, policies, regulations, and standards. These regulations govern all four sustainability factors: planning, performance, risk, and disclosures. Strategic planning processes should mandate staying informed about and compliant with environmental and social regulations and regularly and proactively addressing emerging regulatory changes.

III.3.8 Measuring and Reporting

Sustainability strategic planning should address proper measurement and reporting of both financial ESP and non-financial ESG sustainability performance. It should also address the importance of consistent and substantiated disclosures, strong controls, and robust compliance sustainability programs. The board of directors and executives in charge of the design and implementation of sustainability strategic plans should establish key performance indicators (KPIs) for financial ESP and non-financial ESG sustainability performance, regularly measuring and reporting on sustainability metrics, using data to identify areas for improvement, and periodically revise strategic plans to ensure their effectiveness in supporting the company's profit-with-purpose mission.

III.3.9 Risk Management

Sustainability strategic plans should emphasize the increasing significance of companies disclosing their exposure to climate risks and the need for consistent and transparent risk management and reporting. Companies should set sustainability targets and consider ESG criteria to assess their impact, including disclosing greenhouse gas emissions, establishing industry-specific standards, and improving ESG disclosure. The objective is to provide investors with reliable information for evaluating climate-related risks as well as financial reporting and controls, enterprise risk management, cyber risk, and digital finance transformation. Adequate and effective risk assessment and management should identify and mitigate risks associated with environmental, social, and economic factors and develop contingency plans for potential sustainability changes and challenges.

III.3.10 Innovation and Research

Proper innovation and research enable business entities to effectively integrate ESG factors into strategic planning by addressing the significance of transparency, accountability, and impact in ESG reporting and management. Digital sustainability data plays a significant role in enhancing decision-making and sustainability reporting for companies. Innovation can overcome challenges in effectively managing and analyzing sustainability data, as data fragmentation, lack of standardization, and poor data quality can hinder progress toward strategic planning. Strategic planning should address the potential advantages and risks associated with virtual capabilities and electronic documents in corporate governance and reporting. While these technological tools can enhance decision-making efficiency, their improper use can compromise integrity and expose companies to legal and reputational risks. Effective strategic plans should provide recommendations for effectively leveraging technology while mitigating associated risks by investing in research and development for sustainable products or services and encouraging a culture of innovation to ensure sustainable strategic plans and find new sustainable solutions.

III.3.11 Collaboration and Partnerships

Proper sustainability strategic planning enables maintaining a strong ESG position and brings value to companies through investor attraction, risk reduction, cost savings, brand reputation enhancement, and collaboration and participation with all concerned stakeholders. Assessing and comparing ESG ratings to industry standards and peers helps identify areas for improvement and drives long-term success. Company action items include engaging with shareholders, choosing appropriate metrics, aligning actions with performance, setting goals, and reviewing scorecards. Businesses that implement sustainability strategic plans and programs from the beginning enhance their chances of success. Prioritizing people, profit, and the planet enables businesses to cultivate strong relationships, attract environmentally conscious customers, boost profitability and reputation by collaborating with industry peers and government agencies on sustainability initiatives, and participate in industry-wide efforts to address shared opportunities and challenges.

III. IMPACT INVESTING

The concept of impact investing refers to achieving desired financial returns for shareholders while generating social, community, and environmental impacts that are relevant and important under the stakeholder primacy model. The relationship between financial ESP and non-financial ESG sustainability performance has been extensively yet inconclusively debated in the literature in the past decade, which suggests that investors pay attention to sustainability factors of performance, risk, and disclosure. A growing number of investors are now considering impact investing with a keen focus on financial ESP returns and non-financial ESG sustainability factors and integrating them into their investment strategies. The Global Impact Investing Network (GIIN) explains impact investing (II) as "investments made to generate a positive, measurable, social, and environmental impact alongside a financial return."[26] Although the impact investing concept has often been used interchangeably with socially responsible investing (SRI), the two concepts have important differences. SRI is commonly referred to as the investment strategy that maximizes financial returns while minimizing any negative impact on society or the environment. In contrast, impact investing is a deliberate strategy to achieve financial returns and social and/or environmental impacts.[27]

The distinction between impact investing and SRI investment strategies is important for several reasons. First, investor sentiment plays a role in firms' commitment to impact investing when shareholders place a valuation premium on non-financial ESG sustainability performance. Second, in the aftermath of the COVID-19 pandemic, shareholders and directors have increasingly become attuned to ESG sustainability factors of performance risk and disclosure in allocating scarce resources between impact investing and SRI investments in achieving ESG objectives. Third, shareholders are now paying more attention to ESG initiatives and investments as asset managers of the big three investment families (BlackRock, State Street, and Vanguard) consider ESG risks and opportunities in their investment strategies. Finally, shareholders with stronger ESG preferences focusing on impact investing with portfolios that tilt more toward green assets earn lower expected returns than investors focusing on the SRI strategy of investing in brown assets.

Shareholders typically have incomplete financial ESP and non-financial ESG information about a firm's ESG sustainability performance, and thus, they may not be aware of the firm governance effectiveness, ethical culture, and social and environmental commitments. Lack of knowledge on the part of investors reduces the firm's shareholder base, which in turn makes risk sharing incomplete and inefficient, and thus, stocks of these firms are out of line with their market's fundamentals, which may incentivize firms to obtain certification to influence stock prices. Disclosures of sustainability information, however, make investors aware of the firm's existence and enlarge its investor base, which improves risk sharing and thus makes their stocks closer to their market fundamentals. Stakeholders may attempt to pressure and/or motivate firms to disclose sustainability information about their social, governance, and environmental activities, and releasing such information leads to the disclosure of private information. Managers tend to analyze the costs/benefits of obtaining a sustainability ranking to improve sustainability disclosures and how these disclosures are integrated and observed by capital markets.

Sustainability information on long-term ESP and ESG performance increases the quality and quantity of the firm's disclosures and, thus, allows more focus on long-term and sustainable performance and fewer incentives for short-term performance that could be detrimental to long-term sustainability. Since sustainability-disclosing firms provide fewer incentives and opportunities for short-termism, we expect to find a positive relationship between sustainability disclosure and its rankings and stock prices. Shareholder interest in sustainable investments, products, and services has increased, and policymakers have begun to focus more closely on this area along with a broad set of stakeholders. The demand for sustainability policies and initiatives is gathering velocity and required by some nations. However, other topics must be addressed before discussing the sustainability policies that should be implemented in the business environment. First, a well-regulated sustainable finance ecosystem is needed to support broader sustainability-related policy initiatives at the global level, most pointedly to mobilize the massive amount of capital needed to address climate change. Second, and by no means unrelated, is the concern that robust standards exist to mitigate the risk of "greenwashing" – the risk that either through confusing or outright misleading investment approaches, asset owners cannot make informed choices about the actual sustainability characteristics of their investments.

The investment strategy of impact investing is often considered to be an integration of finance-first and impact-first investment strategies. Finance first is an investment strategy that prioritizes financial returns as the primary and often sole consideration in investment decision-making, with the primary goal being to maximize profitability and financial gain, and other factors such as social or environmental impacts are not even considered or seen as secondary objectives. Impact first represents an investment strategy that prioritizes the social, environmental, or ethical considerations in investment decision-making. In this approach, the primary goal is to positively impact society or the environment, and financial returns are considered a secondary goal.

IV. CONCLUSION

Business sustainability is gaining the attention of investors and regulators as they require sustainability information on financial ESP and non-financial ESG sustainability performance. Investors have also used financial ESP and non-financial ESG sustainability factors of planning, performance, risk, and disclosure in their investment decisions. Investors demand relevant, reliable, consistent, and uniform financial ESP and non-financial ESG sustainability performance information in making sound investment decisions. In meeting investors' expectations and demand for ESG information, public companies should produce and disclose integrated sustainability information. Shareholders are seeking more sustainability information upon which to make investment and voting decisions. Public companies should prepare integrated sustainability reports presenting financial ESP and non-financial ESG sustainability performance information. Public companies, their boards of directors, and executives have responded to investors' demands and regulators' requirements for sustainability information by integrating sustainability into their business environment and corporate culture and decision-making. Companies are now publishing integrated sustainability reports and will continue releasing them to signal their superior and high sustainability performance. Sustainability reports present information on the achievement of financial returns for investors while creating social and environmental impacts. This chapter presents sustainability strategic planning in its capacity to assist business entities in achieving their mission of profit-with-purpose.

V. TAKEAWAYS

- More than 1,300 institutional investors worldwide, representing $59 trillion in assets under management, have signed on to the UN Principles of Responsible Investing, which seek to integrate sustainability concerns into investment objectives.
- Asset managers such as Blackrock, State Street, and Vanguard now invest in sustainable and CSR companies.
- More than 20,000 global public companies disclose their financial ESP and non-financial ESG sustainability performance information.
- More than 6,000 large European companies have been required to disclose ESG and diversity in 2017 and onwards.
- Many public companies have created a board sustainability committee or executive sustainability position to promote and ensure commitment to business sustainability.
- Business sustainability is expected to continue advancing; as investors demand more non-financial ESG sustainability information, society is more concerned about social injustice, environmental initiatives are gaining more attention, and corporations are focusing on their human capital, diversity, and inclusion.
- Shareholders demand relevant, reliable, and consistent financial ESP and non-financial ESG sustainability performance information in making investment and voting decisions.
- Public companies should develop and report integrated sustainability performance information.
- Key performance indicators should reflect both financial ESP and non-financial ESG sustainability performance information.
- Guiding principles and standards should be established for uniform and standardized preparation of relevant, reliable, and consistent sustainability disclosures.
- Investors are most interested in sustainability information relevant to diversity, inclusion, climate change, global warming, and perceived social unrest and injustice.
- Sustainability strategic planning supports the concepts of impact investing and profit-with-purpose missions.

Notes

1 Haanaese, Kurt. 2016. "Why All Businesses Should Embrace Sustainability: Some Top Companies Are Leading the Way." Institute for Management Development. Available at https://www.imd.org/research-knowledge/articles/why-all-businesses-should-embrace-sustainability/

2 Business Roundtable (BRT). 2021. "One Year Later: Purpose of a Corporation." Available at https://purpose.businessroundtable.org/

3 Business Roundtable. August 25, 2019. "Redefined Purpose of a Corporation: Welcoming the Debate." Available at https://medium.com/@BizRoundtable/redefined-purpose-of-a-corporation-welcoming-the-debate-8f03176f7ad8
4 Business Rountable. "One Year Later: Purpose of a Corporation." Available at https://purpose.businessroundtable.org/
5 Morrison, Randi Val. 2020. "BRT Statement of Corporate Purpose: Debate Continues." Harvard Law School Forum on Corporate Governance. Available at https://corpgov.law.harvard.edu/2020/08/28/brt-statement-of-corporate-purpose-debate-continues/
6 Business Roundtable. August 25, 2019. "Redefined Purpose of a Corporation: Welcoming the Debate." 2019. Available at https://medium.com/@BizRoundtable/redefined-purpose-of-a-corporation-welcoming-the-debate-8f03176f7ad8
7 World Economic Forum (WEF). September 2020. *Measuring Stakeholder Capitalism Towards Common Metrics and Consistent Reporting of Sustainable Value Creation*. White Paper. Available at https://www.wlrk.com/docs/WEF_IBC_Measuring_Stakeholder_Capitalism_Report_2020.pdf
8 Ibid.
9 United Nations Principles for Responsible Investment (UNPRI). Available at https://www.unpri.org/about-us/what-are-the-principles-for-responsible-investment
10 World Economic Forum (WEF). 2020. *Measuring Stakeholder Capitalism Towards Common Metrics and Consistent Reporting of Sustainable Value Creation*. Available at https://www3.weforum.org/docs/WEF_IBC_Measuring_Stakeholder_Capitalism_Report_2020.pdf
11 Ibid.
12 Ibid.
13 Ibid.
14 Global Reporting Initiative (GRI). 2021. "Three GRI Standards Come into Effect for Sustainability Reports in 2021." Available at https://www.globalreporting.org/about-gri/news-center/2021-01-13-three-gri-standards-come-into-effect-for-sustainability-reports-in-2021/
15 Patagonia Building Principles. 2023. https://www.patagonia.com/on/demandware.static/-/Library-Sites-PatagoniaShared/default/dw26f3f6c3/PDF-US/Sustainable-Building-Principles.pdf
16 Tesla. 2022. "Tesla's Mission: Accelerating World's Transition to Sustainable Energy." Available at https://energyindustryreview.com/analysis/teslas-mission-accelerating-worlds-transition-to-sustainable-energy/
17 Unilever. 2023. "Leading and Delivering on Sustainability through our Compass Commitments." https://www.unilever.com/news/news-search/2023/leading-and-delivering-on-sustainability-through-our-compass-commitments/
18 Danone. About. https://skatterqviy.web.app/45643/92740.html
19 Google Mission and Vision Statement. Available at https://businessmodelanalyst.com/google-mission-and-vision-statement
20 Walmart Corporate. July 7, 2021. *Engagement in Public Policy.* Available at https://corporate.walmart.com/esgreport/esg-issues/engagement-in-public-policy
21 Deloitte. n.d. "Vision, Values, and Strategy: Distinguishing the Deloitte Culture." Available at: https://www2.deloitte.com/am/en/pages/about-deloitte/articles/vision-values-strategy.html (accessed September 16, 2021).
22 Deloitte. 2021. *A Call for Accountability and Action. The Deloitte Global 2021 Millennial and Genz Survey*. Available at https://www2.deloitte.com/content/dam/Deloitte/global/Documents/2021-deloitte-global-millennial-survey-report.pdf (accessed September 16, 2021).

23 Harvard Law School Forum on Corporate Governance. 2020. "Towards a Common Language for Sustainable Investing." Available at https://corpgov.law.harvard.edu/2020/01/22/towards-a-common-language-for-sustainable-investing/
24 The US SIF Foundation. 2020. *Report on US Sustainable Investing Trends* on November 16, 2020. Available at https://www.ussif.org/trends
25 Davidson, Heath, Daniele Macciocchi, Roni Michaely, and Matthew C. Ringgenberg. 2023. "Does Socially Responsible Investing Change Firm Behavior?" *Review of Finance* Vol. 27, No. 6, November, 2057–2083, https://doi.org/10.1093/rof/rfad002. Available at https://academic.oup.com/rof/article/27/6/2057/7028495
26 Global Impact Investing Network (GIIN). 2019. White Paper. Available at https://thegiin.org/research/publication/impinv-survey-2019
27 Ibid.

Chapter 5

Business Sustainability Performance

I. INTRODUCTION

Sustainability performance is typically classified into financial economic sustainability performance (ESP) and non-financial performance, which is usually grouped into three dimensions of environmental, social, and governance (ESG) sustainability performance, with ethical performance being integrated into both ESP and ESG dimensions of sustainability performance.[1] Although business sustainability continues to evolve, several dimensions of sustainability performance pertaining to social and environmental initiatives have gained widespread global acceptance. These initiatives include an ethical workplace, customer satisfaction, just and safe working conditions, non-discriminatory fair wages, workplace diversity, environmental preservation, clear air and water, minimum age for child labor, safe and quality products, environmental concern, and fair and transparent business practices. It is, however, important to realize that each industry has its own applicable set of sustainability financial and non-financial key performance indicators (KPIs). Each business organization must carefully identify its own social and environmental responsibilities, given the context of the business culture in which it operates. In summary, the financial and non-financial sustainability KPIs list depends on various factors, including industry, legal regimes, cultural diversity, corporate mission and strategy, corporate culture, political infrastructure, and managerial philosophy. The following sections present financial ESP and non-financial ESG sustainability performance.

DOI: 10.4324/9781003437949-5

II. FINANCIAL ECONOMIC SUSTAINABILITY PERFORMANCE

The most important and commonly accepted dimension of sustainability is financial economic sustainability performance (ESP), which consists of various factors relevant to earnings, cash flows, growth, and innovation affected by a firm's financing, investing, and operating activities. The primary goal of any business organization is to maximize firm value by creating shareholder wealth through generating sustainable economic performance throughout the firm life. Business organizations should focus on activities that generate long-term and sustainable corporate performance rather than short-term profit to enhance the overall firm value and increase shareholder wealth. The economic dimension of sustainability performance can be achieved when business organizations focus on long-term sustainability performance and continuous improvement in performance in all areas of effectiveness, efficiency, and productivity. In addition, long-term economic sustainability performance should also be communicated to shareholders through the preparation of high-quality, reliable, relevant, and transparent financial reports that are readily accessible.

Economic sustainability performance reflects a business's ability to achieve and sustain financial success and viability over the long term by managing economic resources efficiently, operating effectively, creating value for stakeholders, and contributing to economic development and prosperity. More broadly, and in compliance with G4 of the GRI and Value Reporting Foundation (VRF) Guidelines, ESP should reflect financial strengths, concerns, and an organization's economic impacts on its shareholders, society, and the environment by showing the changes in the economic status of stakeholders triggered by the organization's activities.[2] Economic sustainability performance can be measured directly through financial activities between an organization and its stakeholders (e.g., returns on investment for shareholders) or indirectly through non-financial costs and benefits of economic relations and their effects on stakeholders achieving social and environmental impacts. Although the conventional financial measures of cash flows, earnings, and return on investment are important in the financial performance of financial capital, they don't necessarily reflect sustainable performance, innovation, future growth, and non-financial capital such as human, social, environmental, and reputational capital.

The key metrics and measures of economic sustainability performance are operational efficiency, talent management, customer satisfaction, and growth and innovation that are derived from internal factors of strategy, strengths and weaknesses, and corporate culture and risk management, as well as external factors of utilization of natural resources, reputation, technology, completion, globalization.[3] In the aftermath of the COVID-19 pandemic, business survival, ongoing concern, continuity, safety, health, and well-being of all stakeholders, particularly investors, customers, employees, and suppliers, have become more relevant and important to business organizations. Business sustainability demands an integrated effort by the board of directors and management and a change in managerial focus from the short-termism of meeting analysts' quarterly earnings forecasts to achieving long-term, sustainable financial and non-financial performance.

The KPMG 2020 Audit Committee Roundtable Report highlights the importance of long-term sustainable performance by suggesting that focusing on achieving quarterly earnings can undermine a firm's long-term sustainable performance.[4] The KPMG report suggests the use of financial and non-financial KPIs and drivers of sustainable performance of operational efficiency, talent management, innovation, and customer satisfaction.[5] The regulatory process and compliance require that each company create and enforce company-level disclosures of economic activities involved in promoting its ESP and ESG sustainability performance.[6] The achievement of financial economic sustainability performance is the main objective function for any business organization to maintain its sustainability. The primary purpose of any business organization is to create shareholder value measured in terms of generating desired returns on investment in maximizing firm value. Economic sustainability disclosure is any financial information related to business organizations' profitability, innovation, and growth. Business organizations have traditionally focused on maximizing profit without considering whether they are producing goods and services that society needs, are not detrimental to society and the environment and have positive impacts on society and the environment.

The main aspects and attributes of financial economic sustainability performance are: (1) financial stability and viability of maintaining a strong and stable financial position, sustaining effective and efficient operations, managing financial risk, and maintaining a sustainable capital structure that supports long-term growth and development; (2) continuous profitability of achieving consistent and reasonable earnings streams, balancing short-term financial profit with long-term value creation, and ensuring that profit margins are sustainable and competitive; (3) revenue diversification of diversifying earnings streams to reduce dependency on a single product and source, exploring new products, services, markets and business opportunities, and adapting to changing consumer preferences, industry directions, and market conditions; (4) cost efficiency and effectiveness of implementing cost-effective and efficient operations and production processes, identifying and eliminating wastes and unnecessary expenses, and adopting continuous improvement strategies; (5) long-term planning of establishing and executing long-term sustainable strategic plans discussed in Chapter 4, balancing short-term financial goals with long-term sustainability, and using economic, social, and environmental factors in decision-making; (6) market positioning of developing competitive advantage and a strong market presence, building customer loyalty and brand equity, and differentiating products or services to create unique market position; (7) innovation and adaptability by investing in research and development to foster innovation, being responsive to changes in the business and market environment, and adapting to technological advancements, industry directions and market trends; (8) compliance and governance by complying with all applicable laws, rules, regulations, corporate governance standards, and ethical business practices, adhering to financial regulations and reporting requirements, and achieving transparency in financial reporting; (9) job creation and economic prosperity by providing fair employment opportunities and contributing to job creation, supporting local, national and global economic development initiatives, and assessing and minimizing negative impacts on local, national and global economies; and (10) stakeholder value creation by maintaining a positive relationship with shareholders through transparent communication, and balancing the interests of different stakeholders including shareholders, creditors, employees, customers and suppliers. Some of the key performance indicators of financial ESP are reported earnings, cash flows, return on assets, growth, research and development, return on investment, total spending on R&D, total spending on information technology, and net investment (capital expenditure less depreciation). These KPIs should be used as benchmarks against which financial ESP is evaluated, and directors and executives are held accountable for generating long-term and sustainable economic performance.

III. NON-FINANCIAL ENVIRONMENTAL, SOCIAL, AND GOVERNANCE SUSTAINABILITY PERFORMANCE

Non-financial dimensions of sustainability performance are divided into environmental, social, and governance (ESG) components, with the ethics component integrated into other ESG components. In the 2020 KPMG audit committee agenda, the board brings attention to the emerging challenges of ESG for the audit committees of business organizations.[7] KPMG highlights seven issues that the audit committees should address in the 2020 audit committee agenda, which include matters such as reassessing the scope and quality of ESG/sustainability reports and disclosures, refocusing standards on ethical compliance and whistleblower programs, and helping ensure that internal auditors stay focused on critical risks, specific for non-financial disclosures. Environmental, social, and governance (ESG) issues and reporting standards have become important for various stakeholders, from customers to employees, suppliers, regulators, and investors. In the aftermath of the 2020 COVID-19 pandemic and recent technological advancements and immediate information in social media, investors are demanding more transparent and higher quality, relevant financial ESP and non-financial ESG reports to make sound investment decisions. Ernst and Young (EY) has also outlined the importance of ESG dimensions for audit committees. The issues that were brought up included prioritizing the most important ESG dimensions, integrating ESG in business strategies and processes, setting proper goals and measurements, and delegating oversight roles among board members. The report also mentioned that it is important for audit committees to understand controls, disclosure requirements, and audits.[8]

The audit committee, as an important board committee, is primarily responsible for protecting investors from receiving materially misstated audited financial and reviewed non-financial reports. The audit committee should work with the company's board of directors to focus on integrating ESG data into corporate reporting. KPMG survey research emphasizes the importance of the tone at the top by directors and the commitment of management to support ESG reporting and disclosures to ensure the company has adequate infrastructure to support ESG issues. In addition, companies should redirect their sustainability focus on climate change, workplace diversity, equity, and inclusion, as well as compliance, whistleblower programs, and ethics, to reduce global regulatory challenges and increase data privacy, financial services, and consumer protection regulations. Implementing tone at the top and "top-down" approaches of compliance with regulatory requirements are common among public companies developing high ethical standards and expectations for their investors. In the age of social media and perceived social injustice, companies must create a culture of integrity, legal compliance, and high ethical values in promoting sustainability.

Furthermore, internal auditors can assist the audit committee in overseeing the assessment and management of sustainability-related capital and risk discussed in chapters 6 and 7. The audit committee should oversee the risk assessment activities of the chief risk officer and chief audit executive (the director of the internal audit department) in identifying the non-financial risks that threaten the company, such as strategic risk, brand reputation, operations, and environmental and social strategies. The following section provides an in-depth discussion and description of ESG dimensions individually.

III.1 Environmental Dimension of Sustainability Performance

Sustainability performance relevant to the environmental dimension has gained significant attention from investors, regulators, the business community, research scholars, and the accounting profession. The move toward addressing global warming, climate change, and the green economy requires reliable, relevant, and transparent information about the impacts of an organization's activities and operations on the environment beyond what is legislated by law. Corporations can no longer solely focus on corporate profitability while ignoring their impacts on society and the environment. The environmental dimension of sustainability performance considers a business's impact on the environment and its efforts to operate to minimize negative impacts on the environment, conserve resources, foster ecological balance, and promote a better environment for the next generations. This includes creating a better work environment, improving air and water quality, reducing the carbon footprint, maximizing the positive effects of an organization, and minimizing the negative impacts on natural resources and the environment. Currently, several global organizations are encouraging corporations to consider their impacts on society and the environment when making business decisions. For example, the Coalition for Environmentally Responsible Economies (CERES) and the UN Environment Program promote environmental initiatives in collaboration with the UN Global Compact.[9] These organizations, among others, undertake initiatives including environmental disclosures related to climate risks and opportunities, climate science policy actions, and law and regulatory enforcement. In short, the current disclosure requirements for environmental risks and threats are inconsistently applied and often permit inadequate information. Governments worldwide are also instituting measures to ensure that the environment is better protected at the behest of society at large. For example, the Chilean government recently canceled a $10 billion dam project in Patagonia due in part to inadequate environmental impact assessments and, in part, pressure from citizens who did not want their land's natural beauty and usability to be devastated.[10] In this case, the government decided to forego the project's economic benefits in consideration not only of the current impact it would have on the environment but also in light of future known and unknown ramifications.

Scholarly research shows that environmental sustainability can strengthen corporate sustainability performance by finding that environmental performance is significantly and positively associated with economic sustainability performance and, thus, firm value.[11] The environmental dimension consists of various topics such as energy use, global warming, climate change, treatment of animals, natural resource conservation, waste, and pollution, which should be properly disclosed in the financial statements. Insufficient environmental information may cause investors not to have sufficient information about the true nature of the firm's environmental sustainability performance and its impact on future bottom-line earnings and firm value. The climate change crisis has extensively been debated among policymakers, regulators, and the business community, and yet the extraction, exploration, and development of new fossil fuel resources have continued globally. Many believe the continuation of growing investment in oil, gas, and coal and the sale of new fossil-fuel cars must end if we want to avoid catastrophic climate change in the future.

The International Standardization Organization (ISO) released ISO 14000, which provides a set of environmental standards that require management to conduct regular evaluations of their environmental management system (EMS) to ensure that the system realizes the set goals and missions of environmental policies.[12] The ISO standards present environmental management, accounting, reporting, and auditing guidelines. The main goal for management's review of the EMS is to identify deficiencies and take proper actions to improve environmental practices in the future. A company will benefit economically and socially through implementing and continuously improving an EMS that is relevant, accurate, and sustainable in monitoring and developing environmental best practices, missions, and goals. Environmental key performance indicators (KPIs), global environmental initiatives, environmental management systems, environmental reporting, environmental assurance and auditing, and environmental best practices should be developed to ensure environmental sustainability performance.

Climate-related sustainability performance and risks can affect financial performance and risks. In October 2018, the Network for Greening the Financial System (NGFS) members acknowledged that "climate-related risks are a source of financial risk. It is therefore within the mandates of central banks and supervisors to ensure the financial system is resilient to these risks."[13] Climate change is one of the many sources of structural change affecting the financial system; however, it has specific risks and must be treated differently than other financial risks. The NGFS goes on to describe these climate change risk characteristics, such as far-reaching impact in breadth and magnitude affecting economies worldwide, the uncertainty of the foreseeable nature, irreversibility of the effects of greenhouse gases combined with lack of matured technology, and dependency on short-term actions without considering the future impacts determined by actions taken today. While we cannot predict the economic future and the financial impacts of climate change, NGFS recognizes that there is a strong risk that climate-related financial risks are not fully reflected in financial statements. Therefore, there is a crucial need for global coordination and a firm willingness to collectively lead the business world into a more sustainable economy.

The NGFS provides six recommendations for professionals to enhance their role in climate change. These are as follows: (1) Integrating climate-related risks into financial stability monitoring and micro-supervision, (2) Integrating sustainability factors into own-portfolio management, (3) Bridging the data gaps between private and public information, (4) Building awareness and intellectual capacity and encouraging technical assistance and knowledge sharing, (5) Achieving robust and internationally consistent climate and environmental related disclosure, and (6) Supporting the development of a taxonomy of economic activities.[14] There is still a significant amount of work to be done within financial systems, and further technical work is being done by the NGFS to help correlate financial risks with climate change. According to its annual report 2020, NGFS won two awards (Central Banking and Climate Bonds Initiative), added 29 new members, published nine reports, and organized more than 20 high-level meetings virtually. By the end of the year, they had recruited 83 members over five continents responsible for 75% of global greenhouse gas emissions and 85% of global GDP.[15]

The Task Force on Climate-Related Financial Disclosures (TCFD) issued a recommendations report in June 2017 to address the growing concern of potentially misleading financial disclosures. One of the most essential functions of financial markets is to set a price for risk using the relevant information to make decisions. However, there has been more focus on financial risks than environmental, social, and governance risks. The Task Force on Climate-related Financial Disclosures recommends four key features as follows: adoptable by all organizations, included in financial filings, designed to solicit decision-useful, forward-looking information on financial impact, and a strong focus on risks and opportunities related to the transition to a lower-carbon economy.[16] In the latest report from the TCFD, they summarized the changes in recommendation guidance in the realms of governance, strategy, risk management, and metrics and targets. The only changes from the 2017 report were in strategy and metrics and targets. As of October 2021, the changes in the strategy realm of climate-related risks include expanding the definition of carbon-related assets, addressing actual financial impacts, and transition planning to low-carbon economies. In the metrics and targets realm, changes include adding or revising disclosures of cross-industry, climate-related metrics, financial intermediary business activities, insurance and investment writings, GHG emissions, and performance targets.[17]

In the past several decades, the SEC has considered whether ESG disclosures are material and relevant for integration into SEC filings by publicly registered companies.[18] The emerging ongoing growth in the use of ESG information by investors has encouraged the SEC to address the mandatory ESG disclosures by (1) providing investors with the material, comparable, and consistent ESG information to make investment and voting decisions (2) presenting public companies with a disclosure framework to disclose useful and material ESG information; (3) creating more comparability and consistency regarding the disclosure of ESG information; (4) making the US, ESG disclosure requirement align with the rest of the world in creating a level playing field among public companies worldwide. The SEC Investor Advisory Committee has held several sessions on ESG disclosures by US issuers.[19] The SEC requires more enhanced climate risk disclosure for the listed public companies in the United States by the end of 2021.[20] The improved climate-related risks will provide investors with consistent, comparable, useful, and relevant information in making sound investment decisions.

Environmental sustainability performance is based on the simple concept of leaving a better environment for future generations. Stakeholders expect business organizations to provide clearer and more complementary information beyond what the law legislates. Interest in environmental sustainability performance is increasing as investors are becoming more concerned about climate change and global warming, and the 2020–2024 Democrat administration has been more in favor of focusing on environmental issues than the previous administration. The United Nations Climate Change Conferences are typically conducted annually to address climate change and global warming. President Biden issued an executive order in January 2021 to rejoin the Paris Agreement to address climate change and global warming. For example, greenhouse gas (GHG) emissions in tons of carbon dioxide equivalent (tCO2e) estimated upstream and downstream GHG emissions are important environmental KPIs.

Climate change is becoming more important to policymakers, regulators, standard-setters, investors, and corporations because extreme global weather interferes with valuable supply chains, affects territories in both developed and developing countries and destroys productive agriculture and aquaculture land. Climate change and global warming issues are central to risk management debates because of governmental and market attempts and initiatives to reduce greenhouse gas emissions. Business organizations are responding to climate change issues and related risks by considering their vulnerabilities and designing related controls to minimize their effects or taking targeted strategic decisions and a holistic approach to identifying and turning climate change challenges into business opportunities. Despite the methods selected by business organizations in addressing climate change, it is predicted that concerns about climate change will continue to accelerate over the next several decades. Public companies, their boards of directors, and executives should commit to addressing the challenges and opportunities relevant to climate change.

The environmental sustainability performance dimension includes reducing an organization's carbon footprint, addressing climate change, creating a better work environment, addressing climate change and global warming, and improving the air and water worldwide. Examples of environmental sustainability key performance indicators (KPIs) are: (1) proper air and water policies; (2) climate changes; (3) beneficial products and services; (4) global warming; (5) pollution policies and ozone-depleting chemicals; (6) recycling; (7) clean energy; and (8) hazardous waste. Energy efficiency and climate change strategies, policies, and procedures should consist of the following:

- Identify and evaluate relevant environmental sustainability factors of performance, risk, and disclosure.
- Assess energy efficiency and climate change risks and opportunities based on an evaluation of company performance.
- Develop key performance indicators (KPIs) relevant to energy efficiency and climate change.
- Design and implement energy efficiency and climate change strategy.
- Periodically review, evaluate, and revise the climate change and energy efficiency policies and procedures.

Climate key performance indicators (KPIs) are:

- **Greenhouse gas emissions (GHG).** An emissions assessment should evaluate the company's emissions compared to peers, industry, or regulatory requirements.
- **Industry climate risk.** Industry climate risk KPIs reflect that some companies are more vulnerable to the future implications of climate change, given the nature of their businesses, industry, or the location of their operations.
- **Climate risk outlook.** Forward-looking KPIs of climate risk performance and disclosure include the company's corporate policies and strategy on climate change and climate change resilience in general.

Energy efficiency and climate change strategies, policies, and procedures should consist of the following:

- Identify and select relevant factors related to energy efficiency and climate change risks and opportunities based on an assessment of company performance.

- Create a methodology for developing key performance indicators (KPIs) for energy efficiency and climate change.
- Implement energy efficiency and climate change strategy.
- Periodically review and revise the climate change and energy efficiency policies and procedures.
- Communicate with all stakeholders the assessment and management of climate change and global warming risks and actions taken to control and minimize such risks.
- Conduct climate risk scenario assessment and planning and design and implement policies and procedures to manage climate-related risks.
- Address climate change challenges and turn them into sustainability opportunities.

The European Union has developed the Taxonomy Regulation, a process of classifying a list of economic activities that lead to environmental sustainability.[21] The European Reporting Lab has also outlined in its Final Report on February 2021 various proposals to improve the EU's sustainability reporting standards. They outlined in their executive summary the importance of having sustainability reporting based on good foundations, strong guidelines, a coherent structure, phased implementation, and enhanced cooperation, among other initiatives.[22]

The United Kingdom seeks to be the first country to implement required climate-related disclosures under the Task Force on Climate-related Disclosures (TCED). They outlined the parameters of this process and everything it entails in the long run through a Roadmap Report published by the UK government.[23] The Bank of England has also established the importance of banks to address climate change, its financial risks, and a strategic approach to manage those risks in its Supervisory Statement from the Prudential Regulation Authority.[24]

In the United States there are multiple actions taken by various systems of government in relation to ESG disclosures. The House of Representatives voted to pass the Corporate Governance Improvement and Investor Protection Act to amend the Securities Act of 1934, mandating that major companies disclose significant information about ESG issues and pushing the SEC to outline the parameters of such issues.[25] President Biden issued an Executive Order to further coherent and accurate disclosures of financial risks associated with the climate crisis. The Order is divided into sections: strategy, assessment, budget outlook, and general provisions.[26]

The State of Vermont reinforced its position on climate change and related disclosures. The main allegation from the State dealt with energy companies withholding key information regarding the environmental impact of certain fossil fuels and how they lead to greenhouse gas emissions, affecting the climate.[27] This and other allegations from other states further the importance of accountability with companies and their responsibilities to keep clients, creditors, and investors informed about climate-related disclosures.

Important and key aspects of the environmental dimension of sustainability performance are: (1) carbon footprint reduction of implementing measures to reduce greenhouse gas emissions, developing targets for carbon neutrality or net-zero emissions, and adopting energy-efficient technologies and renewable energy sources; (2) waste management of adopting the use of recyclable or biodegradable materials, minimizing waste generation through recycling and waste reduction programs, and implementing responsible disposal practices for hazardous materials; (3) water conservation of monitoring water usage and identifying opportunities for conservation, implementing water-efficient practices in operations and production processes, and addressing water pollution and minimizing water waste; (4) ensuring that raw materials and resources are sourced sustainably, assessing suppliers' compliance with environmental standards, and advancing responsible and ethical sourcing practices throughout the supply chain; (5) adhering to environmental regulations, standards, and best practices, proactively addressing potential environmental risks and challenges, and periodically conducting environmental audits to ensure compliance; (6) conducting product lifecycle assessments to reduce the environmental impact of products, developing products with a focus on durability, reduced environmental footprint, and recyclability, and promoting responsible product disposal and recycling; (7) investing in research and development of eco-friendly technologies and products, adopting circular economy principles to minimize resource consumption, and promoting a culture of innovation that prioritizes environmental sustainability (8) biodiversity conservation of evaluating and mitigating the impact of business activities on ecosystems, implementing measures to protect biodiversity and natural habitats, and supporting conservation initiatives and sustainable land use practices; (9) providing education and training to employees on environmental sustainability, raising awareness among stakeholders, customers, and the community, and engaging in environmental advocacy and supporting environmental education initiatives; and (10) disclosing environmental goals and targets, transparently reporting on environmental initiatives and performance, and obtaining assurance on environmental reports to improve credibility of these reports. Business organizations that effectively manage their environmental performance dimension contribute to preserving natural resources, reducing environmental degradation, and ensuring the broader goals of global environmental stewardship.

III.2 Social Dimension of Sustainability Performance

The social dimension of sustainability performance focuses on a business's impact on society and relationships with employees, communities, and broader societal well-being by emphasizing integrating social goals into the business environment, corporate culture, and managerial decisions and practices that benefit all stakeholders of business organizations. Social performance reflects an organization's social goals and alignment with the interests and values of the society in which it operates. The social dimension of sustainability performance can encompass many issues ranging from ensuring the high quality of products and services that are not detrimental to society to improved employee health and well-being and enhanced customer satisfaction to adding a positive contribution to the sustainability of the planet and the quality of life for future generations. Socially responsible investment (SRI) is gaining the attention of both retail and institutional investors and is becoming an increasingly important part of investment asset management. The United Nations Principles of Responsible Investing (PRI) was initiated in 2005 to encourage global investors to integrate ESG into their investment decisions.[28] Under sustainable and socially responsible investing (SRI) principles, investors have been considering various sustainability issues in their investment analysis since SRI increased by more than 22% to $3.74 trillion in managed assets during the 2010–2012 period.[29]

The United Nations Guiding Principles of Human Rights apply to all business organizations worldwide to enhance standards and practices relevant to business and human rights, thus contributing to socially sustainable globalization.[30] These guiding principles address:

1. The responsibilities of states are to protect and fulfill human rights and fundamental freedoms.
2. The role of business organizations in fulfilling their social responsibilities is to comply with all applicable laws, rules, and regulations relevant to human rights.
3. The need for human rights and obligations to be implemented and enforced.

The Securities and Exchange Commission (SEC), in amendments regarding the modernization of Regulation S-K, requires US public companies, on August 26, 2020, disclosure of "a description of the registrant's human capital resources (HCR)."[31] These disclosures include the number of persons employed by the registrant, the nature of the registrant's business, the workforce, and any human capital measures or objectives that the registrant focuses on in managing the business. The final rule is a principle-based approach that relies on materiality, which varies from business to business, and measures or objectives that address personnel development, attraction, retention, and practical effect on corporate disclosure. The SEC-related HCR disclosures encourage the board of directors to oversee management policies and procedures relevant to the assessment and management of HCR. Specifically, the board of directors should:

- Oversee the company's HCR to ensure all board committees review charters and governance principles relevant to HCR management. The board of directors and its compensation committee should assess and manage HCR and the process for recruiting, selecting, promoting, and compensating managers and employees. Board members on the compensation committee should have expertise in HCR assessment and management.
- Evaluating HCR as human capital can constitute a high portion of the total capital for the company, and the cost associated with human capital can be

significant. The board of directors should consider all human capital and employees, including equity, diversity, inclusion, safety, health, and well-being.

- Ensure that the company has the right workforce to meet current and future human capital needs and business strategic plans to meet the human capital needs.
- Review the human capital-related risks, including inequity, bias, discrimination, health-related risks, and unsuitable work environment.
- Review talent management, including employee recruitment, development, promotion, and retention.
- Review employee well-being, health, and safety.
- Review employee fair compensation and benefits, such as minimum wage, paid leave, and pay equity.
- Review the extent of diversity, inclusion, and equity at all levels within the company, from the board of directors to management and employees.
- Review policies and procedures for combating discrimination, harassment, and bullying.
- Review whistleblowing policies and procedures, including the treatment of whistleblowers.

Companies have recently taken it upon themselves to analyze the importance of using their resources for human capital management due to pressure from investors, society, and competitors. Greg Arnold and Andrew Friedlander from Semler Brossy helped develop the HCM Funnel to help steer companies' focus. It starts with Stage 1: Setting HCM Priorities. This includes gathering important topics on what the company should focus on, such as employee engagement, health, diversity, and retention, based on employee, stakeholder, and community interest. Then, they go to Stage Two: Committing to Disclosure. This determines which topics are significant enough to address in various reports, such as the annual report, CSR report, and proxy statement. Finally, companies move to Stage 3: Tying to Compensation. This is the process of incorporating HCM metrics into incentives for executives to bring about certain behaviors and actions within the company.[32]

Ernst and Young put out a report on the importance of the changes in the governance of human capital, along with some key findings from survey results from directors. Some key points revealed in the survey results include the differences in viewpoints within management regarding the importance of human capital and talent issues and whether they should be addressed in management. A large percentage of directors claim that board members spend more time talking about talent strategy. The majority of directors support initiatives to increase skills and training for employees. Directors claim to stay current on human capital trends through frequent briefings. About half of the directors claim that the company's annual reports to stakeholders and the public don't communicate the strategies surrounding human capital.[33]

In 2020, the SEC adopted a new rule requiring companies to disclose key information surrounding their human capital management. Aon PLC conducted research quantifying the types of common disclosures and what companies can do to better communicate these disclosures to customers and stakeholders. According to the research, diversity, geography, and talent development are the three most common disclosure categories. The most common industries reporting on these categories include utilities, materials, and information technology. More than 50% of the disclosures in collective bargaining, turnover/attrition, and diversity are quantitative. The research also revealed that companies with a higher headcount are generally associated with greater numbers of categories disclosed.[34]

The European Union Taxonomy is arguably one of the most significant contributions to the fight for sustainability reporting.[35] This performance threshold tool enables companies, investors, and issuers to meet safeguards for sustainability reporting. The EU Taxonomy has three thresholds referred to as "technical screening criteria," which are as follows: (1) Substantially contribute to one of the six environmental objectives, which include climate change mitigation, climate change adaption, sustainable and protection of water and marine resources, transition to a circular economy, pollution prevention and control, and protection and restoration of biodiversity, and ecosystems; (2) Do no significant harm to the other five environmental objectives and; (3) Meet the minimum safeguards for the OECD Guidelines on Multinational Enterprises and the UN Guiding Principles on business and human rights.[36]

The report demonstrates how social standards should be integrated into OECD Guidelines and in practice. Specifically, the OECD guidance for due diligence and responsible business conduct involves identifying and assessing adverse impacts, mitigating those adverse impacts, tracking the implementation and results, and finally communicating how the impacts were addressed. This cycle should be used to address the social risks of the business continuously. Investors and other stakeholders consider the social safeguards and risks a company faces, including the amount and credibility of available information, the nature of the financial product, and the company's size. Social sustainability performance measures the maximization of positive and minimization of negative impacts on society and how well a company has translated its social goals into practice. Social sustainability performance is about making the company's social purpose a reality and aligning it with the interests of society. Social sustainability performance should be linked to corporate policies that are predominantly community service-driven to improve social conditions.

In recent years, perceived social injustice and social unrest have encouraged business organizations to focus on their racial and ethnic diversity beyond the board of directors and into the broader workplace and how it impacts their social sustainability performance. Examples of social sustainability performance are (1) charitable giving; (2) support of communities; (3) innovative giving; (4) support for housing for low-income individuals; (5) support for education; (6) net employment created; (7)

number of new employee hires; (8) number of employee terminations; (9) women and minority contracting; (10) employment of disabled people; and (11) employee diversity policies. The social sustainability performance dimension ranges from the safety, health, and well-being of employees, customers, and suppliers to positive contributions to the planet's sustainability and improving the quality of life for future generations.

The 2020 COVID-19 pandemic created more opportunities for business organizations to focus on their social responsibility beyond making a profit and what laws and regulations require. While the 2020 COVID-19 pandemic brought on many challenges, including remote work and disruption, stress, and uncertainty, it did cause business organizations to pay attention to rethinking their approach to human capital management, including employee health, safety, and well-being. Investors are also interested in knowing how companies respond to perceived social injustice, changes in employee recruitment, training, development, retention policies and practices, and changes in corporate culture, business environment, and purpose.

Some key attributes and aspects of the social dimension of sustainability performance are:

- **Labor practices and human rights**: achieving fair and ethical labor practices throughout the supply chain, promoting human rights within the organization and its operations, and providing safe working conditions and fair wages for employees.
- **Diversity, equity, and inclusion (DEI)**: promoting DEI in the workplace, enabling equal opportunities for all employees, regardless of gender, ethnicity, race, or other characteristics, and promoting a business culture that values and celebrates diversity.
- **Employee well-being**: emphasizing the health and well-being of employees, providing wellness programs and benefits, and offering a supportive work environment that encourages work-life balance.
- **Employee training and development**: offering opportunities for employee training and skill development, providing continuous learning and career advancement, and empowering employees to reach their full potential.
- **Supply chain and work environment ethics**: ensuring ethical practices throughout the supply chain and work environment, collaborating with suppliers to achieve social responsibility, and conducting due diligence to prevent unethical practices and human rights violations.
- **Health and safety**: providing health and safety measures in the workplace, setting policies and practices to prevent accidents and occupational hazards, and adhering to health and safety laws, rules, regulations, standards and best practices.
- **Social impact assessment**: evaluating the social impact of business activities, addressing potential negative social impacts of business affairs, and monitoring and measuring social key performance indicators (KPIs).

- **Community engagement**: engaging with local and national communities to understand their needs and concerns, contributing to community development initiatives and social programs, and developing positive relationships with local stakeholders.
- **Fair trade practices**: participating in fair trade practices with trading partners and suppliers, ensuring that fair wages are paid to employees and producers in the supply chain, and encouraging fair trade certification standards.
- **Philanthropy and social investment**: encouraging charitable causes and community organizations through philanthropy, aligning corporate giving with the values and needs of communities, and investing in social impact projects that address societal issues and challenges.

Business organizations that engage in the social dimension of sustainability performance contribute to the safety, health, and well-being of employees, promote positive relationships with communities, and play an important role in addressing broader societal issues and challenges, and thus improve the company's reputation and ensure their social license to operate.

III.3 Governance Dimension of Sustainability Performance

Corporate governance is an important dimension of sustainability performance and will continue to be critical in the twenty-first century for addressing economic and business challenges, such as the persistence of financial scandals, business misconduct, the 2017–2019 global financial crisis, and the 2020 global COVID-19 pandemic. Corporate governance measures, both internal (independent board) and external (rules and regulations), have been established by policymakers, regulators, and corporations in terms of best practices to effectively manage corporations and promote economic stability, public trust, and investor confidence in public financial reports. Corporate governance can be defined in several ways; first, it is a process of managing the organization for the benefit of its stakeholders. Second, it is a process of aligning management interests with those of shareholders. Third, it is a process of compliance with a set of laws, rules, regulations, and standards relevant to the operation of public companies. Governance sustainability performance reflects how well corporate governance participants, from the board of directors to executives, financial advisors, accountants, auditors, and legal counsel, fulfill their responsibilities in creating shared value for all stakeholders and protecting their interests.

Corporate governance performance reflects the way business organizations are managing and operating to generate shared value for all stakeholders and whether their decision-making processes contribute to sustainable practices. Corporate governance plays an essential role in shaping business organizations' policies, strategies, and actions that influence their environmental and social impact. The corporate governance structure consists of principles that guide corporate participants and gatekeepers in fulfilling their responsibilities; corporate governance functions that define the roles and responsibilities of corporate participants from directors to executives, auditors, legal counsel, and financial advisors; and mechanisms that determine corporate governance measures.[37] Corporate governance functions are oversight functions delegated to the board of directors to protect shareholder interests, managerial functions given to executives for managing the organization for the benefit of shareholders, and other functions such as internal and external auditing, legal and advisory compliance, and monitoring functions. Corporate governance mechanisms are internal and external multidimensional measures, and it is important to consider all measures when examining governance sustainability performance. The corporate governance landscape has also changed significantly after the global 2007–2009 financial crisis. The lack of effective corporate governance has frequently been an overriding factor in the global financial crisis. For example, a a rising trend in corporate governance is "say on pay." As businesses become more transparent regarding their inner workings, not to mention adapting to the stark realization of the income gap brought to light throughout the Great Recession, shareholders are asking for more say in how companies reward their executives.

The 2020 COVID-19 pandemic and the recent move toward social justice and environmental consciousness have changed the landscape of corporate governance with a focus on protecting the interests of shareholders and creating shared value for all stakeholders. The 2020 COVID-19 pandemic has changed and continues to affect all operating and governance attributes of business organizations, from the oversight function of the board of directors to the managerial function of management, the audit function of auditors, and the monitory function of policymakers and regulators. These functions have been significantly changed, and their effectiveness has been compromised as business organizations are required to focus on the safety, health, and well-being of their customers, suppliers, and employees. In addition to the traditional shareholder governance concept with a focus on stakeholders, the stakeholder governance concept has recently been debated in the governance and accounting literature with pros and cons.[38]

Proponents of stakeholder governance support stakeholder capitalism, which determines the roles and responsibilities of corporate gatekeepers that focus on benefiting all stakeholders. Opponents of stakeholder governance argue that stakeholder governance does not directly benefit all stakeholders and may impose additional costs on shareholders and society. Recently, the World Economic Forum (WEF, 2020) supported the stakeholder governance concept in the context of stakeholder capitalism and has developed the stakeholder governance principles to protect the interests of shareholders, employees, customers, suppliers, governments, and society.[39] The stakeholder governance concept underscores the importance of business survival and continuity in the short term in response to the challenges brought on by the COVID-19 pandemic and sustainable value creation for all shareholders in the long term in response to sustainable strategic planning. The stakeholder governance concept promotes corporate governance as coordination and collaboration among all corporate governance participants, from shareholders to other stakeholders and boards of directors executives, to achieve financial ESP and non-financial ESG sustainability performance in creating shared value for all stakeholders. The emerging stakeholder governance concept enables business organizations to redefine their purpose of achieving financial, social, and environmental impacts and better realize their responsibility for the safety, health, and well-being of employees, customers, and suppliers. The stakeholder governance concept should be driven by a new comprehensive and coherent set of guiding principles, a new set of governance functions redefining the fiduciary duties of directors and executives to all stakeholders, and a new set of corporate governance mechanisms and measures.

In recent years, different internal and external corporate governance mechanisms and measures have been established by policymakers and regulators to improve the quality of corporate governance. As a result, these establishments enhance stakeholders' trust and investors' confidence in sustainable corporate performance and reporting. The governance dimension of sustainability performance is affected by regulatory, legal, internal, and external mechanisms and best practices to create shareholder value while protecting the interests of other stakeholders. Effective corporate governance sustainability performance promotes accountability for the board of directors and executives, enhances sustainable operational and financial performance, improves the reliability and quality of financial ESP information and non-financial ESG disclosures, and strengthens the integrity and efficiency of the capital markets.

Corporate governance measures are established and implemented to provide guidelines for corporate gatekeepers from the board of directors to management, accountants, auditors, regulators, policymakers, financial advisors, and legal counsel to fulfill their responsibility of working together in improving corporate governance performance. The effectiveness of corporate governance performance determines an organization's success in pursuing sustainable strategic planning to achieve shared value for all stakeholders. The EU Taxonomy addresses governance metrics by recommending that companies apply corporate governance practices drawn from the G20/OECD Principles of Corporate Governance.[40] This endorsement includes focusing the company's attention on compliance with emerging topics, such as human and labor rights, and combating bribery extortion and social injustice encountered in recent years. Some key performance indicators relevant to governance are (1) board independence; (2) reasonable compensation for directors and executives; (3) composition of the highest governance functions; (4) ownership structure; (5) transparency; (6) composition of company share ownership and voting rights; (7) stock ownership by directors and officers; and (8) executive compensation disclosures (ratio of CEO compensation to non-CEO). While business organizations have adopted these corporate governance KPIs in the past several decades, many of these KPIs are descriptive and historical. Thus, stakeholders, especially investors, expect a move towards forward-looking corporate governance KPIs demonstrating accountability, commitment, and progress toward best business sustainability practices. Corporate governance measures and effectiveness are gaining the attention of policymakers, regulators, investors, other stakeholders, and the business community.

As representatives of shareholders fulfilling their fiduciary duties, the board of directors should be engaged in effective corporate governance strategies and adopt strategies beyond just compliance with some rules and regulations. Public companies, in improving the quality and effectiveness of their corporate governance framework, should consider the following measures:

- Focus on long-term and sustainable strategic plans.
- Ensure compliance with all applicable laws, rules, regulations, and standards.
- Improve board diversity and representation.
- Engage stakeholders in the board oversight function.
- Address sustainability factors of performance, risk, and disclosure.

Some of the main attributes and aspects of the governance dimension of sustainability performance are: (1) shareholders' participation in the election of directors; (2) effective board oversight of sustainability initiatives, appointing competent and ethical management to manage the company for the benefits of its shareholders, setting the overall direction of the company, and demonstrating commitment to sustainability; (3) integrating sustainability into business environment, corporate culture and the core business strategy and decision-making processes to ensure long-term sustainability; (3) engaging with and considering the interests of all stakeholders from shareholders to employees, customers, communities, and suppliers, society and the environment; (4) preparing and publishing integrated sustainability reports that provide stakeholders with comprehensive information on their financial ESP and non-financial ESG; (5) promoting ethical behavior and a culture of sustainability within the company to foster sustainable practices and values throughout the company; (6) incorporating risk management processes that identify, assess and mange sustainability-related risks that are presented in Chapter 7; (7) focusing on long-term goals and outcomes rather than short-term gains; (8) holding management responsible and accountable for stewardship of all sustainability capitals presented in Chapter 6; and (9) ensuring compliance with all applicable laws, rules, regulations, standards, and best practices of corporate governance.

Overall, the governance dimension of sustainability performance reflects the need for stakeholder engagement, effective leadership by the board of directors, strategic integration of sustainability, transparency, and ethical decision-making by management to ensure that organizations contribute positively to economic viability and environmental and social impacts.

IV. IMPORTANCE AND RELEVANCE OF SUSTAINABILITY PERFORMANCE

Integrating financial ESP and non-financial ESG sustainability performance dimensions into corporate culture, strategic planning, business environment, and managerial decisions and actions can create sustainable performance and thus create shared value for all stakeholders. This integration enables companies to pursue the mission of profit-with-purpose, optimize production processes, identify product innovations, achieve cost efficiency and effectiveness, conserve scarce resources, increase productivity, promote corporate reputation, and create shared value for all stakeholders. However, engaging in sustainability activities is not without costs and may require considerable resource allocation that could conflict with shareholder wealth maximization objectives and force management to invest in sustainability initiatives that do not directly benefit shareholders. Management engagement in non-financial ESG sustainability activities performance can be viewed as value-increasing or value-decreasing for investors. On the one hand, companies that effectively manage their business sustainability improve ESG performance, enhance their reputation, promote customer satisfaction, fulfill their social responsibility, ensure environmental impacts, and promote a corporate culture of integrity and competency.

On the other hand, companies can only survive and generate sustainable performance when they continue to generate profits and create shareholder wealth. Nonetheless, financial ESP and non-financial ESG sustainability performance supplement and complement each other and are not mutually exclusive and not competing. Companies with effective non-financial ESG sustainability performance are expected to produce sustainable performance, create shareholder value, and gain investor confidence and public trust. Sustainability has gained the attention of global financial institutions and investors as they began considering how ESG risks affect their investment portfolio value.

Properly establishing and implementing sustainable strategic planning requires identifying all stakeholders and integrating all financial ESP and non-financial ESG dimensions of sustainability performance into the business environment, corporate culture, and managerial processes. Business sustainability enables management to focus on long-term and enduring financial and non-financial performance and disclose high-value and forward-looking information to all stakeholders. Under business sustainability management, managers can gather and use relevant financial ESP and non-financial EESG information for planning and forecasting purposes. Through business sustainability strategic planning, management can better focus on sustainable value-deriving activities and use sustainability information to effectively communicate the company's sustainability performance, creating shared value for stakeholders. Business sustainability promotes the mission of profit-with-purpose, business strategy, planning and decision-making, supply chain, and financial and non-financial management. It is important to communicate sustainability performance information regarding business profit, processes, people, and the planet (the environment) to all stakeholders in an integrated sustainability report. Sustainable strategic planning focusing on achieving sustainable performance suggests that management must extend its focus beyond maximizing short-term shareholder profit by considering the impact of its operation and entire value chains on all stakeholders, including the community, society, and the environment. Disclosure of financial ESP and non-financial ESG dimensions of sustainability performance while signaling management commitments to sustainability and establishing legitimacy with all constituencies poses a cost–benefit trade-off that has implications for investors and business organizations. In creating stakeholder value, management should identify potential social, environmental, governance, and ethical issues and integrate them into their strategic planning and managerial processes.

There are many reasons and justifications why management should integrate sustainability performance into its processes and practices, including the pressure of the labor movement, the development of moral values and social standards, and the change in public opinion about the role of business, environmental matters, governance, and ethical scandals. Companies that are, or aspire to be, leaders in sustainability are challenged by raising public expectations and increasing innovation, continuous quality improvement, effective governance measures, high standards of ethics and integrity, and heightened social and environmental problems. Thus, management should develop and maintain proper sustainability programs that provide a common framework for the integration of financial ESP and non-financial ESG dimensions of sustainability to their management processes that consist of:

- Development of the mission of profit-with-purpose to focus on creating shared value for all stakeholders.
- Integration of financial and non-financial sustainability KPIs into the business and investment analysis, supply chain management, and decision-making process.
- Communication of the company's management sustainability strategies, practices, and expectations to major stakeholders, suppliers, and customers to mitigate risks and foster corporate values and culture.
- Continuous assessment of the company's sustainability initiatives and related managerial processes to monitor and improve sustainability performance and identify challenging areas and risks that need further improvements.
- Promotion of product innovation and quality, customer retention and attraction, employee satisfaction, talent attraction, and productivity through management sustainability processes.
- Development of environmental, social, ethical, and governance initiatives that will impact the company's ability to generate sustainable financial performance for shareholders and create value for all stakeholders.
- Establishment of financial and non-financial KPIs relevant to ESP and ESG dimensions of sustainability performance that support management strategic decisions and actions.
- Develop integrated sustainability reports to ensure that relevant financial and non-financial sustainability performance information is disclosed to all stakeholders.
- Prepare periodic certifications of both financial and non-financial sustainability KPIs, issue integrated sustainability reports, and secure external assurance reports on financial ESP and non-financial ESG dimensions of sustainability performance.

Business sustainability requires organizations to refocus their business purpose to create shared value for all stakeholders. Business organizations should expand their mission to generate profit, create shareholder value, and ensure shared value for all stakeholders. The concept of shared value challenges how we think about profits, philanthropy, sustainability, and development. Sustainable shared value creation enables business organizations to integrate financial ESP with non-financial ESG into business culture and the corporate environment. Shared value initiatives can be created in three ways: (1) producing products and services that increase shareholder wealth and meet societal needs, including improved nutrition, education, health, and general well-being; (2) redefining productivity in the supply chain by investing in training and resources to create high-quality suppliers and improve ESP and ESG sustainability performance; and (3) developing material indicator taxonomies to effectively measure revenue, costs, and value of organizations.

Emerging business sustainability requires management to consider divergent economic, governance, social, ethical, and environmental issues simultaneously. Stewardship theory enables management to effectively exercise stewardship over a broader range of financial and non-financial assets and capitals, including financial, physical, human, social, and environmental capital. Stewardship, among other theories, enables firms and their management to translate ESG sustainability performance to financial performance and, thus, firm value creation. The relationships between business, society, and the environment are complex and often tense, and management must find ways to address the potential tension and maximize both financial and ESG sustainability performance. However, a single, cohesive, and integrated theory of business sustainability is lacking in explaining the multidimensional and conflicting aspects of sustainability performance. Management is generally responsible for stewarding corporate resources, including assets and capital, with an ethical vision toward benefitting the broader range of stakeholders, including society and the environment. Thus, management should not impose its vision of "good" on society but instead seek compliance with regulatory measures and the best sustainability practices in creating shared value for all stakeholders. Regardless of which theory is more relevant to a particular firm or whether integrated theories can be more effective, management should address climate change and other environmental challenges effectively.

As stewards of business resources and capital, management are responsible for minimizing capital utilization, including financial, manufacturing, strategic, human, social, environmental, and reputational capital, as discussed in Chapter 6. Management's primary role is to design and implement sustainable strategic planning that creates shared value for all stakeholders by improving sustainability performance. Sustainability enables management to continuously improve performance by addressing business challenges in managing opportunities and risks. However, a stewardship mindset requires management strategies and actions to continuously improve both financial ESP and non-financial ESG components of sustainability performance. Specifically, the rationales for the promotion of management stewardship in business sustainability are:

1. Business sustainability tends to align with the goal of long-term shared value creation for all stakeholders.
2. Sustainability can be achieved through effective practices of corporate operations, risk management, governance, and compliance.
3. Ineffective stewardship and unsustainable performance can contribute to losing value for all stakeholders, including shareholders.

In summary, business sustainability has gained significant attention from global investors, regulators, the business community, public companies, academics, and the accounting profession. More than 20,000 public companies worldwide are issuing sustainability reports on their financial ESP and non-financial ESG dimensions of sustainability performance, and this number is expected to increase worldwide. Proper measurement of sustainability performance, accurate and reliable disclosure of sustainability performance information, and effective assessment of sustainability risks remain major challenges for business organizations. Different dimensions of business sustainability performance are considered in isolation, without effective integrations of both financial ESP and non-financial (ESG) sustainability performance and disclosures/reporting. Many business organizations have failed to establish the link between financial ESP and non-financial ESG and the integrated relationship with the bottom-line earnings. A proper link should be established to convince investors of the importance of ESG sustainability performance, communicate good ESG stories to all stakeholders, and show compliance with all mandatory sustainability initiatives.

Business sustainability is a multidisciplinary and multidimensional concept with multiple users. This chapter addresses financial ESP and non-financial ESG dimensions of business sustainability when analyzing their impacts on business practices and outcomes holistically by considering the reciprocal relationship among all related parties. Business sustainability has traditionally been defined only in terms of one aspect of CSR and thus ignores regulations and practices related to other dimensions of sustainability. These incomplete definitions of business sustainability could not provide a full picture of the underlying business practice and may provide incomplete yet biased conclusions. Attention should be given to the interactions of both financial ESP and non-financial ESG dimensions of sustainability performance and possible tensions among these dimensions. Financial ESP is the primary dimension that should be emphasized, and its link to non-financial ESG sustainability performance should be addressed. Business sustainability describes current sustainability reporting and assurance practices and how these practices can enhance the overall concept of business sustainability practice and performance. In this context, a business sustainability model should incorporate activities that generate financial (long-term earnings, growth, and return on investment) and non-financial ESG sustainability performance that concern all stakeholders. In practice, business sustainability should be viewed as a collection of procedures that improve both financial ESP and non-financial ESG sustainability performance dimensions which create shared value for all stakeholders. This chapter presents sustainability financial and non-financial performance reporting and assurance in detail.

V. CONCLUSION

An ever-increasing interest in business sustainability in the past several decades has led to a growth in the literature addressing the theoretical and practical implications of various dimensions of business sustainability. Business sustainability focuses on corporate activities, including supply chains that generate long-term financial ESP of firm value maximization in creating shareholder value, as well as other activities that result in the achievement of non-financial ESG sustainability performance that protects the interests of all stakeholders. Business organizations worldwide recognize the importance of sustainability factors in planning and performance. Business sustainability suggests that a firm must fulfill its stewardship responsibilities to all stakeholders, including shareholders, creditors, the community, society, and the environment. Disclosure of ESP and ESG sustainability performance dimensions while signaling management commitments to sustainability and establishing legitimacy with all constituencies poses a cost–benefit trade-off that has implications for investors and business organizations. In creating shared value for all stakeholders, management should identify potential financial, social, environmental, governance, and ethical issues and integrate them into its decision-making, strategic planning, and managerial processes, including supply chain management.

Business sustainability indicates that the main objective function of business organizations is to create shareholder value by maximizing firm financial performance through continuous improvements of both financial ESP and non-financial ESG sustainability performance. The ESP and ESG sustainability performance dimensions are interrelated and complement/complete each other, and thus, they should be integrated into the corporate environment and business culture. The focus of business sustainability should be on creating long-term and sustainable shared value for all stakeholders. Integrating ESP and ESG into business culture indicates that management realizes the importance of sustainability in supply chain management and business operations.

VI. TAKEAWAYS

- More than 1,300 institutional investors worldwide, representing $59 trillion in assets under management, have signed on to the UN Principles of Responsible Investing, which seek to integrate sustainability factors of performance and risk into investment objectives.

- Business sustainability is advancing from greenwashing and branding to, very recently, business imperative with integration into the business model, corporate culture, and strategic plan.
- There is a growing demand from investors for relevant and reliable non-financial ESG information for making investment decisions in the aftermath of the 2020 global COVID-19 pandemic.
- Build awareness of growing sustainability opportunities and challenges.
- Integrate ESP and ESG dimensions of sustainability performance into company's strategic plans, business processes, and supply chain.
- Incorporate the sustainability performance strategy into the overall corporate strategy, including operational processes.
- Tell company's success sustainability performance stories and best practices of sustainability performance.

Notes

1 Much of the discussion and materials for this section and the next two sections come from Rezaee, Z. 2015. *Business Sustainability: Performance, Compliance, Accountability and Integrated Reporting*. Greenleaf Publishing Limited.

2 Global Reporting Initiative (GRI). 2013. *G4 Exposure Draft. Frequently Asked Questions about the G4 Exposure Draft and the Second G4 Public Comment Period*. Available at https://www.globalreporting.org/resourcelibrary/G4-ED-PCP2-FAQs.pdf

3 KPMG. 2013. *Beyond Quarterly Earnings: Is the Company on Track for Long-term Success?* Spring 2013 Audit Committee Roundtable Report. Available at auditcommittee@kpmg.com

4 Ibid.

5 Ibid.

6 TEG. March 2020. Final Report on Financing A sustainable European Economy. EU Technical Expert Group on Sustainable Finance. Taxonomy.

7 KPMG. 2020. "On the 2020 Audit Committee Agenda Board Leadership Center." *Summer 2020 Audit Committee Roundtable Report*. Available at https://boardleadership.kpmg.us/content/dam/boardleadership/en/pdf/2019/on-the-2020-audit-committee-agenda.pdf

8 EY Center for Board Matters. September 8, 2020. *What Audit Committees Should Consider at the End of 2020 and Beyond. 2020.* https://assets.ey.com/content/dam/ey-sites/ey-com/en_us/topics/board-matters/ey-what-audit-committees-should-consider-at-the-end-of-2020-and-beyond.pdf

9 Coalition for Environmentally Responsible Economies (CERES). 2024. *Sustainability is the Bottom Line*. Available at https://www.ceres.org/

10 Ng, A. and Rezaee, Z. 2018. "The Emergence of Business Sustainability: Educational, Practical and Research Implications." In *Research Handbook of Finance and Sustainability*. Edward Elgar Publishing, Cheltenham, UK. doi: https://doi.org/10.4337/9781786432636.00034

11 Alsayegh, M. F., Abdul Rahman, R. and S. Homayoun. 2020. "Corporate Economic, Environmental, and Social Sustainability Performance Transformation through ESG Disclosure." *Sustainability* Vol. 12, No. 9. Available at https://www.mdpi.com/2071-1050/12/9/3910

12 International Standardization Organization (ISO). ISO 14000 Family: Environmental Management. https://www.iso.org/iso-14001-environmental-management.html.

13 Network for Greening the Financial System (NGFS). April 2019. *A Call for Action Climate Change as a Source of Financial Risk. Network for Greening the Financial System Executive Summary First Comprehensive Report.*

14 Ibid.

15 Network for Greening the Financial System. March 2021. *Annual Report 2020.* Available at https://www.ngfs.net/sites/default/files/medias/documents/ngfs_annual_report_2020.pdf

16 Financial Stability Board (FSB). June 2017. *Final Report: Recommendations of the Task Force on Climate-Related Financial Disclosures.* Available at https://www.fsb-tcfd.org/wp-content/uploads/2017/06/FINAL-2017-TCFD-Report-11052018.pdf

17 Task Force on Climate-Related Financial Disclosures. October 2021. *Implementing the Recommendations of the Task Force on Climate-Related Financial Disclosures.* https://assets.bbhub.io/company/sites/60/2021/07/2021-TCFD-Implementing_Guidance.pdf

18 Securities and Exchange Commission. August 8, 2019. Modernization of Regulation S-K Items 101, 103, and 105, Release No. 33–10668.

19 SEC Investor Advisory Committee. "Discussion Regarding Whether Investors Use Environmental, Social, and Governance (ESG) Data in Investment/Capital Allocation Decisions." https://www.sec.gov/spotlight/investor-advisory-committee- 2012/iac110719-agenda.htm

20 Securities and Exchange Commission (SEC). July 28, 2021. Speech by Chair Gary Gensler. Prepared Remarks Before the Principles for Responsible Investment "Climate and Global Financial Markets" Webinar. Available at https://www.sec.gov/news/speech/gensler-pri-2021–07–28

21 European Commission (EU). 2023. EU Taxonomy for Sustainable Activities. Available at https://finance.ec.europa.eu/sustainable-finance/tools-and-standards/eu-taxonomy-sustainable-activities_en

22 European Reporting Lab. February 8, 2021. *Proposals For A Relevant And Dynamic EU Sustainability Reporting Standard Setting.* https://ec.europa.eu/info/sites/default/files/business_economy_euro/banking_and_finance/documents/210308-report-efrag-sustainability-reporting-standard-setting_en.pdf

23 HM Treasury. November 2020. *A Roadmap Towards Mandatory Climate-Related Disclosures.* https://assets.publishing.service.gov.uk/government/uploads/system/uploads/attachment_data/file/933783/FINAL_TCFD_ROADMAP.pdf

24 Bank of England Prudential Regulation Authority. April 2019. Supervisory Statement, *SS3/19 Enhancing Banks' and Insurers' Approaches to Managing the Financial Risks from Climate Change.* https://www.bankofengland.co.uk/-/media/boe/files/prudential-regulation/supervisory-statement/2019/ss319

25 The Investor Protection Act is comprised of several smaller bills: ESG Disclosure Simplification Act, Shareholder Political Transparency Act, Greater Accountability in Pay Act, Climate Risk Disclosure Act, Disclosure of Tax Havens and Offshoring Act, Workforce Investment Disclosure Act, Preventing and Responding to Workplace Harassment, Cybersecurity Disclosure, Improving Corporate Governance Through Diversity Act, Uyghur Forced Labor Disclosure Act, and Study and Report on Small Business and ESG Disclosures.

26 Press Release, Executive Order on Climate-Related Financial Risk. May 20, 2021. https://www.whitehouse.gov/briefing-room/presidential-actions/2021/05/20/executive-order-on-climate-related-financial-risk/

27 State of Vermont V Exxon Mobil Corporation, ExxonMobil Oil Corporation, Royal Dutch Shell Plc, Shell Oil Company, Shell Oil Products Company Llc, Motiva Enterprises Llc, Sunoco LP, Sunoco LLC, Etc Sunoco Holdings Llc, Energy Transfer (R&M) Llc, Energy Transfer LP, and Citgo Petroleum Corporation. ZCC_(002).pdf (wlrk.com)

28 United Nations Principles of Responsible Investing (UN PRI). 2005. *The Freshfields Report*. Available at www.unepfi.org/fileadmin/documents/freshfields_legal_resp_20051123.pdf

29 Social Investment Forum (SIF). November 2012. 2012 Report on Sustainable and Responsible Investing Trends in the United States. US SIF foundation: The forum for sustainable and responsible investment.

30 United Nations Human Rights. 2011. *UN Guiding Principles on Business and Human Rights*. Available at https://www.ohchr.org/documents/publications/guidingprinciples businesshr_en.pdf

31 Securities and Exchange Commission (SEC). August 26, 2020. "Amendments Regarding the Modernization of Regulation S-K, Final Rules." Available at https://www.sec.gov/rules/final/2020/33–10825.pdf

32 Arnold, Greg and Friedlander, Andrew. September 2, 2021. The HCM Funnel: Board Considerations. Semler Brossy. https://semlerbrossy.com/insights/the-hcm-funnel/

33 Ernst and Young. 2020. *How the Governance of Human Capital and Talent is Shifting: Key Findings from a Survey of Public Company Directors*. A Corporate Board Member/ EY Center for Board Matters Report.

34 Allen, Wanlass, and Harden. January 2021. "Analysis of New Human Capital Disclosures by U.S. Public Companies." Aon PLC. https://humancapital.aon.com/insights/articles/2021/analysis-of-new-human-capital-disclosures-by-u-s-public-companies

35 EU Technical Expert Group on Sustainable Finance. March 2020. *Financing a Sustainable European Economy. Technical Report. Taxonomy: Final Report of the Technical Expert Group on Sustainable Finance*. Available at https://ec.europa.eu/info/sites/info/files/business_economy_euro/banking_and_finance/documents/200309-sustainable-finance-teg-final-report-taxonomy_en.pdf

36 European Commission. "EU Taxonomy for Sustainable Activities: What the EU is doing to create an EU-wide classification system for sustainable activities." https://ec.europa.eu/info/business-economy-euro/banking-and-finance/sustainable-finance/eu-taxonomy-sustainable-activities_en

37 Rezaee, Z. March 2018. *Corporate Governance in the Aftermath of the Global Financial Crisis*, four volumes. Business Expert Press.

38 Rezaee, Z. and R. Y. Rezaee. 2021. "Modified Corporate Governance for the Hospitality Industry in Aftermath of the COVID-19 Pandemic." *Journal of Tourism Studies and Hospitality Research* Vol. 2, No. 2, 1–11.

39 The World Economic Forum (WEF). June 2020a. *Integrated Corporate Governance: A Practical Guide to Stakeholder Capitalism for Boards of Directors*. White Paper. Available at http://www3.weforum.org/docs/WEF_Integrated_Corporate_Governance_2020.pdf

The World Economic Forum (WEF). April 24, 2020. "World Economic Forum Pledges to Stand by Stakeholders in the COVID-19 Era." Available at https://www.weforum.org/agenda/2020/03/world-economic-forum-launches-covid-action-platform/

40 Ibid.

Chapter 6

Corporate Sustainability Capital

I. INTRODUCTION

Business organizations have typically utilized financial capital to generate profit to create value for shareholders. The recent move toward adopting business sustainability encourages organizations to pay attention to other types of capital in creating shared value for all stakeholders.[1] The magnitude of environmental, social, governance (ESG) sustainability-focused investment was $37.8 trillion at the end of 2020 and is predicted to reach $53 trillion by 2025.[2] Investors investing in and holding ESG funds require that corporations define their purpose of generating desired financial returns and achieving social and environmental impacts. Globalization, technological advances, and financial crises have forced corporations to focus on the short-termism of meeting or beating analysts' forecast expectations. However, corporations are now experiencing pressures from social activists and stakeholders to pay attention to long-term strategic sustainability planning to create shared value for all stakeholders and protect the interests of customers, suppliers, employees, society, and the environment. Achievement of financial economic sustainability performance (ESP) and non-financial environmental, social, and governance (ESG) sustainability performance, discussed in Chapter 5, requires business organizations, their boards of directors, and executives to utilize financial and non-financial capitals presented in this chapter effectively.

II. TYPES OF SUSTAINABILITY CAPITALS

Business organizations have generally employed financial capital, both equity and debt capital, in their financing, investing, and operating activities in generating

DOI: 10.4324/9781003437949-6

revenues; giving less attention to non-financial capital. The recent move toward sustainability requires business organizations to utilize all types of financial capital (equity, debt) and non-financial (strategic, reputational, human, social, and environmental) to generate shared value for all stakeholders. Sustainability capitals represent all various aspects crucial for achieving long-term economic, environmental, and social goals. These capitals are interconnected and play a role in sustaining financial viability and maintaining and enhancing the well-being of both present and future generations. Figure 6.1 presents the sustainability capital structure and all related capital, including strategic, financial, human operational, social, environmental, reputational/trust, intellectual, and manufactured capital. The IIRC suggests six capitals: (1) financial capital, (2) manufactured capital, (3) intellectual capital, (4) human capital, (5) social and relationship capital, and (6) natural capital, that organizations can utilize in creating shared value for all stakeholders.[3] Management is the steward of strategic, financial, human, social, and environmental capital and the active and long-term oriented steward of all stakeholders, including shareholders. Some capitals are interrelated, but all collectively create shared value for all stakeholders.

The ever-increasing importance of business sustainability and the related ongoing issues require management to consider divergent economic, governance, social, and environmental issues simultaneously. The focus on sustainability capital enables management to effectively exercise stewardship over a broader range of business capital (financial, environmental, social, and reputational) to ensure business continuity and sustainability of non-financial human capital in protecting the safety, health, and well-being of investors, employees, customers, and suppliers. The relationship between business, society, and the environment is complex and often tense, and it has become more relevant in recent years because management is now required to be a good steward of all capital, including financial, human, environmental, and social. The following subsections present several sustainability capitals in alphabetical order as illustrated in Figure 6.1.

II.1 Environmental/Natural Capital

The environmental/natural capital, including air, water, land, biodiversity, and ecosystems, is relevant to the environmental impacts of the operation either through the use of natural resources and non-renewable assets as an input to the supply chain, or production, or through harmful releases into the environment that could affect bottom-line financial earnings. Sustainable practices are intended to preserve and regenerate natural capital to ensure a healthy environment. Environmental capital is crucial to business organizations' long-term sustainability, growth and innovation, and worldwide economic prosperity, leaving a better environment for the next generations. Environmental/natural capital represents natural resources and ecosystems that provide valuable goods and services to humans because nature has intrinsic value and is important in supporting human well-being and existence. Natural resources consist of both renewable resources like plants and clean air and non-renewable

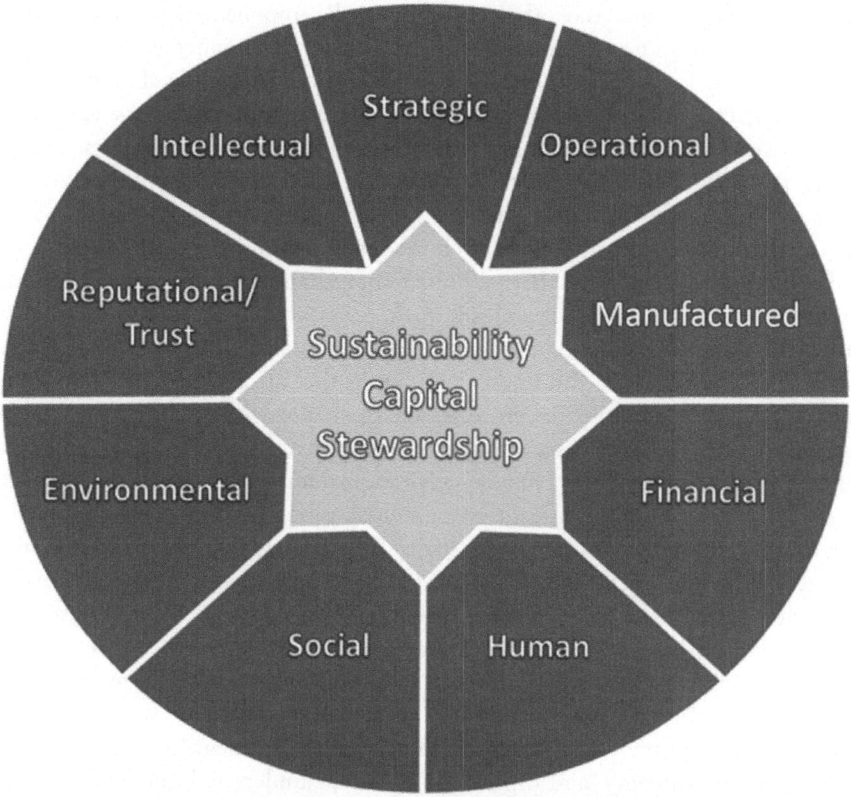

Figure 6.1 Sustainability capitals

assets like oil and gas. Environmental capital is a measure of the impact of an organization's operation on the environment, including negative values such as contamination, pollution, and desertification.

Natural capital is a part of the environment, including fertile soils, geology, air quality, clean water, and all living organisms, which affect the triple bottom line of people, profit, and planet. Organizations should preserve the environment and try to leave a better one for the next generations. It is important to understand that even though the organizations affect the environment the most, with their responsible or irresponsible behavior, the consumers are the key element here. Without the support of consumers, organizations would not be able to earn enough revenue to be profitable. That is why consumers need to demand a certain standard, but it is also crucial for organizations to adhere to it by training their employees and strictly following rules and regulations.[4]

Environmental capital often refers to the ecosystems and natural resources that provide crucial services to societies. Environmental capital consists of the air, water, soil, biodiversity, and other environmental components that contribute to the well-being of human communities and ecosystems in supporting economic and social activities. The important components of environmental/natural capital consist of (1) biodiversity of different species, genetic diversity, and ecosystems; (2) ecosystem services, including clean air and water, pollination of crops by insects, cultural and recreational services, regulation of climate; (3) renewable resources that can be regenerated naturally including sunlight, forests, wind and water that should be managed responsibly; (4) non-renewable resources including fossil fuels (coal, oil, and natural gas) and minerals that are finite resources and their use can have material environmental impacts; (5) air and soil quality that contributes to the air purification and agriculture and food production; (6) water and climate resources including rivers, lakes, and aquifers and forests and oceans that are essential for human survival, agriculture, and industrial processes and their effective management is vital for sustaining natural capital. Assessing and managing environmental capital is essential for sustainable development. Human activities, including agriculture, industrialization, and urbanization, can affect environmental capital, and any over-exploitation of resources, excessive pollution, deforestation, and climate change can degrade environmental capital. Any initiatives and efforts to promote environmental sustainability, including strategies to conserve and restore environmental capital, measures to protect biodiversity, reduce pollution, promote sustainable resource management, and address climate change, can preserve environmental capital. The environmental strategies should ensure that current and future generations can continue to benefit from the important services provided by the environment. Thus, individuals, businesses, governments, and organizations should understand and recognize the importance of integrating environmental considerations into decision-making processes. Effective recognition and management of environmental capital is important for economic growth and sustainable development. Conservation and sustainable management of natural capital are vital for maintaining the well-being of current and future generations. Any degradation of natural capital triggered by deforestation, over-exploitation of resources, and pollution can negatively affect society and the environment.

II.2 Financial Capital

Financial/economic capital consists of assets, monetary resources, and wealth that business entities, governments, and individuals use to generate earnings and support economic and business activities. Financial capital represents financial and economic resources, including infrastructure, financial systems, and wealth, to generate sustainable economic development and to balance economic growth with social and environmental considerations; for business organizations, financial capital refers to equity and debt capital. Debt capital consists of borrowing money through loans or bonds, paying interest, and the return of principal at maturity. Equity capital represents ownership in a company's shares by shareholders who have a claim on the company's assets and earnings. Efficient allocation of financial capital is important for economic efficiency and development. Effective financial capital management is vital for economic stability and growth. Effective and reliable financial management practices, efficient and transparent financial markets, and prudent and robust regulatory frameworks are important in efficiently allocating economic and financial resources.

Financial/economic sustainability performance can be achieved by continuously improving capital productivity by optimizing supply chains, cost reengineering focused on reducing operating, production, and compliance costs, improving employee productivity and efficiency, and focusing on activities that create long-term, enduring, and sustainable financial performance. Focusing on economic sustainability can also create opportunities for business innovation and growth by promoting sustainable products and services, new customer relationships, and new markets through environmentally friendly and socially acceptable products and services. Economic sustainability performance is measured in terms of long-term, accounting-based measures (return on equity, sales), market-based measures (stock returns, market-book value), and long-term investments (R&D and advertising) and is disclosed through a set of financial statements disseminated to shareholders assessing the risk and return associated with their investments. Economic capital is commonly referred to as investment capital consisting of debt and equity, but what is more important is that companies prefer raising financial capital by using equity rather than debt since it is less risky for them. One of the key ratios for determining how much and in which way the company is leveraged is the debt-to-equity ratio. This ratio is specifically important to investors when determining the riskiness of the business.[5]

When discussing financial capital, it is important to distinguish between financial and economic capital; where financial capital focuses on assets needed to provide goods and services, economic capital represents the estimated funding for potential future losses.[6] Financial capital includes cash, money and currency, bank deposits, real estate, investments, loan and debt instruments, and business ownership. Financial capital is a critical driver of economic growth, prosperity, and development by facilitating investment in productive activities, enabling innovation, and creating jobs. Sufficient financial capital is essential for businesses and individuals to start or expand operations, make investments, and generate income. Financial markets, including banking systems, stock exchanges, financial institutions, and bond markets, play an important role in allocating and distributing financial capital. Governments and central banks also influence financial capital, which is influenced by the country's monetary policies, interest rates, regulatory frameworks, and social norms, including issues of wealth distribution, income inequality, and access to financial services.

II.3 Human Capital

Human capital is the education, knowledge, skills, abilities, and other intangible assets possessed by individuals that can contribute to their productivity and economic value. Human capital is an important component of an individual's overall capabilities that can contribute to economic growth and development through education, training, and health investment. Human capital is an asset of skills possessed by the labor force that can be utilized to generate other assets by investing in people's education, health, skills, and overall well-being. The OECD defines human capital as "the knowledge, skills, competencies and other attributes embodied in individuals or groups of individuals acquired during their life and used to produce goods, services or ideas in market circumstances."[7] Human capital (HC) is defined as attributes of labor that increase productivity and is viewed as an investment in labor, including education, training, skills, capacity, health, and ability to adapt to achieve productive capacity goals, maintain innovation, and create economic value. As part of non-financial environmental, social, and governance (ESG) sustainability, human capital factors are relevant and material to investors. Human capital supports sustainable development by enhancing the capabilities and quality of life of individuals who contribute to business sustainability and success.

The important components of human capital are education, skills and knowledge, training, health and well-being, creativity and innovation, expertise and experience. Investment in human capital by focusing on improving education, healthcare, and workforce training can lead to long-term economic benefits and prosperity. Widely considered the most important asset in today's business world, human capital is still not disclosed as it should. Under the current wave of demands for non-financial ESG disclosure, stakeholders would also want to know more about human capital factors and how organizations handle them to determine if the human capital is adding to the company's long-term value. In 2018, the Embarkment Project for Inclusive Capitalism (EPIC), put together by the Coalition for Inclusive Capitalism and Ernst & Young, after defining talent as one of the key components of the long-term value creation, produced a set of metrics regarding human capital disclosure and what they call human value to propose a disclosure solution to the organizations and allow investors and other stakeholders to easily compare major factors including human capital deployment, organizational culture, and employee health across the organizations. A specific set of metrics was developed for each one of the major factors, and these include, but are not limited to, workforce cost, training, learning and development, workforce composition and diversity, lifestyle management, access to healthcare and insurance, performance and well-being, ethics, and integrity, alignment with purpose and values, teaming, and adaptability.[8] This targeted some key aspects that the major stakeholders wanted to see in the new reports, but they still did not cover some of them. In response to rising concerns, in 2019, the SEC proposed *Modernization of Regulations S-K Items 101, 103, and 105* to improve the description of the business and disclosure measures, which hadn't been updated for 30 years, focusing mainly on removal of repetition and disclosure of immaterial information. Changes such as the elimination of five-year and three-year disclosure timeframes, updated disclosures in the subsequent filings, disclosure about business strategy, and addition of information regarding the description of the business and its resources regarding human capital are only some of them.[9]

Even though the intent was there, the new SEC disclosure updates failed to reach the desired potential since they did not manage to address the main concerns and issues. In November 2020, the SEC's proposed updates were made effective, requiring organizations to provide information about human capital resources and management, but without necessarily including any specific metrics. New measures were supposed to provide all the necessary information to the stakeholders that are considered material and provide further understanding of the organization's business from the material point of view. However, problems arise when the companies follow a new set of requirements but do not provide any concrete information, meaning that the disclosure adds to the length of the 10K annual report but not the true value. Areas that were most commonly disclosed include diversity and inclusion, employee development, safety, and compensation practices, as well as other voluntarily disclosed areas such as employee engagement efforts, strategy employee turnover, culture, recruiting practices, mental health, pay equity, and succession planning. In addition, only 43% of the companies provided one or more quantitative metrics, while the other 57%did not include even one in their reports and strategy, strictly focusing on qualitative language and non-value-adding information. Therefore, even though the new SEC requirements were made to satisfy the demand for transparency and improve the understanding of how human capital adds to overall business value and strategy, only a few companies managed to fulfill this.[10]

Human capital is becoming more important as a valuable and productive asset for public companies, while employees are becoming important stakeholders for several reasons. Corporate boards increasingly prioritize human capital due to market shifts, worker expectations, and ESG demands. Topics like culture, hybrid work, diversity, and well-being are now on board agendas. The pandemic accelerated these discussions, but digital transformation and talent competition were already driving change. Regulatory drivers and investor expectations call for more human capital disclosure. Boards need to widen their view of workforce risk, enhance oversight, and address upcoming shifts like worker expectations and human–technology collaboration.[11]

First, employee participation in the production and service processes is essential as employee productivity improves corporate performance. Second, employees become shareholders by investing in the company's shares through 401K, 529 plans, and direct investment. Third, employees in many countries are given the opportunity to be represented on the board of directors of public companies. Finally, the COVID-19 pandemic has caused business organizations to assess the human capital risk by making the safety, health, and well-being of employees, customers, and suppliers a prerequisite for reopening businesses. Human capital issues are relevant to the company's human resources management as key assets to delivering long-term value. These issues affect the company's bottom line through employee productivity, labor relations, and the health and safety of employees. Human capital is an important asset that contributes significantly to long-term and sustainable value creation and protection. There is a need for proper identification, measurement, recognition, and reporting of human capital.

One of the greatest concerns regarding human capital is whether or how companies should get their stakeholders, especially their employees, involved in making important corporate-level decisions rather than pursuing the shareholder primacy model in which the benefits of shareholders are maximized. Some advantages of shared governance (also known as co-determination) include better coordination, information flows between board and employees, employees' loyalty and motivation, implicit contracts enforcement, and alignment of shareholders' and employees' interests. In the working paper *Labor in the Boardroom* in 2019, Jäger, Schoefer, and Heining exploit a 1994 reform experiment in Germany that mandated the representation of worker-elected directors in the boards of some stock corporations while eliminating board seats of workforce representatives in others. The results of the experiment show that workers' participation in the board of directors increases capital by increasing production output per worker and reducing outsourcing. Despite no clear effect on financial capacity and profitability, shared governance reduces interest payments over debt by an insignificant amount, making firms with worker-elected directors seem slightly less risky. It has also been found that the lack of workforce representatives on the board tends to cause underinvestment, while co-determination can increase investment. However, too much worker bargaining power may result in inefficiencies such as overinvestment. On top of that, if worker-elected directors only compose the minority of board seats, they tend to be more moderate in building rapport with other shareholders rather than excessively voicing demands.[12]

The co-determination model is typically promoted in European countries, especially Germany. The publicly listed companies in Germany have supervisory boards overseeing their executive boards. These supervisory boards must have workforce representatives composing one-third or half of the seats if the companies have more than 500 employees, according to Article 4(1) of the German Law on One-Third Participation and German Co-Determination Act of 1976. Article 96(2) of the German Stock Corporation Act also mandates companies with more than 2000 employees to assign at least 30% of board seats to directors of each gender. The worker-elected directors are either employees working at the firms for at least one year, company trade union members, or managerial staff. On top of the supervisory board, worker's participation is represented in works councils. Works councils function similarly to trade unions, but their members are not necessarily trade union representatives. The number of work council members is proportionate to the number of company employees, excluding senior managers (represented by other bodies), the distinguishment of manual and non-manual employees, and gender equality. Compared to workers' representation on the board, worker's participation through company shares is less popular as German regulations discourage employee equity-based incentives with a tax exemption threshold of €360 (which is significantly lower than the threshold of other countries in Europe, ranging between €2,065 and €6,000). At the "Ownership Day" conferences in 2015 and 2017, companies and experts signed an appeal to increase the tax exemption threshold to €3,000, remove dividends, interests, and taxes, and simplify regulations. According to the appeal, only 14% of Germans are shareholders, and only half of DAX 30 corporations provide their employees with equity-based incentive plans.[13]

Unlike in most European countries, shareholder primacy is more popular in the United States. As shareholders' benefits are maximized, no workers are involved in corporate decision-making, and riskier investments are usually made. Even with the help of the labor union, worker bargaining power is still low if the issues are beyond the terms and conditions of the National Labor Relations Act (NLRA). Amendments to labor laws should be made on both state and federal levels to help workers express their opinions and voice their concerns through participation in the board of directors. Recently, there have been proposals from the Reward Work Act and the Accountable Capitalism Act to mandate one-third to 40% of board seats to be assigned to employees. These proposals encourage the stakeholder theory to replace the shareholder primacy model even though implementing a co-determination policy can be challenging in the United States.[14] Business organizations recognize the importance of human capital management and disclosures intended to attract, develop, and retain a skilled and motivated workforce as part of their broader context of ESG initiatives in promoting ethical and sustainable practices in managing human resources.

II.4 Intellectual Capital

Intellectual capital refers to the intangible assets that contribute to a company's bottom-line earnings, long-term sustainability performance, business continuity, survival, and competitive advantage. Intellectual capital presents resources and intangible assets consisting of organizational investments and processes in developing intellectual capital, the expertise of employees, and all the effort knowledge contained within the organization. Intellectual capital consists of non-material resources that are not easily measurable but essential for a business's success and innovation. Intellectual capital of knowledge, innovation, and intellectual property can be classified into three main components: human capital, customer/relational capital, and organizational/structural capital presenting structural capital, including the non-physical infrastructure, processes, and databases and information technology platforms of the organization that enable other capitals, including operational, financial, and human, to function effectively. Structural capital consists of policies, processes, patents, trademarks, the organization's image, information infrastructure, proprietary software, databases, information technology platforms, innovation, and research and developments. One of the questions that arises when it comes to intellectual capital is how organizations measure it. There have been multiple approaches to this question, but only two stand out: component and holistic methods. Component method separates given elements of the intellectual capital, measures them, and then calculates the total value. On the other side, a holistic approach focuses on the market value and, based on that, determines the intellectual capital value. Both methods have been criticized, but newer research tries to answer past criticisms by combining these two methods.[15] Something important to note is that an organization's size plays a significant role in determining the disclosed amount of intellectual capital, based on the research conducted in 2020. The bigger the organization is, the higher its disclosed capital could be. This provides large organizations an opportunity to disclose potentially higher intellectual capital and minimize their business risk in case they are in debt. Profitability and leverage also positively affect the disclosure amount of intellectual capital, but these two components do not affect it as much as the company's size.[16]

Business recovery and transformation are essential to strategic planning for coping with growing challenges caused by the COVID-19 pandemic. Under the board of directors' oversight, executives, and management teams of business organizations should consider all possibilities and scenarios under which an organization can survive, recover, and continue sustainable performance by utilizing existing information technology. Business risk assessment and supply chain management can play important roles in recovery. Many business organizations have made significant modifications and adjustments to business operations and practices, using intellectual capital and information technology in response to challenges brought on by the COVID-19 pandemic. These organizations are also changing their communication, reporting, and control systems, using their intellectual capital, information technology, and virtual platforms. The finance function is better positioned to evaluate the available intellectual capital and virtual platforms and make suggestions for their adoption. Intellectual capital should be considered a strategic asset contributing to an organization's long-term success and sustainability.

II.5 Manufactured Capital

Manufactured capital is a broad descriptor and consists of issues relating to financial, environmental, human, and social integration into the company's value-creation and protection processes. Manufactured capital is the tangible assets created by humans through the manufacturing process of production. The development and maintenance of manufactured capital is essential in the achievement of business sustainability. Manufactured capital usually refers to the financial resources and assets invested in producing goods, including funds available for buying equipment, machinery, technology, raw materials, labor, and other factory overhead costs relevant to the manufacturing process. Manufactured capital is also referred to as built capital, which represents the infrastructure, buildings, manufacturing, and physical assets that support economic activities and community life. Thus, manufactured capital investments consist of financial, physical, technology, and human capital. The effectiveness of manufactured capital is typically measured by operational effectiveness, maximum utilization of resources, and return on investment (ROI).

Manufactured capital is a key component of industrial economies, where the production of tangible goods plays a significant role. It represents the financial foundation that enables companies to set up and operate manufacturing facilities, develop new technologies, and expand production capacities. Manufactured capital deals with issues of resource recovery, product innovation, use phase and disposal of products, and efficiency and responsibility in the design that determines accountability and stewardship for the broad base of capital (financial, manufactured, intellectual, human, social and relationship, and environmental) and emphasizes their interdependencies. Manufactured capital is often interchangeable with operational capital in describing activities and related resources relevant to customer relationships, trademarks and trade names, supplier relationships, franchises, and licenses. A business organization establishes the value of relationships with its customers. Employees can contribute to the maintenance of manufactured capital that can be used in producing goods and services and thus contribute to the long-term sustainability of the business. With global warming being one of the most important topics of the twenty-first century, organizations specifically pay attention to manufacturing processes and their toxicity and try to follow industrial ecology policies. As the Earth's population grows daily, the manufacture of new products and materials does so, too. Emphasis is put on training the employees or, more recently, automating the manufacturing process and toxic gas and material emissions since those are two of the biggest concerns. Innovative technologies such as augmented reality and 3D printing are only some instruments implemented before mass production.[17]

II.6 Operational Capital

Operational capital usually refers to the financial resources needed to fund day-to-day operations and pay for various operational expenses, including raw materials, labor, rent, utilities, and other ongoing costs for conducting business activities. A firm's operational capital reflects an organization's resources in producing goods and services demanded by their constituencies and stakeholders that are not detrimental to society and the environment. The key components of operational capital are cash flow and cash management, working capital (the difference between current assets and current liabilities), inventory management, cost management, benefit management, operating expenses, and contingency funds. The corporate culture of integrity and competency plays a significant role in establishing policies, procedures, and processes to maximize operational capital. Effective management of operational capital is crucial for maintaining business sustainability, economic growth, and prosperity. Inadequate operational capital can create challenges of lack of business continuity and ongoing concern, liquidity problems, difficulties in meeting obligations, and delays in payments, among others, whereas excess operational capital may indicate inefficient use of resources.

Business organizations should balance managing their operational capital with effective and efficient use of scarce resources to ensure smooth daily operations and long-term financial health. The board of directors, as the representative of shareholders, should design directions for operational efficiency and effectiveness and guide management to implement and maintain policies and procedures to achieve both financial economic sustainability performance and non-financial environmental, ethical, social, and governance performance in creating shared value for all stakeholders including shareholders, creditors, employees, customers, suppliers, communities, society, and the environment. The board of directors should oversee that the organization is pursuing the goal of sustainable performance and compliance with all applicable laws, rules, regulations, standards, and best practices. While the board of directors should avoid micromanaging operations, it should provide strategic directions for management to continuously improve efficiency and effectiveness. Effective corporate governance measures should be implemented to promote vigilant oversight function by the board of directors, effective managerial function by management, and accountable and responsible actions by other corporate gatekeepers, including auditors and financial advisors. All the measures and actions should be proactively planned. Well-run and vigilant boards usually schedule major topics that they must discuss at a certain time of the year. This is important because it gives the board some time to think about the consequences and concerns regarding the upcoming topic. Additionally, board committees, particularly the audit committee, should be engaged in better and more efficient decision-making. By strictly following decision protocols and ensuring the right governance culture, organizations can strive for long-term financial and non-financial sustainability while enhancing their organizational capital.[18]

II.7 Reputational/Trust Capital

Reputational capital, also known as trust and cultural capital, reflects the intangible value an organization earns through trust, credibility, and positive perception with its stakeholders and constituencies, including customers, employees, suppliers, investors, and society. Reputational capital represents the trust, goodwill, and positive reputation built over time through consistent ethical practices, positive behavior, and commitments to delivering on promises that can improve relationships and contribute to long-term success and sustainable business. Important components of reputational capital are cultural heritage, traditions, knowledge and creativity, brand image, credibility, customer satisfaction, ethical workplace, credibility, trustworthiness, corporate social responsibility, and employee relations. Reputational capital is an asset built over a long time and can be challenging to rebuild once damaged; thus, its sustainability is essential for maintaining diverse identities and enhancing a sense of community. It plays an essential role in attracting and maintaining talented employees, creating customer satisfaction and attraction, building professional relationships with suppliers, and maintaining positive relationships with other stakeholders. Business organizations should invest in activities and strategies that create and sustain their reputational capital, including competent and ethical business practices, corporate social responsibility initiatives, fairness, and transparent communication disclosures.

The evolution of trust in the stakeholder era of capitalism has grown increasingly difficult to manage. Research examines global governance and the rule of law with the changing face of leadership, ethical technology, and more.[19] Corporations are structured to make trust and reputational strength difficult to achieve. Business purpose should be molded into an applied enterprise instead of a static set of promises. Corporations should begin investing in aligned and effective governance, leadership, employee engagement, and ethical sourcing for green investment decisions and responsible tax policies to build up their reputation and trust capital. A good reputation with stakeholders, including shareholders, employees, creditors, customers, suppliers, and communities, can take many years to build and can be easily and immediately destroyed with unintentional mistakes and irregularities and intentional fraud to deceive stakeholders.

One of the main reasons reputation has been so easily affected in recent years is that every piece of information about an organization can be found online. A big part of an organization's reputation depends on online reviews written by customers and partners. According to research, 97% of new consumers look at the reviews online and consider an organization's reputation before engaging in any relationship with them. Good online reviews are worth a lot, but bad reviews can have an even stronger effect on consumers. Statistics show that after reading a negative review, 60% of the potential customers decided not to use the service or business.[20] Some of the organizations even hire teams to write positive reviews for them and, in that way, raise their review score.[21] Search engine optimization is also one of the things that organizations invest in highly to improve their reputation, attract more consumers, and bring in better potential employees. Anecdotal evidence and scholarly research suggest that many factors can positively or negatively affect reputation. Indeed, the reputation–reality gap, changing beliefs and expectations, and weak internal coordination are the three major ones responsible for a potential organization's reputation downfall.[22] It is important for an organization to treat each relationship with caution but also to stick to its core values regardless of challenges and opportunities.

Corporate culture plays a crucial role in trust capital. Speaking of culture, Wilcox states:

> There are, however, three proverbial certainties that have developed around corporate culture: (1) We know it when we see it – and worse, we know it most clearly when its failure leads to a crisis. (2) It is a responsibility of the board of directors, defined by their "tone at the top." (3) It is the foundation for a company's most precious asset, its reputation.[23]

Several business metrics, such as worker retention, customer satisfaction, legal issues, etc., can be used to assess a company's culture.[24] Regarding the popularity of shareholder primacy in the United States, management aims to maximize shareholders' benefits. This principal–agent model usually leads to the misalignment of interests, which can be detrimental to trust or reputational capital. Therefore, a reduction in the power of shareholders or an increase in the power of other stakeholders, especially employees, can be the solution to problems related to integrity in corporate cultures.[25] Moreover, stakeholders now require more transparent communication, which challenges the board of directors to maintain a balance among transparency, confidentiality, and independence.[26]

II.8 Social Capital

Social capital is an important asset that reflects the value of the networks of relationships among individuals, communities, and social groups based on norms of trust, reciprocity, social relationships, interactions, and cooperation. Social capital can be earned through (1) bonding social capital of the close relationships among individuals who share similar values, identities, or experiences or (2) building social capital of relationships and connections with different individuals, groups, diverse communities, organizations, or networks. Social capital is defined by the Organisation for Economic Cooperation and Development (OECD) as "networks together with shared norms, values, and understandings that facilitate cooperation within or among groups."[27] In this definition, the networks are broadly considered real-world links between groups or individuals, including friends, family, colleagues, and local, national, and international communities. The shared values reflect respect for people's safety, security, health, and well-being of others. The important elements of social capital are norms and values, trust, networks and connections, community engagements, and reciprocity. These elements create networks of relationships and strong ties among individuals, social groups, and communities. Social capital impacts individuals and businesses by creating economic development and social networks to exchange information, resources, support, and community well-being. Establishing and sustaining social capital requires continuous investments in relationships, community building, social trust, and communication.

Social capital is relevant to the company's management of relationships with key outside stakeholders, including suppliers, customers, local communities, the public, and the government. Social capital includes human rights, responsible business practices, local economic development, customer privacy, and other social matters. In recent years, perceived social injustice and unrest have made social capital more relevant and important to business organizations. Social capital involves the effective functioning of social groups through interpersonal relationships, a shared sense of identity, understanding, norms, values, trust, cooperation, and reciprocity. Social capital is a measure of the value of resources, both tangible (e.g., public spaces, private property) and intangible (e.g., actors, human capital, people), and the impact that these relationships have on the resources involved in each relationship and on the larger groups. It is generally seen as a form of capital that produces public goods for a common purpose.

Social capital has been used to explain the improved performance of diverse groups, the growth of entrepreneurial firms, superior managerial performance, enhanced supply chain relations, the value derived from strategic alliances, and the evolution of communities, including the positive impacts of human interaction. The positive impacts of social capital are tangible or intangible factors such as useful information, future opportunities, innovative ideas generated from personal relationships, and networks outside and within an organization that enable a productive work environment that adds to bottom-line earnings. Social capital is a set of shared values that enables individuals to work together to effectively achieve a common purpose and goal that helps them all. Social capital can be attributed to the factors and characteristics that describe how people are able to band together in society to live harmoniously. In business, social capital can contribute to a company's success and sustainable performance by promoting shared values, mutual respect, and common goals.

Social capital is not a new term, and the relationships that compose it are crucial for long-term sustainability. Even though one can see and understand how important social capital really is, managers and organizations tend to ignore the importance and relevance of social capital. Management has often focused on efficiency and profit, forgetting the human side. This way of thinking can be costly since social awareness is one of the most important topics in the twenty-first century. Like with reputational capital, employees find it hard to stay with an organization that does not support their core beliefs and values. If an organization is not careful about the social aspect of the business processes, its operations, and relationships within and outside the organization, long-term sustainability will be almost impossible. In today's world, when information travels faster than ever before, and a small incident can ruin years of hard work, it is important to highlight social awareness or discuss it and implement it in daily operations and relationships. Social awareness must become a part of the organization's culture to enhance the creation of social capital and support long-term sustainability.

II.9 Strategic Capital

Strategic capital reflects management strategic planning and consists of strategic plans, decisions, and actions. Strategic planning is establishing purpose and mission, making decisions, taking action in documenting and communicating plans throughout the organization to those affected by actions, evaluating compliance with actions, and holding individuals accountable. The strategic plans enable organizations to document their purpose, mission, values, and vision and establish goals and action plans to implement them. The economic order, stakeholder expectations, corporate culture, and business environment are changing in the post-COVID-19 era, and how business organizations define their purpose and measure the achievement of their success is changing, too. Purpose determines why the organization exists, its mission, who the stakeholders are, and its objectives and strategies in achieving them. The main objective function of any business organization is to create shared value for all stakeholders, including shareholders, creditors, customers, suppliers, employees, government, society, and the environment. Changes in the purpose, mission, objectives, and strategies for business organizations in the aftermath of the COVID-19 crisis are important for the organization's long-term sustainability. Without a clear purpose and mission, organizations are finding it difficult not only to manage the pressures from outside stakeholders but also in the position of re-establishing their core values to deal with external pressures. Organizations not only have to understand all potential issues and challenges regarding long- and short-term sustainability, but prioritization among the objectives becomes a major factor in challenging times. How businesses operate, and the circumstances under which the operation process is done have drastically changed since the 2020–2022 pandemic and will be considered key components when discussing future objectives.

Every company should have its unique purpose determined in its charter of incorporation to maximize its positive impacts on all stakeholders, including society and the environment, and to minimize the negative impacts on multi-stakeholders. In case of nonexistence of and/or inadequate statement of purpose, all executives in the C-suite under the oversight function of the board of directors and approval by majority shareholders should establish an appropriate stakeholder-inclusive statement of purpose. The purpose of profit maximization and shareholder wealth creation has changed to create shared value for all stakeholders. To effectively achieve this new purpose, corporations are expanding their performance to both financial/quantitative economic performance (ESP) and non-financial/qualitative environmental, ethical, social, and governance (ESG) sustainability performance. Sustainability has become an economic and strategic imperative with the potential to create business opportunities and risks.

The mission reflects the organization's determination to stay with its purpose and its short-, medium-, and long-term achievement. Companies are now adopting the corporate mission of profit to create shared value for all stakeholders by shifting their goals to create shareholder value while fulfilling their social, environmental, and governance responsibilities. Corporate objectives have sustainably changed in the post-COVID-19 pandemic era to survival in the short term, medium-term continuity, and long-term sustainability. The board of directors pays more attention to the well-being, safety, and health of their employees, customers, and suppliers.

Strategic capital is very broad and can encompass political and technological capital. Political capital refers to the institutions, governance structures, and political systems that can affect decision-making and are vital for achieving sustainability goals. Technological capital represents technological advancements that can contribute to ESP and ESG sustainability performance by improving efficiency and addressing environmental issues and challenges. One of the additional factors to consider is the increased technology usage due to COVID-19. Even before the pandemic, the way organizations operated was creating an enormous amount of data. With most companies going completely online, data creation is higher than ever. The rise of online data not only represents the potential opportunity for better strategic decisions and capital allocation but also poses a risk of leakage of data and/or exposure of confidential information and strategic objectives. The rise of the data analytics field and its implementation in a considerable number of business processes in recent years just shows how dependable companies are on it and how most strategic decisions will be made with respect to data analysis in the future.

Following a financial crisis, it is not uncommon for investors to lose confidence in firms. The board of directors can rebuild trust by focusing on more long-term goals. While the board has fiduciary duties to carry out, they often fall prey to pressures of obtaining immediate results, which may deviate from the long-term picture. Instead, strategies should be implemented to allow the firm to withstand short-term pressures. The board's priorities should be the focus. That can be achieved by delegating duties that do not require the board's full attention to the committees, allowing the board to focus on the companys priorities. To rebuild trust, directors must always act in the company's best interests, even if it means disagreeing with shareholders and risking reelection. Effective communication with shareholders should be established in order to understand their concerns, ideas, feedback, and any potential disconnection in their views. Strategic capital reflects the organization's value, vision, culture, purpose, mission, goals, objectives, plans of action, and accountability and can reflect strategic financial, human, social, and intellectual capital.

III. CONCLUSION

Management has traditionally assumed stewardship of an organization's resources and capital in making strategic decisions that protect the interests of all stakeholders. As the steward of all business capital, management should focus on long-term interests and sustainability goals. Multi-stakeholders' well-being is relevant and applicable to corporate governance in the post-COVID-19 era, as business organizations are more concerned about the safety, health, and well-being of their employees, customers, suppliers, and other stakeholders. Management, as the steward of business resources and related capital discussed in this chapter, has the primary role of improving sustainability performance, managing related risks, and maximizing utilization of all capital from strategic to financial, reputational, manufactured, human, social, and environmental to create shared value for all stakeholders. Stakeholder interests in a firm are equity capital, human capital, social capital, and compliance capital. Thus, management is the steward of strategic, financial, human, social, and environmental capital and the active and long-term oriented steward of all stakeholders, including shareholders.

IV. TAKEAWAYS

- Management should consider all capital, from strategic to financial, reputational, manufactured, social, environmental, and human, in creating accountability and stewardship for all capital and stakeholders.

- As the steward of business resources, management has the primary role of improving sustainability performance and managing related risks, maximizing utilization of all capital from strategic to financial, reputational, manufactured, human, social, and environmental to create shared value for all stakeholders.
- Management should assess and manage all capital affecting the bottom-line earnings and minimize contingent and actual corporate liabilities.
- All nine sustainability capitals presented in this chapter are crucial to achieving ESP and ESG sustainability performance. All the different forms of capital are interconnected and interdependent and collectively contribute to financial success and stability and ensure social and environmental impacts.
- A holistic and integrated approach to business sustainability enables synergies and trade-offs between these capitals to achieve a balanced and resilient financial system.
- Business organizations, policymakers, and investors should use the holistic capital framework to guide their policies, strategies, and decision-making processes toward more sustainable outcomes.

Notes

1 Much of the discussion in this chapter comes from Rezaee, A. 2021. *Corporate Sustainability: Shareholder Primacy Versus Stakeholder Primacy*, Chapter 2. Business Expert Press. New York.
2 Bloomberg Intelligence. September 2021. "ESG Assets May Hit $53 Trillion by 2025, a Third of Global AUM." *Bloomberg*. Available at https://www.bloomberg.com/ professional/blog/esg-assets-may-hit-53-trillion-by-2025-a-third-of-global-aum/#:~:text=Assuming%2015%25%20growth%2C%20half%20the%20pace%20of%20the,trillion%20in%202018%20from%20%2422.8%20trillion%20in%202016.
3 International Integrated Reporting Council (IIRC). 2013. *Capitals Background Paper For IR*. Available at https://integratedreporting.ifrs.org/wp-content/uploads/2013/03/IR-Background-Paper-Capitals.pdf
4 AllThingsNature. 2021. "What Is Environmental Capital?" Available at https://www.allthingsnature.org/ what-is-environmental-capital.htm
5 The balance. 2021. "What Is Financial Capital?" Available at https://www.thebalance.com/what-is-financial-capital-3305825#:~:text=Key%20Takeaways%201%20Financial%20capital%20is%20money%2C%20credit%2C,debt%2C%20equity%2C%20and%20specialty%20capital.%20More%20items...%20
6 Investopedia. 2019. "Understanding Financial Capital vs. Economic Capital." Available at https://www.investopedia.com/ask/answers/031715/what-difference-between-financial-capital-and-economic-capital.asp#:~:text=Key%20Takeaways%201%20Financial%20capital%20is%20a%20broad,is%20referring%20to%20financial%20capital%2C%20not%20economic%20capital.
7 Organisation of Economic Co-operation and Development (OECD). 2018. "Human Capital – The Value of People." Available at https://www.oecd.org/insights/humancapital-thevalueofpeople.htm

8 Inclusive Capitalism. 2017. *Embarkment Project for Inclusive Capitalism*. Available at https://coalitionforinclusivecapitalism.com/wp-content/uploads/2021/01/coalition-epic-report.pdf

9 Security and Exchange Commission (SEC). 2019. *Modernization of Regulation S-K Items 101, 103, and 105*. Available at https://www.sec.gov/corpfin/modernization-regulation-s-k-compliance-guide

10 Amit Batish, Andrew Gordon, John D. Kepler, David F. Larcker, Brian Tayan, and Courtney Yu. 2021. Stanford Closer Look Series. *Human Capital Disclosure- What Do Companies Say About their" Most Important Asset?* Available at https://www.gsb.stanford.edu/ faculty-research/publications/human-capital-disclosure-what-do-companies-say-about-their-most

11 Strine, Jr., Leo E., Restoration: The Role Stakeholder Governance Must Play in Recreating a Fair and Sustainable American Economy - A Reply to Professor Rock (December 15, 2020). Business Lawyer, Vol. 76 . Available at https://papers.ssrn.com/sol3/papers.cfm?abstract_id=3749654

12 MIT Economics. 2020. *Labor in the Boardroom*. Available at https://dspace.mit.edu/bitstream/handle/1721.1/133704/Labor_in_the_Boardroom_QJE.pdf

13 Harvard Law School Forum on Corporate Governance. 2020. *Worker Participation: Employee Ownership and Representation*. Available at https://corpgov.law.harvard.edu/2020/01/23/worker-participation-employee-ownership-and-representation/#:~:text=There%20are%20two%20main%20forms,on%20the%20board%20of%20directors.

14 Harvard Law School Forum on Corporate Governance. 2019. *Worker Representation on U.S. Corporate Boards*. Available at https://corpgov.law.harvard.edu/2019/12/30/worker-representation-on-u-s-corporate-boards/#:~:text=Thus%2C%20a%20federal%20legislation%20solution,one%2Dthird%20of%20board%20seats.

15 Carlos M. Jardon and Xavier Martinez-Cobas. 2021. "Measuring Intellectual Capital with Financial Data." *PLoS ONE*. Available at https://pubmed.ncbi.nlm.nih.gov/33939709/

16 Septiana and Subowo. 2020. *Accounting Analysis Journal*. The Effect of the Firm's Size, Profitability, and Leverage on the Intellectual Capital Disclosure with Audit Committee as Moderator. Available at https://eds.b.ebscohost.com/ eds/pdfviewer/pdfviewer?vid=3&sid=dde47c95-82c7–4614-ac42-1f7e017286d7%40sessionmgr102

17 Weisz, H., S. Suh, and T. E. Graedel. 2015. *Industrial Ecology: The Role of Manufactured Capital in Sustainability*. Available at https://doi.org/10.1073/pnas.1506532112

18 Useem, Michael. 2006. "How Well-Run Boards Make Decisions." *Harvard Business Review*. Available at https://hbr.org/2006/11/ how-well-run-boards-make-decisions

19 Harvard Law School Forum on Corporate Governance. 2020. "The Evolution of Trust in the Era of Stakeholder Capitalism." Available at https://corpgov.law.harvard.edu/2020/04/23/the-evolution-of-trust-in-the-era-of-stakeholder-capitalism/

20 Campbell, Kent. 2021. *Reputation X*. Online reputation management statistics. Available at https://blog.reputationx.com/online-reputation-management-statistics

21 Schaer, Brianne. 2021. *Reputation X*. What is Reputation Capital? Available at https://blog.reputationx.com/ what-is-reputation-capital#:~:text=Definition%20of%20reputation%20capital%20Reputation%20capital%20is%20the,products%20and%20services%2C%20stock%20price%2C%20and%20company%20valuation.

22 Eccles, Robert G., Scott C. Newquist, and Roland Schatz. 2007. "Reputation and Its Risks." *Harvard Business Review.* Available at https://hbr.org/2007/02/reputation-and-its-risks

23 Wilcox. K. 2020. *Leading Through Culture: How Real Leaders Create Cultures that Motivate People to Achieve Great Things.* Waterside Productions. Available at https://www.goodreads.com/book/show/52196897-leading-through-culture

24 Harvard Law School Forum on Corporate Governance. 2020. "Corporate Purpose and Culture." Available at https://corpgov.law.harvard.edu/2020/02/21/corporate-purpose-and-culture/

25 Harvard Law School Forum on Corporate Governance. 2019. "The Effects of Shareholder Primacy, Publicness, and 'Privateness' on Corporate Cultures." Available at https://corpgov.law.harvard.edu/2019/09/23/the-effects-of-shareholder-primacy-publicness-and-privateness-on-corporate-cultures/

26 Harvard Law School Forum on Corporate Governance. 2020. "Corporate Purpose and Culture." Available at https://corpgov.law.harvard.edu/2020/02/21/corporate-purpose-and-culture/

27 Organisation for Economic Cooperation and Development (OECD). 2020. Social Capital. Available at https://www.oecd-ilibrary.org/economics/how-s-life-2020_aa436802-en

Chapter 7

Business Sustainability Risk

I. INTRODUCTION

Sustainability risks reflect the probability that an organization is not meeting its sustainability performance targets of achieving financial economic sustainability performance (ESP) and non-financial environmental, social, and governance (ESG) sustainability performance. Sustainability risks reflect the potential adverse effects of business activities on the environment and society. They are conditions that can negatively impact business organizations' ability to meet their present and future needs while maintaining economic, environmental, and social sustainability. Sustainability risks can arise from various sources and may affect different ESP and ESG dimensions of sustainability performance. Identifying, assessing, and managing sustainability risks is vital for promoting resilience and sustainable development. Several risks are relevant to business sustainability, including strategic, operations, compliance, financial, and reputation.

The 2020 US Government Accountability Office (GAO) report indicates that many of the surveyed institutional investors integrate ESG factors of performance and risk into their portfolio decisions to better understand risks associated with financial performance and information.[1] Investors generally use ESG disclosures provided by public companies to monitor management and assessment of ESG risks and make investment and voting decisions. This chapter explains the scope of business sustainability risks, risk management, and mitigation. This chapter discusses enterprise risk management (ERM) and the COSO ERM framework. This chapter discusses risk factors within corporate annual reports (10K) and how corporate accountants work with their legal and tax departments to disclose and analyze risk factors, particularly as they relate to ESG. The most important risks relevant to business sustainability

DOI: 10.4324/9781003437949-7

are strategic and financial risks. Strategic risk is the probability that an organization will fail to achieve its strategic sustainability plans and goals (e.g., focus on climate change and reducing GHG emissions). This risk should be identified, assessed, and managed to minimize its negative effects on operational and financial performance and build up on the opportunities provided by addressing this risk.

The operation risk is relevant to financial ESP and non-financial ESG sustainability performance. The operation risk should be assessed at all levels of business activities and integrated into all sustainability performance dimensions, starting from operating activities across operational units, operation technology, supply chain, and information technology to other functional areas. Many companies face the challenges of complying with ever-increasing regulations, and non-compliance may cause significant risks of interruption, penalties, and/or discontinuation of their business. Litigation and compliance risks must be assessed and managed, and their negative impacts on sustainability performance should be minimized. To address regulatory and compliance risks, many companies have created a board compliance committee or an executive chief compliance and risk officer position.

All financial ESP and non-financial ESG sustainability performance dimensions are affected by customer satisfaction, business reputation, and the employee workplace. A company's reputation and related risks should be assessed and managed continuously, and any damage to its reputation should be minimized. The financial risk of issuing materially misstated financial reports is detrimental to corporations' financial viability and sustainability. Sustainability reports are expected to be value-relevant to both external and internal users of such reports. Cyber hacking and security breaches of information systems are becoming a reality for many businesses (e.g., Sony, Target, Morgan Chase), and their risk assessment and controls demand significant I.T. investment and commitment by directors and offices to prevent their occurrences. Sustainability risks can be classified into several general categories: environmental, social, governance, market, regulatory, and supply chain risks. Assessing, managing, and mitigating sustainability risks requires adopting sustainable business practices and integrating ESG initiatives into decision-making processes. Businesses that effectively manage and mitigate sustainability risks are better able to create long-term shared value for their stakeholders, have desirable social and environmental impacts, and contribute to a more sustainable future. This chapter presents sustainability risks as depicted in Figure 7.1. Each risk is explained alphabetically in the next section.

II. TYPES OF SUSTAINABILITY RISKS

Sustainability risks reflect potential adverse impacts of both financial ESP and non-financial ESG factors that can have detrimental effects on the long-term sustainability and performance of economies, businesses, and individuals. Sustainability risks have recently gained the attention of policymakers, regulators, businesses, and investors as more robust sustainability initiatives have been implemented. Sustainability risks can be classified into financial, environmental, governance, compliance, and social risks discussed in this section.

Businesses are constantly changing and becoming more volatile, unpredictable, riskier, and complex, particularly during and in the aftermath of the COVID-19 pandemic. In this challenging and ever-changing business environment, identification and assessment of risks are crucial to business survival, continuity, and sustainability. Investors typically consider sustainability risks when integrating financial ESP and non-financial ESG sustainability performance into their investment decisions. The majority of investors responding to a survey in 2020 believe that consideration of non-financial ESG sustainability issues reduces investment risk, and other drivers are enhancing performance and avoiding firms with unsustainable performance and unethical conduct.[2] The survey suggests that investors are now considering non-financial ESG risks and opportunities in their investment strategies and decisions with a keen focus on climate change risk factors, reputational risk, and human capital management. At the board level, as well as engagement with management, it is considered by investors to be the most effective way to impact an organization's decision-making and new policies while simultaneously evaluating a corporate purpose. Full non-financial ESG disclosure, an effective and honest relationship between investors and the board, and understanding of the organization's culture are the key points for a better understanding of financial performance in the past and prediction of the same in the future.[3] Among several sustainability risks investors consider are strategic, financial, regulatory non-compliance, cyberbanking, reputational, changes in consumer preferences, operational, social unrest, and pandemic risk. These and other sustainability risks are presented in this section.

The International Organization for Standardization (ISO) published its new standards, *ISO 31000: Risk Management – Guidelines* in 2018 and *ISO 31010: Risk Management Assessment Techniques* in 2019, providing new risk management guidelines and risk assessment techniques.[45] These ISO 31000 and ISO 31010 risk guidelines and assessment techniques assist business organizations in developing, implementing, maintaining, assessing, monitoring, and continuously improving their risk management system in minimizing the negative effects of strategic, operations, financial, compliance, and reputation risks.[6] These risks are interrelated and, thus, should be properly assessed and managed. For example, an excessive strategic risk can also cause operational, financial, compliance, and reputational risks. The compliance risk directly or indirectly associated with business sustainability, including non-compliance with regulatory reforms, health and safety, human rights and labor laws, corporate governance measures, anti-bribery, and environmental risks, can vary among organizations and across countries. For example, environmental risks can include direct effects (e.g., emissions trading cost exposures) and indirect consequences (e.g., energy price increases and accompanying reporting and compliance costs) of non-compliance with environmental laws, rules, and regulations. Business organizations also assess and manage their financial risk of producing and

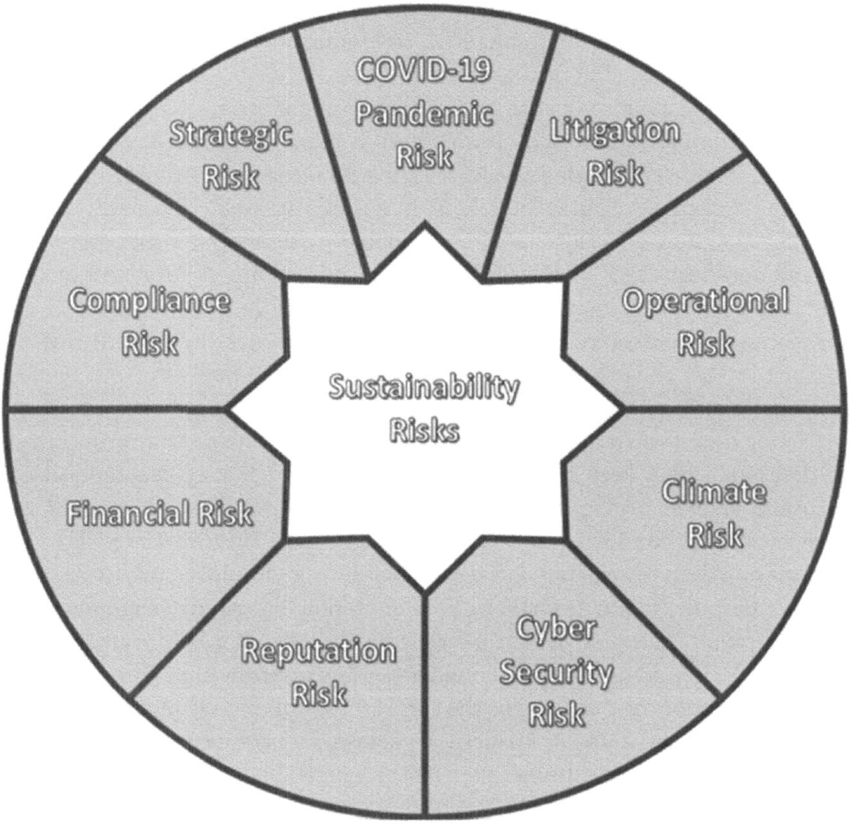

Figure 7.1 Sustainability risks

disclosing materially misstated financial reports. Minimizing the reputational risk is vital to the success of sustainability programs and related performance, as stakeholder satisfaction is essential to sustainable business. To effectively manage sustainability risks, business organizations adopt enterprise risk management policies and practices, conduct robust and thorough ESP and ESG assessments, engage with stakeholders, and integrate sustainability factors of performance and disclosure into their decision-making processes to mitigate risks and ensure long-term shared value creation for all stakeholders. Investors also consider sustainability opportunities and risks in making their investment decisions. The following subsection examines nine sustainability risks in detail in alphabetical order, as depicted in Figure 7.1.

II.1 Climate Change Risk

Climate change risk generally is the failure to address the potential adverse effects of climate change on various aspects of business, society, the economy, and the environment that have been caused by changing climate patterns of extreme weather events, sea-level rise, and rising temperatures. Climate change is often caused by human activities that increase the concentration of greenhouse gases in the atmosphere, which could trigger global warming and related changes in weather patterns. The risk results from the physical impacts of climate change. The global initiatives relevant to climate change are real, and the expected transitions to a net-zero carbon economy could put more pressure on the economic sustainability of many countries and their business organizations. Climate change risks include the detrimental effects of (1) global greenhouse gas (GHG) emissions; (2) rising temperatures of about 1.8 F degrees since the mid-twentieth century; (3) natural disasters of catastrophic flooding, wildfires, storms, and droughts; (4) extreme weather events (hurricanes, droughts, floods, wildfires, and heatwaves); (5) rising sea levels that can lead to damage to coastal communities, infrastructure, and ecosystems; (6) legal and liability risks associated with climate change; and (7) other climate changes and environmental related issues that could have detrimental effects on business operations. Several initiatives can be taken to assess, manage, and mitigate climate change risks, including acknowledging the changing climate, reducing greenhouse gas emissions, setting emission reduction targets, adopting sustainable business practices to address climate change, integrating climate risk assessment and management into strategic planning processes, establishing and implementing international agreements that address climate change risks, incorporating climate risk considerations into investment decisions and recognizing the importance of climate-related financial disclosures.

The initial 2019 Carbon Disclosure Project (CDP) survey and subsequent surveys in 2020 and 2021 show that 215 of the world's largest public companies could suffer financial losses of about $1 trillion of climate-related risk in the next five years.[7] The 2021 survey revealed that over 13,000 companies (64% of global market capitalization) and over 11,000 cities disclosed their environmental data. This represents a 35% growth when compared to 2020, and it just shows how seriously organizations took the survey results from 2019.[8] However, this does not come as a surprise considering the CDP's five-year strategy, *Accelerating the Rate of Change*, which focuses on improving transparency, tracking the results reported, and implementing strategies.[9] The CDP climate change programs are intended to mitigate climate change risk and reduce greenhouse gas emissions. The climate change risk can be assessed and managed, and its negative impacts can be minimized if business organizations:

1. Acknowledge that climate change poses risks to their operational effectiveness, financial market stability, and financial sustainability.
2. Adopt sustainable business practices that establish emission reduction targets.
3. Integrate climate risk assessments into their strategic planning processes.
4. Explore the integration of climate risk into all aspects of business, from operational to financial and supply chain.

5. Integrate climate change into their strategic planning, decisions, corporate culture, and business environment.
6. Assess the adequacy and effectiveness of internal controls in responding to climate risks.
7. Disclose the climate risk properly and transparently to all stakeholders.
8. Comply with international agreements and regulations aimed at addressing climate change risks.
9. Recognize the importance of climate-related financial disclosures and incorporate climate risk considerations into investment decisions.

Proper disclosure of climate change by business organizations is important in addressing the global climate change risk. This disclosure can be included in financial reports, sustainability reports, or a separate report by management to inform stakeholders about the organization's efforts to address and adapt to climate change and related risks. In March 2022, the Securities and Exchange Commission (SEC) proposed new rules for disclosing climate-related financial risks in SEC filings by requiring public companies to discuss their climate risk management and disclose greenhouse gas emissions in their annual reports.[10] SEC rules would be a significant step towards mandatory reporting in the US. The success of the global economy, depends on governments, companies, and households working together to eliminate or absorb carbon. Simple steps can be taken such as measurement and annual reporting. Much progress has been made in measurement and reporting, but public companies do not disclose this information. Also, a small number of private companies do this, and there is no specific framework or method for measurement and reporting. Carbon emission information is essential given the critical weather conditions. The first but necessary step is to require public and private companies to publish carbon emission reports. Carbon emissions alone will not solve climate crises, but they will help accelerate solutions, as companies are encouraged to change their emissions from previous years by releasing carbon emissions reports.

II.2 Compliance Risk

Technological advances and globalization require business organizations to comply with local, national, and international laws, rules, regulations, standards, and best practices. Compliance risks are failures to comply with these local, national, and international laws, rules, regulations, and standards which apply across governance ranging from financial reporting to climate change, social responsibility, and financial activities.[11] Many companies are experiencing the challenges of complying with the ever-increasing regulatory measures, and non-compliance with these regulations may cause significant risks of interruption, paying fines, and/or discontinuing their business operation. Major components of compliance risk are failure to comply with (1) regulatory compliance; (2) data privacy and security policies and procedures; (3) internal policies and procedures to ensure operational efficiency and ethical conduct;

(4) financial compliance with financial regulation and accounting standards; (5) anti-money laundering and counter-terrorism financing to prevent illegal financial activities; and (6) ESG mandatory and voluntary initiatives by conducting ESG statement inventory, providing regular training on ESG matters, reviewing and clarifying ESG policies, maintaining accurate records, and assessing the ESG compliance policies and disclosures to avoid misrepresentation and greenwashing.

Compliance risks need to be assessed and managed, and their negative impacts on financing, investing, and operating activities minimized. Many companies have created either a board compliance committee or an executive position of compliance and risk officer to achieve this objective. The compliance committee usually comprises executives who can assist the compliance officer in making important decisions regarding compliance with many obligations, regulations, and laws. Even though the company's strategic risks, goals, and tasks differ from one organization to another, the main goal of the committee, as well as the compliance officer, remains the same. Chief financial officer, chief accounting officer, HR director, IT director, and general counsel are some key executives who should be inside the compliance committee and try to reduce any potential compliance risk. The committee should work with leaders and managers from different departments to minimize and maintain complete control over the risk. Some organizations do not have a compliance committee but only a compliance officer. While the compliance officer does not work directly on emerging issues, he or she works closely with other executives and managers and navigates them throughout the compliance process. With the greater number of responsibilities assigned to only one person to oversee, there is a greater chance of compliance risk becoming a serious threat, and organizations must be aware of it.

Governance, risk management, and compliance reporting (GRC) has evolved to mitigate the rising economic challenges. GRC refers to the strategy the organization implements when dealing with these three components while also assisting the company in achieving its goals and meeting its objectives. It comprises a set of practices that must be followed to ensure that risks are reduced and visibility of the same is increased, business objectives are met, segregation among the departments is minimal, costs are lower, and information is gathered more efficiently and used more appropriately. Specifically, compliance risk has increased due to the widening business complexity, the need to reduce risk exposure, and the mission to improve the firm's performance. Companies and their boards of directors and top executives should give considerable attention to compliance risk or face consequences such as fines, public scrutiny, regulatory intervention, or discontinuation of their operations.

II.3 COVID-19 Pandemic/Health Risk

Health risk, in general, is associated with diseases, pandemics, and health emergencies that can have widespread economic and social consequences. The 2020 COVID-19 pandemic brought on many challenges for organizations of all types and sizes and particularly caused devastating social, environmental, human, governance, and economic consequences worldwide. Economic shutdown, home lockdowns, social distancing triggered by the COVID-19 pandemic, and travel restrictions left organizations with the option of either suspending all business activities until the pandemic was over or modifying their operations. Business organizations were forced to modify their business purpose of protecting the interests of all stakeholders, including investors, customers, suppliers, employees, and communities, and adapt the new normal governance measures to ensure business continuity and prospects. The COVID-19 pandemic risk is the failure of business organizations to modify their corporate governance measures and sustainability practices in response to the pandemic and to minimize its detrimental effects on their financing, investing, and operating activities as well as going concern and continuity of their operations. The COVID-19 pandemic caused several risks that can impact individuals, businesses, and societies. Pandemic risks are (1) health and safety risks of individuals contracting and spreading the disease; (2) economic risks of lockdowns, restrictions, and disruptions to supply chains; (3) operational risks of remote work challenges and supply chain disruption; (4) financial and market risks of market volatility because of uncertainties surrounding the pandemic; and (5) other risks of disruptions to education systems, and resistance or hesitancy to vaccination. These pandemic risks have evolved and may change if new variants emerge and vaccination activities progress.

Managers need to provide the board with accurate and flexible analytical information to implement strategies following the pandemic and its economic consequences. The pandemic has created several new challenges, such as employee serendipity and return-to-work strategies. Some of these challenges have led companies to thrive no matter what happens in the future. This era has focused on many issues, such as crisis management, succession planning, etc. One of the benefits of this pandemic in many companies was that managers increased the speed of decision-making, increased trust between team members and managers, and increased transparency between them. The coronavirus has accelerated some digital businesses and helped start many startups. It is doubtful that those businesses that survived will to return to their previous normality, and the shadow of the disease will last longer.

This COVID-19 systemic risk has continued destabilizing global capital markets, financial systems, and the broader economy. The COVID-19 pandemic risks need to be identified, assessed, and managed because these risks could have disruptive and significant negative effects on asset valuations, global financial markets, and economic stability. The overwhelming costs and regulatory requirements, including the cost of mandatory vaccination, can impose significant financial burdens on companies in many countries and threaten their business sustainability. Thus, companies worldwide must scrutinize pandemic risk when making strategic sustainability planning and decisions and take appropriate actions to protect their shareholders and other stakeholders during and in the aftermath of the COVID-19 pandemic.

There are multiple ESG sustainability factors to consider in assessing and managing pandemic risks, such as board oversight of risk management, incident, and systemic risk management, business model resilience, supply chain resilience, executive compensation, business continuity scenario analyses, human capital issues, customer welfare and impact on communities, shareholder engagement, dividend payouts, and stock buybacks, and critical ESG disclosures. The first ESG factor is the board oversight of risk management related to the COVID-19 pandemic. In light of a crisis like COVID-19, every firm should prepare to address the concerns of their shareholders, creditors, employees, suppliers, customers, and other stakeholders. This requires the boards of the companies to fully understand the risks involved and control activities that should be in place to mitigate their negative impacts. Regular communication between directors and management about pandemic risk and its possible impacts on operations and stakeholder-related issues is important. The boards should also reassess both short-term and long-term strategic sustainability plans to maintain business continuity, emphasizing issues such as capital allocation, public relations, credits, and compliance with new regulations. If it is feasible and cost-effective, the board of directors should consider establishing a separate risk oversight committee in response to a pandemic. Alternatively, to effectively manage various pandemic risks, all the standing board committees, including the audit committee, nominating and governance committee, and compensation committee, can oversee the assessment and management of pandemic risks. However, when facing special situations like the COVID-19 pandemic, boards with a separate risk committee can gain insights into such unique circumstances and focus resources and attention on managing the risks. This board committee can be an ad hoc committee that meets on short notice to discuss pandemic issues, take actions related to the crisis, and improve the quality of the corporate oversight function and business sustainability.

The second factor to consider is critical incidents and management's immediate response to the pandemic in identifying, assessing, managing, and minimizing negative effects. Pandemics such as COVID-19 show the vulnerability of companies and industries to incidents and can cause negative impacts in the long term. These critical events have detrimental effects on operating cash flow, shareholder relationships, stock prices, credit ratings, capital access, supply chain, employee well-being, customer relationships, and corporation reputation. Therefore, companies need to implement more dynamic and comprehensive risk management to maintain business sustainability and continuity. The virtual platform and long-distance working through technology during the pandemic should alert companies to be more cautious and skeptical about collecting, storing, and sharing sensitive data on their computer systems to avoid hackers and other cybersecurity threats.

An important ESG factor affected by the pandemic is human capital issues such as employee health, safety, and well-being. Implementation of effective safety measurements and good communication is important during pandemics. Companies should implement employee safety protocols and effectively communicate with employees to get vaccinated to limit the spread of the virus. Furthermore, firms should provide employees with sufficient safety, vaccination, protective gear, sick pay, financial assistance, flexibility at work, and technological assistance for working from home. Corporations should evaluate their employees' competence to meet workforce demands in the post-COVID-19 era. It is also important to consider the business model's and supply chain's resilience. During and in the aftermath of the pandemic, the supply chain also suffered from many problems, such as a shortage of medical supplies, inadequate vaccination, lack of infrastructure, and panic buying behaviors. Therefore, global companies need to determine and improve the weaknesses of the supply chains to deal with any future disruptions.

Other relevant ESG factors include executive compensation, dividend payouts, and stock buybacks. It is advisable for companies to update their executive compensation plans to reflect economic difficulties and cashflow shortages. Executive compensation limits are encouraged in the Coronavirus Aid, Relief, and Economic Security Act (the "CARES Act"). Similarly, the CARES Act limits the amount of dividend payouts and stock buybacks for businesses participating in the federal assistance program. In fact, a lot of companies had to avoid paying dividends and repurchasing stocks to maintain liquidity.

Consumer welfare and its impact on local communities should also be evaluated during the pandemic as only a few industries, including transportation and shipping services and healthcare providers, grocery chains, and banks, operate at the frontline. These businesses greatly facilitate the fight against the pandemic by protecting the health of citizens while meeting their basic needs during the pandemic. Another ESG factor is to effectively address shareholder engagement among firms. Investors and other stakeholders need sufficient reassurance during the pandemic as they become much more anxious about their investments during a crisis. Therefore, companies should engage shareholders with transparent and regular communication about the status of operations and their approach to multiple issues. A company's board of directors and management should focus on short-term strategic plans to ensure business continuity and ongoing concern, as well as long-term sustainable strategic plans to ensure long-term well-being and value creation for all stakeholders. The board of directors and management should effectively communicate with their shareholders and other stakeholders about the impact of the pandemic on the firm's short-term, medium-term, and long-term strategies and their strategic sustainability planning in addressing significant ESG issues.

Finally, non-financial ESG sustainability performance disclosures are crucial during the post-pandemic era. Regarding the severe impacts of a pandemic such as COVID-19, companies should have extensive disclosures about their resilience, responses, and strategies for dealing with the pandemic. In the aftermath of the COVID-19 pandemic, business organizations will be able to evaluate their weaknesses, vulnerabilities, and strengths in the short term. At the same time, shareholders become more concerned about the long-term sustainability and resilience of businesses, which can lead to the need for additional ESG disclosures. More importantly, corporations should take lessons from the pandemic to form future policies and disclosures about ESG issues.

II.4 Cybersecurity Risk

An ever-increasing number of cyberattack incidents is detrimental to companies' operations and business sustainability. Cybersecurity risk is the potential harm caused by unauthorized access, use, disruption, modification, destruction, or disclosure of information, networks, and systems that are material to individuals, businesses, and governments. Risks related to data breaches and cyberattacks can have detrimental effects of disrupting operations and compromising sensitive information. Technological advances enable hackers to access information systems, creating significant challenges for individuals, organizations, and governments. Destructive cyberattacks, like the ones of Sony Pictures, Target, Yahoo, JPMorgan, Chase, Uber, Home Depot, Equifax, and Facebook, have been devastating and are recorded as the most damaging cyberattacks outside the norms of cyber practices. Technological advancements have pushed cybersecurity to the top of the agendas of public companies' boards of directors and executives. For example, the Equifax cyber breach is one of the largest data breaches in history, affecting nearly half of the population in the US (about 143 million Americans).[12] A new report shows a substantial increase in cyberattacks, including online scams, phishing, data-harvesting malware, malicious domains, disruptive malware, misinformation, and ransomware since the onset of the 2020 COVID-19 pandemic because of the increase in digital remote work and the uncertainty or fear caused by the unstable social and economic environment.[13] There are many reasons for and aspects of these cyberattacks and related cybersecurity risks, including threats of malware of software viruses, ransomware, and spyware, deceptive emails or messages, vulnerabilities or weaknesses in software, employees or individuals with access to sensitive information, hackers gaining access to sensitive data, and lack of a robust incident response plan. To mitigate cybersecurity risks, business organizations should implement robust and comprehensive security measures, including regular software updates, the use of encryption technologies, employee training, network monitoring, and a proactive and adaptive cybersecurity posture.

The US government is considering a "proportional response" against those who are responsible for the Sony cyberattack.[14] There are three losses relevant to cyberattack incidents. The first loss is the direct economic loss, including destruction of assets, loss of trade secrets, operational impairment, and cost of remedial measures. The second loss pertains to reputational damages and lost revenue following the disclosure of cyberattacks and the loss of negative impact on the trading price of the company's stocks. The third loss is any fine and sanction levied on firms that announce cyberattack incidents by regulators.

Cyber hacking can be detected and prevented using effective and efficient cybersecurity processes and procedures driven by information security management systems (ISMS). Cybersecurity standards enable organizations to manage the security of assets such as financial information, human capital, intellectual property, employee information, or information entrusted to the entities by third parties.[15] ISMS is a systematic approach to managing sensitive information and maintaining its integrity and confidentiality. ISMS can also help identify the risks to valuable information and design appropriate controls to reduce the risk. It includes measures, people, processes, and information technology systems by applying a risk management process. These standards are available to help any size and type of organization, whether small, medium, or large businesses in any industry. There are several policies and procedures for managing sensitive data in companies. The purpose of this system is to minimize the risk of safety violations.

Information security management systems (ISMS) can be implemented in various ways, such as controlling access to customer data. Comprehensive systems can usually deal with employee behavior with relation to company data. ISMS could be different from organization to organization because not all are subject to the same risk. Regardless, some of the same policies, regulations, procedures, and workflows should be implemented to prevent information asset theft and limit potential setbacks caused by it. Controls set by the organizations must be followed and reviewed regularly for efficiency to ensure that controls go along with the company's objectives. To ensure controls are effective, organizations must separate the data by its value and importance and appropriately use risk assessment to determine the right set of controls for each set of organizational data. Rather than just creating ISMS and continuing with their everyday operations, organizations should strive to incorporate it by making it part of the company culture, training their employees, and raising their awareness about potential threats and risks.[16] One of the best ways to effectively implement ISMS while demonstrating to your clients that a strong set of controls is being executed is by following ISO/IEC 27001:2013. Even though it is not mandatory, most organizations decide to follow this set of effective requirements while obtaining certification to ISO/IEC 27001:2013 and, in that way, build up their stakeholders' confidence in the organization.[17] Some key benefits include reduced risk of cyberattacks while securing the information in any given form, faster response to security threats, a central framework managing all the information in one place, and improving the company's culture while raising its reputation.

In March 2022, the SEC proposed legislation to reduce cyber risks and increase the standardization of public company disclosure and risk management for cybersecurity, and on July 26, 2023, adopted rules requiring registrants, including foreign private issuers, to disclose material cybersecurity incidents they experience as well as material information regarding their cybersecurity risk management, strategy, and governance on an annual basis.[18] In the past several years, the SEC has been actively considering cybersecurity threats to financial markets and protecting sensitive information. The SEC rules address (1) disclosure requirements of disclosing material information related to cybersecurity risks and incidents; (2) guidance on cybersecurity disclosures to assist public companies in preparing disclosures about cybersecurity risks and incidents; (3) internal controls and policies for establishing and maintaining internal controls and procedures to ensure disclosures of adequate information pertaining to cybersecurity risks; (4) board oversight of the establishment of cybersecurity policies and procedures of cybersecurity risk assessment and management; and (5) examination and enforcement to assess the implementation of adequate cybersecurity measures and risk management by public companies.

II.5 Financial/Economic Risk

Financial risk is related to investments in unsustainable activities or exposure to liabilities associated with environmental or social issues. Is the probability that investors and users of corporate financial statements receive materially misstated financial reports that will adversely affect their financial and investment decisions? Financial risks are often triggered by economic instability, market uncertainties, and fluctuations in commodity prices that can negatively affect businesses and industries. Receiving materially misstated information is usually due to management incompetence, weak internal controls, a rapidly changing environment, or poor accounting systems and information recording, and organizations should try to devote additional attention to all of these factors. It is important to understand that not only investors and outside users could be affected by false or incomplete accounting information, but also executives and internal users, having their decision-making and strategic goals based on the wrong or insufficient information, not understanding the full scope of the situation, and leading an organization to the disastrous outcome. Non-financial dimensions of sustainability performance, including environmental, social, and governance (ESG), can also affect financial performance. The financial risk of issuing materially misstated financial reports negatively affects investors' confidence and public trust in financial information and, thus, is detrimental to the overall sustainability of corporations.

Further, integrated sustainability reports are expected to be useful, reliable, and value-relevant to both external and internal users of such reports. Investors and other stakeholders, including suppliers, employees, customers, government, and society, can have more transparent information about financial ESP and non-financial ESG sustainability performance, enabling them to make more informed decisions. Sustainability reporting improves internal management decision-making, actions, and practices by enabling companies to establish better relationships with their investors, customers, employees, suppliers, regulators, and society.

Sustainability reporting can be used as a tool for more effective risk assessment and management to identify opportunities and risks associated with financing, investing, and operating activities. Thus, more transparent sustainability disclosures on financial ESP and non-financial ESG sustainability performance create opportunities to identify and correct operational inefficiencies, reputational damages, and financial risks that would improve financial or economic performance. Best practices of sustainability suggest that companies which ignore their financial ESP and non-financial ESG sustainability performance issues and responsibilities encounter the risk of: (1) not maintaining sustainability in the long term; (2) being subject to higher scrutiny and intervention by regulators; (3) losing their license to operate;

(4) having less of an analyst following and forecasting, that may affect their market valuation; (5) not attracting socially responsible investors with long-term horizons; (6) encouraging managerial practices of not committing to the long-term sustainability of multidimension stakeholders; (7) not setting an appropriate tone at the top by directors and executives in promoting sustainability and ethical, accountable, socially, and environmentally responsible behaviour and practices; (8) losing customers and customer confidence in products and services; (9) not being able to attract and retain most qualified and talented human capital and workforce; (10) incurring a higher cost of capital both in debt and equity; and (11) preventing proper growth and development.

II.6 Litigation Risk

Litigation risk is the probability that a company becomes subject to legal proceedings that could result in adverse outcomes, including financial losses, damage to reputation, or other negative consequences. Litigation risk can arise from various sources and for various reasons, including changes in laws and regulations that may impact business operations and compliance, and could involve civil, criminal, or regulatory actions. Risks arise from changes in laws and regulations that may impact business operations and compliance. Litigation risks could arise in ESG reporting issues because of lack of compliance with applicable ESG-related laws, rules, regulations, and standards. Arise in litigations has occurred because of the lack of compliance and the newly increased availability of ESG sustainability information. Financial reports show outside users are now able to see information that was not previously disclosed, use it, and drive conclusions based on it. For example, when using scenario analysis to understand future business performance through various potential climate-based scenarios, disclosing these results and analysis, or lack thereof, gives way to possible litigation issues. This explains the rise in litigations in recent years (2020–2023) and makes companies aware of both potential benefits and risks regarding non-financial ESG sustainability reporting.

Risks could come from inadequate climate-based scenarios or working papers regarding scenario analysis and could be used to commence litigation. Inaccurate or misleading material information from these scenarios and lack of adequate attention to environmental, social, and governance measures can also pose an immense potential litigation risk. Investors and other stakeholders are looking for transparent and sufficient information that can be utilized for effective decision-making. Information and disclosures of a company should include all material matters to prevent the risks of litigation resulting from inadequate reports and inappropriate assumptions used in preparing ESG sustainability reports. These risks stem from a lack of preparation for future events such as the COVID-19 pandemic, giving rise to a potentially misleading set of financial statements. Business organizations can implement several strategies to manage litigation risk, including risk assessment and management policies and procedures, comprehensive and robust compliance programs, retaining legal counsel, obtaining adequate insurance coverage, focusing on ethical business practices, adopting proactive measures to address and prevent potential issues before they escalate into legal disputes, and conducting regular legal reviews, compliance audits. A focus on this can contribute to minimizing litigation risk.

II.7 Operational Risk

Operational risk is the likely failure of internal processes, systems, people, and external events to generate desired outcomes and production that can cause potential challenges for business organizations to successfully conduct their business and operations. Operational risks can be triggered by a lack of resources, such as materials, water, minerals, and energy sources, and often are relevant to both financial ESP and non-financial ESG sustainability performance dimensions. Operational risk should be integrated into all sustainability performance dimensions as well as operating activities across operational units, information technology, operation technology, supply chain, and other functional areas. One of the important challenges for business organizations in implementing their strategic sustainability planning is effective collaboration and integration across operational business units and key functional areas. Operational risks are relevant to both conventional financial key performance indicators (KPIs), such as earnings and return on investment, and non-financial KPIs, such as social, environmental, and natural performance. Risks such as internal or external fraud, employee mistakes, business processes, controls-related risks, and technology risks are only some operational risks that can highly influence financial and non-financial KPIs. After these risks are identified, they need to be accurately assessed and managed, and their negative impacts on both financial ESP and non-financial ESG should be minimized. Operational risks are related to the business operation's impact on sustainability performance, including those risks pertaining to IT, supply chain, and production facilities. Strategic sustainability planning can be used as a tool for more effective risk assessment and management and in identifying challenges and opportunities associated with operations. The more transparent disclosure of operational risk, the lower the risk of regulatory actions, higher employee satisfaction, higher customer confidence, and more effective management activities and practices within the organization.

Some of the important aspects of operational risk are (1) inadequacies or failures in internal processes, systems, and controls that may result in financial loss or harm to the organization's sustainability; (2) failure of employees triggered by inadequate training, employee turnover, misconduct that can impact operational performance and create vulnerabilities; (3) failures or disruptions in information technology systems that can have material detrimental operational and financial consequences; and (4) inadequate or non-compliance with applicable laws, rules, regulations and industry standards that can result in legal and regulatory actions with potential financial penalties, operational disruptions and reputational damage. As business sustainability and its reporting evolve, the board of directors and executives will have to give considerable attention to operational risk management and its overall effectiveness and efficiency. Even though many organizations implement the Enterprise Risk Management (ERM) approach, there are some organizations that, in addition to it, use the Operational Risk Management (ORM) perspective, which comes with fewer risks compared to ERM. That is why ORM is considered a subset of ERM, excluding strategic, reputational, and financial risks.[19] ORM strictly focuses on day-to-day operations and minimization of operations-related risks while trying to implement the right set of controls that could aid in risk prevention. One of the most effective approaches to ORM is to divide risks into groups and, in that way, diminish the risk. If implemented correctly, ORM can create stronger stakeholder confidence, better business risk anticipation, more accurate financial forecasting, more efficient operations on a daily level, improved quality of the product/service and its recognition, as well as providing executives with better visibility of the processes. Using the ERM and ORM in managing operational risk requires identifying, assessing, and mitigating potential risks by implementing effective and strong internal controls, risk management frameworks, monitoring systems, and adequate insurance coverage. A robust and comprehensive management of operational risk contributes to the success of an organization and its business sustainability.

II.8 Reputation Risk

Reputation is the most important asset for any profit and non-profit organization; it can be earned through much effort and dedication over many years and can be easily destroyed overnight. Reputational risk is the potential for damage to the reputation of an individual, company, or institution that can have adverse consequences on its brand, business operations, and customer trust. Reputation risk may result from the perception of customers, employees, investors, regulators, and the public. A negative reputation can cause business loss, sustainability damage, legal or regulatory issues, and challenges in attracting and retaining talent. Sustaining a good business reputation and meeting and exceeding the expectations of corporate stakeholders, from investors to creditors, customers, employees, suppliers, community, society, and the environment is a major challenge for many businesses. Reputational risks are growing increasingly and present a significant risk to the financial and operational of a company.

Many factors can contribute to reputational risk, including problems with products or services, quality control challenges, supply chain disruptions, unethical behavior, non-compliance with applicable laws, rules, regulations, and legal issues, loss of customer data triggered by cyberattacks, executive misconduct, and leadership failures. The business sustainability performance of financial ESP and non-financial ESG is relevant to business reputation, customer satisfaction, suppliers, the ethical workplace, and upholding high ethical standards and compliance with regulations. Reputational risks can be triggered by (1) brand damage of perceived or actual negative impacts on the environment, society, or ethical behavior and (2) consumer activism of ill-informed awareness and activism among consumers pertaining to sustainable practices. The company's reputation risk should be evaluated and managed on an ongoing basis, and any damage to the reputation must be minimized. The social risk theory suggests that every company faces an unavoidable reputational risk relevant to CSR initiatives. Research shows that many companies understand the importance of social risks and their impact on reputation, but they do not necessarily report them openly.[20] Public companies pay close attention to risks affecting their shareholders, such as financial risks and those risks that are perceived as most prevailing. From the perspective of CEOs, one of the biggest threats to reputation in the technology-evolving world is the threat of online reviews and unwanted search results. Analysis of company reports shows many executives believe this factor can significantly affect an organization's earnings. Hand in hand with the organization's reputation image goes the CEO's reputation. Having an ethical person at the top of the company representing it correctly and with integrity can significantly decrease reputation risks. Additional factors and events that organizations must tackle promptly are often related to negative articles, social media, services and pricing, data loss, and regulation changes.[21] Reputational risk management is an important integral component of overall risk assessment and management strategy for organizations that requires a robust, comprehensive, and proactive approach to maintain trust and credibility.

II.9 Strategic Risk

Strategic risk is the potential uncertainties and threats caused by unsound strategic decisions made by individuals or organizations. Unlike other risks, such as operational or financial risks that are more tangible and measurable, strategic risks are typically more subjective. They are associated with consequences of choices regarding business decisions in achieving intended goals, objectives, and the allocation of resources. Important aspects of strategic risks are: (1) ever-increasing technological advances that can create challenges and opportunities for organizations and their failure to adapt or invest sufficiently in information technology; (2) changes in market conditions such as the emergence of new competitor and shifts in consumer preferences and the risk of not responding or adjusting to these changes; (3) new rules and regulations and changes in government policies can pose strategic risk of non-compliance; (4) failing to innovate or adapt to new trends of establishing market positioning; (5) risks associated with poor working conditions, unfair labor practices, and violations of human rights; (6) risks related to the displacement of communities triggered by industrial activities, development projects, or environmental changes; (7) risks caused by unequal distribution of resources, opportunities, and benefits within societies. Effective management of strategic risks, including proper oversight function by the board of directors and proper planning and adaptability, can contribute to business success and sustainability. Strategic risk management is an integral component of enterprise risk management that enables organizations to effectively manage their strategic risks and better position themselves to adapt to changes, capitalize on opportunities, and achieve long-term and sustainable success.

Business organizations are taking many initiatives and guidelines, including board risk oversight function, managerial strategies, adequate IT investment, and cybersecurity infrastructure to ensure the integrity of IT systems and the effectiveness of cyber infrastructure in minimizing cybersecurity risk and dealing with potential cyberattacks and cybersecurity breaches.

The achievement of both financial ESP and non-financial ESG sustainability performance requires business organizations to assess and manage all risks, particularly those that threaten strategic sustainability planning. There are several strategic risks triggered by business sustainability performance, reporting, and assurance, including threats to survival and achievement of long-term performance, business continuity, uncertainty with marketing position and volatility in security prices, risks relevant to strategic investments, stakeholder communications, investor relations, abnormal changes in consumer demand, and changes in global trends. Technology advancements and globalization underscore the importance and relevance of these risks. Executives consider new technology risks, including social media, data mining, and analytics, to be the most disruptive for the business model and able to significantly affect business strategic sustainability. The risk and compliance board committee should oversee the managerial approach in assessing and managing the risk and determine the risk tolerance and a plan of action to respond to the risk quickly and efficiently.[22] Business continuity and threats to survival, especially since the COVID-19 pandemic started, are among the main risks to consider. In this new world where organizations rely heavily on their software and business processes being online, factors such as software failure, data non-compliance, or even human vulnerability, including human-made mistakes, could play a huge role in business continuity, affecting business strategic goals. Due to the accelerated lifestyle and progress in almost all scientific and technology fields, it is not a surprise that global trends also happen at a faster pace. Considering the speed at which the information travels, companies may be under threat or, if they react appropriately, at an advantage to reach their strategic goals. While these strategic risks provide many challenges, they may also create opportunities for possible improvements in investing, financing, and operating activities to create shared value for all stakeholders. Strategic risks affecting strategic sustainability planning should be identified, assessed, and managed with a keen focus on minimizing their negative effects and building on the opportunities provided by addressing these risks. Recent research highlights the importance of enterprise risk management (ERM) in assessing and managing the strategic risk relevant to sustainability performance implementation and sustainability reporting to deliver on the quality and quantity of sustainability reporting and assurance.[23]

III. SUSTAINABILITY RISK ASSESSMENT AND MANAGEMENT

Sustainability risk assessment and management are integral components of overall sustainability strategic planning and practices, which enable business organizations to identify, assess, and manage the potential economic, social, and environmental risks and opportunities associated with their operations. Identification of sustainability risks, discussed in the previous section, is the first step in the sustainability risk assessment, management, and control. Effective and comprehensive sustainability risk assessment and management require the use of an integrated approach in evaluating the relationships between economic, governance, environmental, and social factors to develop a risk mitigation strategy to minimize risks and maximize opportunities for long-term business resilience and success. The approach to effective assessment and management of sustainability risks consists of the identification of risks, development of risk evaluation tools and metrics, integration with enterprise risk management (ERM), performing scenario analyses, materiality assessment, development of risk mitigation and management strategies, engagement of stakeholders, compliance with regulations and standards, and conducting the review, adaptability, and continuous improvement.

The Committee of Sponsoring Organizations' (COSO) enterprise risk management (ERM) framework is an excellent guide in assessing and managing sustainability risks.[24] All eight components of the COSO ERM framework should be considered including: (1) internal environment of setting the tone at the top of an organization in promoting sustainability factors of performance, risk, and disclosure; (2) objective setting of achieving short-, median-, and long-term strategic sustainability planning; (3) risk identification of risk exposures relevant to sustainability issues; (4) risk assessment of determining risk root cause, sensitivity analyses of the drivers, and pathways of organizational risks; (5) risk responses of addressing the drivers of sustainability risks; (6) control activities designed to manage sustainability risks; (7) information about the organization's responses and efforts in assessing and managing sustainability risks and proper communication with all affected stakeholders; and (8) monitoring of risks and ensuring that an organization is achieving its sustainability objectives, managing related sustainability risks and monitoring and evaluating its sustainability activities.[25]

The COSO ERM framework also suggests several tips for raising sustainability awareness in the organization including (1) getting leadership (the board of directors and executives) involved by embedding sustainability into corporate culture and business environment, making sustainability part of strategic planning; (2) engaging stakeholders (investors, employees, suppliers, customers) in sustainability initiatives and activities; (3) integrating sustainability into the business strategies; (4) identifying, assessing and managing material sustainability risks; (5) looking for sustainability achievements and quick wins; (6) properly communicating sustainability good, bad, and ugly stories; (7) selecting appropriate measurement tools by using balanced scorecards.[26]

The COSO revised its 1992 issue of *Internal Control-Integrated Framework* in 2013 and then in 2022 to address internal controls for both financial and non-financial ESG activities. The COSO 2023 internal control framework, *Achieving Effective Internal Control over Sustainability Reporting* (ICSR), was published in

March 2023 to tailor internal controls for sustainability reporting.[27] Business organizations can promote a culture of sustainability and accountability, revisit their mission of profit-with-purpose, integrate the COSO internal control framework into both financial reporting and sustainability reporting, and focus on the assessment and management of risks associated with financial economic sustainability performance (ESP) and non-financial environmental, social and governance (ESG) sustainability performance.

It is important to understand that sustainability risk management is not a matter of only one component but effectively dealing with multiple threats and risks. To expand on the previously given tips, the board of directors and executives must lead by example and try to implement the right sustainability measures in the corporate culture while being held accountable for their actions or lack thereof. By creating the right culture, objectives, and strategy, organizations can present to their stakeholders what they stand for and what aptitude such organizations with implemented long-term sustainability strategies have. Organizations should give an opportunity to their lower-level stakeholders and employees to express their concerns, ideas, preferences, and critiques and, by listening and executing, engage them in a value-adding process. When working on long-term sustainability goals, rather than focusing strictly on long-term strategy, organizations should try to achieve short-term goals and show often and consistently that they are serious about the organization's sustainability. Finally, progress in achieving sustainability should be measured accordingly and frequently to ensure the organization is on the right track.[28] The International Organization for Standardization (ISO) published its new standard, *ISO 31000: Risk Management–Principles and Guidelines*, in 2009, which provides principles and guidelines on risk management.[29] These ISO 31000 risk guidelines assist business organizations in developing, implementing, maintaining, assessing, monitoring, sustaining, and continuously improving their risk management system in minimizing the negative effects of strategic, operational, financial, compliance, environmental, and reputation risks.[30] These risks are interrelated and, thus, should be properly assessed and managed. For example, an excessive strategic risk can also cause operational, financial, compliance, and reputational risks. The compliance risk directly or indirectly associated with business sustainability, including non-compliance with regulatory reforms, health and safety, human rights and labor laws, corporate governance measures, anti-bribery, and environmental risks, can vary among organizations and across countries. For example, environmental risks can include direct effects (e.g., emissions trading cost exposures) and indirect consequences (e.g., energy price increases and accompanying reporting and compliance costs) of non-compliance with environmental laws, rules, and regulations. Business organizations should also assess and manage their financial risk of producing and disclosing materially misstated financial reports. Minimizing the reputational risk is vital to the success of sustainability programs and related performance, as stakeholder satisfaction is essential to sustainable business.

IV. CONCLUSIONS

The risks relevant to sustainability factors of performance and disclosures should be identified, assessed, managed, monitored, and controlled, and their negative impacts on financial, investment, and operational activities be minimized. Business sustainability requires a complete understanding of both performance and risks and their relationship and integration into the business environment, corporate culture, and all management strategies, decisions, and actions. Several risks are relevant to both financial ESP and non-financial ESG business sustainability performance, including strategic, operations, compliance, financial, climate change, litigation, compliance reputation, the COVID-19 pandemic, and cybersecurity. These risks can adversely affect business operations, finance the investing activities of business organizations, and destabilize capital markets. Proper assessment, management, control, and disclosure of those risks are becoming increasingly important and play an effective role in achieving both financial ESP and non-financial ESG sustainability performance in creating shared value for all stakeholders. Effective assessment and management of sustainability risks require the use of proactive measures, including conducting risk assessments, implementing robust governance frameworks, adopting sustainable business practices, and developing resilience strategies.

V. TAKEAWAYS

- Business sustainability factors of planning, performance, risk, and disclosure should be integrated into investment objectives and decisions.
- By addressing sustainability risks presented in this chapter, individuals and organizations can contribute to a more sustainable and resilient future.
- The use of enterprise risk management (ERM) in assessing and managing sustainability risks discussed in this chapter can turn sustainability challenges and risks into sustainability opportunities and performance.
- Move toward sustainability reporting and risk assessment that underscores the importance of an adequate ERM in improving the effectiveness of both financial ESP and non-financial ESG sustainability performance.
- Use *ISO 31000: Risk Management–Principles and Guidelines* (2009), which provides principles and guidelines on risk management.
- Properly disclose assessment and management sustainability risks and their possible impacts on operational, investment, and financial activities and related performance.

Notes

1 United States Government Accountability Office (GAO). July 2020. Report to the Honorable Mark Warner US Senate. *Public Companies Disclosure of Environmental,*

Social and Governance Factors and Options to Enhance Them. Available at https://www.gao.gov/assets/710/707949.pdf

2 PricewaterhouseCoopers (PwC). May 2014. Sustainability Goes Mainstream: Insights into Investor Views. http://www.pwc.com/us/en/pwc-investor-resource-institute/index.jhtml

3 Harvard Law School Forum on Corporate Governance. 2020. *Institutional Investor Survey*. Available at: https://corpgov.law.harvard.edu/2020/03/25/institutional-investor-survey-2020/#:~:text=Morrow%20Sodali's%20survey%20explores%20how%20ESG%2C%20as%20a,an%20appetite%20for%20a%20separate%20vote%20on%20sustainability.

4 International Organization for Standardization (ISO). 2018. *ISO 31000: Risk Management–Guidelines, 2018. ISO*. www.iso.org (accessed October 6, 2021).

5 International Organization for Standardization (ISO). 2019. *ISO 31010: Risk Management – Risk Assessment Techniques, 2019. ISO*. www.iso.org (accessed October 6, 2021).

6 Ibid.

7 CDP. June 4, 2019. "World's Biggest Companies Face $1 Trillion in Climate Change Risks. 2019. Available at https://www.cdp.net/en/articles/media/worlds-biggest-companies-face-1-trillion-in-climate-change-risks

8 CDP. October 14, 2021. "CDP Reports Record Number of Disclosures and Unveils New Strategy to Help Further Tackle Climate and Ecological Emergency." Available at https://www.cdp.net/ en/articles/media/cdp-reports-record-number-of-disclosures-and-unveils-new-strategy-to-help-further-tackle-climate-and-ecological-emergency

9 CDP. 2021. *Our Five-year Strategy – Accelerating the Rate of Change*. Available at https://www.cdp.net/ en/info/about-us/our-five-year-strategy

10 Securities and Exchange Commission (SEC). March 21, 2022. "SEC Proposes Rules to Enhance and Standardize Climate-Related Disclosures for Investors." Available at https://www.sec.gov/news/press-release/2022–46

11 Brockett and Rezaee. 2015. *Corporate Sustainability: Integrating Performance and Reporting*. Wiley. Available at: https://books.google.com/books?hl=en&lr=&id=EK1NFc8kWZIC&oi=fnd&pg=PP13&dq=Operations+Risk+egsee+sustainability+performance&ots=8wiMqc3Hig&sig=OtcLSX8reP_VQNrju9zJnT-X_q0#v=snippet&q=Operations%20Risk%20&f=false

12 Sternberg, L. J. 2017. "Surviving the Equifax Data Breach." Available at https://blog.aicpa.org/2017/09/surviving-the-equifax-data-breach.html#sthash.Stida706.dpbs

13 Bitsight. 2021. "Ransomware: The Rapidly Evolving Trend." Available at https://www.bitsight.com/hubfs/eBooks/Ransomware_The%20Rapidly%20Evolving%20Trend.pdf

14 Banker, P. December 18, 2014. "US Weighs Response to Sony Cyberattack, with North Korea Confrontation Possible." *New York Times*. http://www.nytimes.com/2014/12/19/world/asia/north-korea-confrontation-possible-in-response-to-sony-cyberattack.html?_r=0.

15 *ISO 27001: Information Security Management*. http://www.iso.org/iso/home/standards/management-standards/iso27001.htm.

16 Klassen Matt. 2018. *What is an Information Security Management System (ISMS) & How Should It Be Implemented?*. Cherwell. Available at: https://www.cherwell.com/security-management/library/blog/what-is-an-information-management-security-system/

17 ISO/IEC 27001:2013. 2013. Information technology – Security techniques – Information Security Management Systems – Requirements. Available at https://www.iso.org/ standard/54534.html

18 Securities and Exchange Commission (SEC). July 26, 2023. "SEC Adopts Rules on Cybersecurity Risk Management, Strategy, Governance, and Incident Disclosure by Public Companies." Available at https://www.sec.gov/news/press-release/2023–139

19 Auditboard. What is Operational Risk Management? The Overview. Available at https://www.auditboard.com/blog/operational-risk-management/

20 Jacob, C. 2012. "The Impact of Financial Crisis on Corporate Social Responsibility and its Implications for Reputation Risk Management." *Journal of Management and Sustainability*. https://heinonline.org/HOL/Page?handle=hein.journals/jms2&id=491&collection=journals&index=

21 Sickler Jonas. 2021. *What is Reputational Risk and How to Manage it*. ReputationManagement.com. Available at https://www.reputationmanagement.com/ blog/reputational-risk/

22 Deloitte. 2013. *Exploring Strategic Risk*. Available at https://www2.deloitte.com/content/dam/Deloitte/global/Documents/Governance-Risk-Compliance/dttl-grc-exploring-strategic-risk.pdf

23 Shad, M., F. Lai, C. Flott, J. Kremes, and A. Bokhan. 2019."Integrating Sustainability Reporting into Enterprise Risk Management and its Relationship with Business Performance: A Conceptual Framework." *Journal of Cleaner Production* Vol. 208, January 20, 415–425. Available at: https://www.sciencedirect.com/science/article/abs/pii/S0959652618331366

24 Committee of Sponsoring Organizations of the Treadway Commission (COSO). May 2013. *Demystifying Sustainability Risk*. Available at https://www.coso.org/documents/COSO-ERM%20Demystifying%20Sustainability%20Risk_Full%20WEB.pdf

25 Ibid.

26 Ibid.

27 The Committee of Sponsoring Organizations of the Treadway Commission (COSO). 2023. *Achieving Effective Internal Control Over Sustainability Reporting (ICSR)*. Available at https://www.sustainability-reports.com/coso-releases-new-achieving-effective-internal-control-over-sustainability-reporting-icsr-supplemental-guidance/

28 Ibid.

29 International Organization for Standardization (ISO). 2009. *ISO 31000: Risk Management –Principles and Guidelines*. www.iso.org (accessed July 31, 2011).

30 Ibid.

Chapter 8

Sustainability Disclosure and Reporting

I. INTRODUCTION

Sustainability disclosure and reporting effectively and transparently communicate organizations' financial economic sustainability performance (ESP) and non-financial environmental, social, and governance (ESG) sustainability to their stakeholders. The sustainability disclosure process involves providing information about the organization's financial performance (profit) and impact on the planet, people, and its governance practices. Sustainability disclosure and reporting are integral components of corporate accountability and responsibility. There are two aspects of non-financial environmental, social, and governance (ESG) sustainability. These aspects are ESG sustainability performance and ESG sustainability disclosure, which are interrelated. Sustainability disclosures indicate that "more sustainable" firms have incentives to disclose ESG information to differentiate themselves from "less sustainable" firms with no focus on ESG sustainability performance. Sustainability performance reflects an organization's commitment to and achievement of financial ESP and non-financial ESG sustainability initiatives and goals.

Global business organizations are currently dealing with the challenges of adopting a proper sustainability reporting framework to effectively present both financial ESP and non-financial ESG sustainability performance. Business sustainability has recently evolved from focusing on short-term financial and economic performance and fulfillment of corporate social responsibility (CSR) to achieving long-term financial ESP and non-financial ESG sustainability performance in creating shared value for all stakeholders. Many public companies in Europe and Asia are now required to disclose their non-financial ESG sustainability performance information. It is expected that public companies in other countries follow suit in requiring disclosure

DOI: 10.4324/9781003437949-8

of sustainability information on both financial ESP and non-financial ESG. This disclosure requirement is intended to support investors, consumers, policymakers, and other interested stakeholders in evaluating the non-financial ESG sustainability performance. This chapter presents both mandatory and voluntary disclosure of sustainability information, including sustainability reporting.

II. CORPORATE REPORTING

Corporate reporting and disclosure, mandatory on ESP information and voluntary on ESG sustainability performance information, are vital to the financial markets, economic growth, and value-relevant to investors and other stakeholders. The type and extent of corporate voluntary reporting have recently received considerable attention as many public companies worldwide disclose information on various ESG dimensions of their sustainability performance. Corporate disclosure, mandatory on ESP or voluntary on ESG, is intended to provide investors and other stakeholders with useful, transparent, reliable, and relevant financial and non-financial information in making sound investment decisions. Thus, it is the backbone of the financial markets and the economy. Public companies in the United States have disclosed a set of financial statements to their shareholders under the corporate mandatory disclosure regime, and they also communicate with shareholders and other stakeholders through various channels, including voluntary corporate disclosures on ESG information. Anecdotal evidence suggests that investors value meaningful and reliable voluntary disclosures and use them to make investment decisions and utilize mandatory disclosures to verify voluntary disclosures.[1] Thus, given the limited resources and other legal and compliance considerations, management often trades off the relative costs of mandatory and voluntary disclosures and may adjust the voluntary disclosure level according to the mandatory disclosure level in providing relevant, useful, and reliable financial ESP and non-financial ESG information.

Management may be more inclined to disclose mandatory financial ESP information than disclose voluntary ESG information or act in a similar or opposite direction regarding disclosing ESG information. Investors and other corporate stakeholders may view mandatory ESP information and voluntary ESG information as complementary or contradictory. Voluntary ESG disclosures are based on management discretion of what information to disclose, for what purposes, and to what extent to disclose such information. Public companies in the United States are required to disclose mandatory financial information, whereas they may choose to disclose the type and extent of non-financial ESG disclosures in striking the right balance between enhancing long-term shareholder value and creating shared value for all stakeholders. Sustainability ESG disclosures are largely not mandated, and management may opportunistically determine its disclosure strategies and practices.

There has been an ongoing argument in the business community that conventional financial reports do not portray a comprehensive and complete picture of a company's financial health, sustainability, and risk factors. Thus, corporate reporting should reflect both financial ESP and non-financial ESG sustainability performance.[2] Sustainability reporting is measuring, classifying, and recognizing financial ESP and non-financial ESG sustainability performance and disclosing such information to all stakeholders. Investors and other external stakeholders, including suppliers, customers, governments, society, and the environment, can now have more transparent information about companies' commitment to sustainability. Management can use sustainability reporting to improve managerial and strategic decisions by integrating sustainability into the business environment, corporate culture, and supply chain management. Sustainability performance reporting and assurance can provide management and external stakeholders with improved confidence in the credibility and trustworthiness of sustainability information.

Sustainability initiatives are designed to maximize corporate social benefits while minimizing the conflicts between corporations, society, and the environment caused by differences between private and social costs and benefits and to align corporate goals with those of society. Nonetheless, the proper measurement, accurate and reliable disclosure of sustainability performance, and effective assessment of sustainability risks remain major challenges for organizations of different types and sizes because of inadequate disclosure guidelines. Several organizations worldwide, including the Global Reporting Initiative (GRI), International Integrated Reporting Council (IIRC), Sustainability Accounting Standards Board (SASB), and International Sustainability Standards Board (ISSB), have issued guidelines regarding voluntary/mandatory disclosure of sustainability information. Almost all public companies worldwide have considered these guidelines in producing stand-alone integrated sustainability reports.

There are two ESG reporting regimes: mandatory (European, some Asian, and South African countries) and voluntary/semi-mandatory (US and some other countries). Disclosure of sustainability performance information is expected to affect the firm's performance and corporate governance. First, investors typically have incomplete financial ESP and non-financial ESG sustainability performance, and thus, they may not be aware of the firm's governance effectiveness, ethical culture, and social and environmental commitments. Lack of knowledge on the part of investors reduces the firm's investor base, which in turn makes risk sharing incomplete and inefficient, and thus, stocks of these firms are out of line with their market's fundamentals, which may incentivize firms to obtain certification to influence stock prices. Disclosures of sustainability information, however, make investors aware of the firm's existence and enlarge its investor base, which improves risk sharing and thus makes their stocks closer to their market fundamentals.

Second, the costs and benefits of sustainability disclosures are often uncertain, and the extent to which sustainability disclosures lead to the release of private information on firms' governance, environmental, and social initiatives is unknown. Stakeholders may attempt to pressure and/or motivate firms to disclose sustainability information about their social, governance, and environmental activities, and releasing such information leads to the disclosure of private information. Managers tend to analyze the costs/benefits of obtaining sustainability disclosure to improve sustainability disclosures and how these disclosures are integrated and observed by capital markets. Third, sustainability information on long-term economic and ESG performance increases the quality and quantity of the firm's disclosures and, thus, focuses more on long-term and sustainable performance and has fewer incentives for short-term performance that could be detrimental to long-term sustainability. Given that sustainability disclosing firms experience fewer incentives and opportunities for short-termism, there should be a positive relation between sustainability disclosures and stock prices.

II.1 Mandatory Sustainability Reporting

Mandatory sustainability disclosure and reporting are the requirements imposed on business organizations by regulators and standards-setters worldwide to disclose information about their ESG performance and initiatives. Mandatory sustainability reporting requirements typically cover various sustainability topics, from environmental impact to labor conditions, human rights, social practices, and governance. Investors have recognized the importance of sustainability disclosures in their decision-making, and regulators have mandated sustainability requirements and standards. Sustainability reporting regulations often imposed by government or regulatory bodies on business organizations are intended to improve accountability, transparency, and the integration of sustainability initiatives and considerations into business practices. For example, in recent decades, many countries, including Australia, Austria, Canada, Denmark, France, Germany, Malaysia, Netherlands, Sweden, Hong Kong, and the United Kingdom, have adopted mandatory reporting on non-financial ESG sustainability performance.[3] Regulators in other countries are expected to follow suit, moving toward mandatory sustainability performance reporting and assurance. Stock exchanges worldwide either require or recommend that their listed companies report sustainability information (e.g., Singapore Stock Exchange, 2011; Toronto Stock Exchange, 2014; Hong Kong Stock Exchange, 2015), and more than 6,000 European companies are required to disclose their non-financial ESG sustainability performance and diversity information for their financial year 2017 and onwards.[4] The Hong Kong Exchange has announced that an integrated sustainability and corporate governance report will be required for Hong Kong-listed companies starting in 2015.[5] This guide requires environmental, social, and governance disclosures. The Exchange encourages an issuer to identify and disclose additional ESG issues and KPIs relevant to its business. An issuer may adopt a higher level of ESG reporting based on international guidance standards, such as IIRC and GRI. In the United States, the Securities and Exchange Commission (SEC) released its climate change proposed rule on March 21, 2022, that would require public companies to disclose certain climate-related risks that are considered to have material impacts on their business, results of operations, or financial condition, as well as other climate-related financial statement metrics such as greenhouse gas emissions.[6] The SEC released its final rules on climate change in March 2024 that require additional disclosures of climate change issues.[7]

The global standard setters and initiatives can also require mandatory sustainability reporting. For example, the European Union's Non-Financial Reporting Directive (NFRD) requires certain large European companies to disclose non-financial ESG information, that may drive global efforts toward mandatory sustainability reporting. In September 2014, the European Commission adopted the Council of the Directive on disclosure of non-financial sustainability information for more than 6,000 companies for their financial year 2017.[8] The directive provides non-binding guidelines in facilitating non-financial environmental, social, anticorruption, and diversity information disclosure by large public companies. The directive also allows large companies to disclose non-financial information as a separate or integrated report along with financial information. The primary objectives of the directive are to (1) increase transparency in sustainability reporting in the areas of environmental, social, governance, employee-related issues, human rights policies, and anticorruption and bribery issues; (2) increase sustainability performance on social and environmental matters; and (3) contribute effectively to long-term economic growth and employment. In January 2023, the EU Corporate Sustainability Reporting Directive (CSRD) was issued, requiring mandatory sustainability reporting for European companies that could apply to their counterparts and trading partners worldwide.[9] The CSRD is intended to complement existing sustainability-focused regulations and voluntary frameworks and standards of the GRI and the ISSB and will have a global implication. The CSRD requires covered companies to disclose historical and forward-looking information relevant to sustainability matters, including ESG issues and information about sustainability risk management, metrics, and value chain due diligence for EU companies.

Mandatory sustainability reporting requirements typically focus on identifying and disclosing material ESG sustainability issues considered most relevant to business organizations and their stakeholders. Noncompliance with mandatory sustainability reporting may cause penalties or other consequences, as regulatory bodies oversee financial and corporate reporting and usually monitor and enforce compliance. Sustainability reporting regulations are evolving as sustainability reporting practices have advanced. Mandatory ESG sustainability reporting can encourage positive environmental, social, and governance practices among business organizations and contribute to shared value creation for all stakeholders and the broader goals of sustainable development, generating desired financial performance and having social and environmental impacts. Mandatory ESG sustainability reporting is expected to be integrated with mandatory financial reporting to provide a more comprehensive and holistic approach to corporate reporting.

Regulators worldwide have issued sustainability disclosure and reporting regulations, standards, and guidelines. For example, in the United States, the Task Force on Climate-related Financial Disclosures (TCFD) regulates sustainability disclosure on climate-related financial risks by requiring companies to disclose climate change information in their financial filings. The SEC has considered regulations on climate change and human capital. In Europe, the EU Non-Financial Reporting Directive requires large companies to disclose non-financial ESG information in their management reports, and the CSRD requires disclosure of ESG historical and forward-looking information. Regulators in Asia, Australia, Canada, and the United Kingdom have issued rules on sustainability reporting, climate change, human capital, and environmental matters.

The International Financial Reporting Standards (IFRS) Foundation's consultation on establishing a global non-financial ESG reporting framework has highlighted the need for global sustainability reporting standards and received strong support from investors, the corporate sector, accounting professionals, policymakers, regulators, and central banks.[10] These sustainability disclosure initiatives, whether mandatory or voluntary, are intended to reflect the financial, social, and environmental impacts of a company's business operation and, thus, provide relevant and reliable financial and non-financial information for all stakeholders, including investors. There are debates among policymakers and scholars that international accounting standard-setters, such as the Financial Accounting Standards Board (FASB) and International Accounting Standards Board (IASB), and the ISSB of the International Financial Reporting Standards (IFRS) are in the process of issue accounting standards for proper disclosure of ESG sustainability information, which will be discussed in the next section.

II.2 Voluntary Sustainability Reporting

Voluntary sustainability reporting is the practice of disclosing ESG information voluntarily. Business organizations typically initiate voluntary sustainability reporting as part of their commitment to sustainable business practices and to demonstrate their commitment to corporate responsibility. Voluntary sustainability reporting provides a platform and mechanism for business organizations to communicate with stakeholders on a broad range of economic, social, environmental, and governance matters and share their sustainability efforts, initiatives, and achievements. In recent years, many companies in the United States and other countries have issued voluntary integrated sustainability reports on both financial ESP and non-financial ESG sustainability performance. Voluntary disclosures, such as management earnings forecasts and non-financial ESG, are often released by management on a discretionary basis. Voluntary ESG sustainability reporting demonstrates an organization's commitment to ethical and sustainable business practices by contributing positively to society, minimizing environmental impact, and building trust and reputation with stakeholders, including investors, customers, employees, and suppliers. Voluntary reporting is gaining global attention and acceptance as a best practice in corporate reporting and governance.

Currently, there are several voluntary sustainability disclosures and reporting initiatives to guide business organizations worldwide in disclosing their ESG performance information. These initiatives provide frameworks and structured processes for companies to communicate their ESG sustainability efforts and activities to their stakeholders. Chapter One presented several organizations worldwide, including the Global Reporting Initiative (GRI), the International Integrated Reporting Council (IIRC), the Sustainability Accounting Standards Board (SASB), the Value Reporting Foundation (VRF), International Sustainability Standards Board (ISSB), the United Nations Global Compact (UNGC), the International Organizations for Standardization (ISO, 26,000) that have issued guidelines regarding voluntary disclosure of sustainability information.

Over 40,000 public companies have considered these frameworks in producing stand-alone integrated sustainability reports, and companies choose these guidelines that align best with their stakeholder expectations, business models, and industry specifications. These voluntary sustainability initiatives are essential for enhancing transparency and accountability and contributing to the long-term value creation for all stakeholders. For example, the fourth generation (G4) of GRI's Guidelines covers economic, governance, social, and environmental performance, globally accepted sustainability standards emphasizing both financial ESP and non-financial ESG sustainability performance. In 2011, the GRI developed version 4.1, or the fourth generation (G4) of guidelines, which covers economic, governance, social, and environmental performance, and in 2016 established globally accepted sustainability standards (GASS) which focus on financial and non-financial sustainability disclosures. GASS creates a coordinated set of guidelines for businesses and organizations to correctly and consistently report their impacts related to sustainability measures. The reports of these impacts help cater to the needs of stakeholders, investors, and policymakers.[11] In October 2021, The GRI launched its 2021 Universal Standards, representing the most important update on ESG standards for sustainability reporting. The 2021 Universal Standards strengthen the basic foundations of all sustainability reporting through GRI, focusing on transparency, due diligence, and material topics that impact the economy, environment, and people for global organizations of all types and sizes. The 2021 updated GRI standards include a consolidated set of GRI standards, including GRI 1 Foundations, GRI 2 General Disclosures, GRI 3, Material Topics, GRI 11, Oil and Gas Sector, GRI 201 Economic Performance. GRI 202 Market Presence, GRI 203 Indirect Economic Impacts, GRI 204 Performance Practices, and GRI 205 Anticorruption.

The International Integrated Reporting Council (IIRC) issued the Integrated Reporting (IR) framework that suggests processes for making a comprehensive sustainability report framework that merges financial ESP and non-financial ESG sustainability performance information into an "integrated" format that is relevant to all corporate stakeholders. The 2020 revision for the IIRC welcomes the identifying metrics that support effective and long-term sustainability value creation and shows the universal need for financial and non-financial ESG standards. The Sustainability Accounting Standards Board (SASB) has established sustainability accounting standards based on the US Securities and Exchange Commission's (SEC) reporting, which mandates material disclosures for 88 industries in 10 sectors as part of mandatory filings with the SEC.

The International Sustainability Standards Board (ISSB) was created as a non-profit organization by the International Financial Reporting Standards (IFRS) in 2021 and, by August 2022, integrated the VRF, GRI, SASB, and IIRC to become a primary sustainability organization in establishing frameworks and standards for sustainability reporting.[12] The ISSB has issued two standards (IFRS S1 and IFRS S2) that improve accountability, trust, and confidence in sustainability matters and create a framework for disclosing sustainability performance information, including the risks and opportunities associated with climate change.[13] IFRS S1 provides disclosure requirements for companies to communicate sustainability-related risks and opportunities to their investors. IFRS S2 establishes specific guidelines relevant to climate-related disclosures and is intended to be used with IFRS S1. ISSB's sustainability reporting standards are akin to IRFS standards to ensure the interconnectedness of corporate reporting tailored to industry-specific details as part of general reporting and emission control targets to be set by entities themselves based on their situation and reporting of progress with reference to those standards.

III. BEST PRACTICES OF SUSTAINABILITY REPORTING

Global trend toward business sustainability planning, performance, risk, disclosure, reporting, and assurance encourages and ultimately rewards companies that focus on financial ESP and non-financial ESG dimensions of sustainability performance and disclose their sustainability performance in sustainability reports and assurance. Business organizations worldwide now recognize the importance of ESP and ESG sustainability performance and the link between bottom-line profitability and ESG sustainability. Justifications for ESG sustainability performance are social responsibility, moral obligation, maintaining a good reputation, environmental impacts, ensuring sustainability, licensing to operate, and creating shared value. Corporations identify potential social and environmental issues of concern in a shared value approach and integrate them into their strategic planning. There are many reasons why a company should pay attention to non-financial ESG sustainability performance, such as the pressure of the labor movement, the development of moral values and social standards, the development of business education, and the change in public opinion about the role of business. Companies that are, or aspire to be, leaders in sustainability are challenged by rising public expectations, increasing innovation, continuous quality improvement, and heightened social and environmental problems. Businesses should fulfill social responsibility and environmental initiatives because of the public image, consumer movements, government requirements, and investors' education, avoidance of environmental violations and obligations and tax benefits, better relations with stakeholders, employee satisfaction, a sense of pride, and an appropriate way to improve quality.

In the past two decades, global progress has been towards integrated mandatory or voluntary sustainability reporting and assurance. More than 40,000 business organizations worldwide have started to issue sustainability reports on the various dimensions of their sustainability performance.[14] About 20% of the S&P 500 companies produced non-financial ESG sustainability reports in 2011, whereas in 2012, more than 53%, about 72% in 2013, 86% in 2018, and more than 90% in 2019.[15] This steady growth in public companies publishing integrated sustainability reports is expected to continue. Several global professional organizations, including the Global Reporting Initiative (GRI), the International Integrated Reporting Council (IIRC), the Sustainability Accounting Standards Board (SASB), and the Value Reporting Foundation, have promoted integrated sustainability reporting and assurance in the past decade. Global accounting standard-setters, such as the International Accounting Standards Board (IASB) and the Financial Accounting Standards Board (FASB), are currently considering whether and how to establish accounting guidelines to properly recognize and disclose all five dimensions of sustainability performance information.

Sustainability disclosure and reporting are essential for promoting transparency, accountability, and responsible business practices by providing stakeholders with the information they need to assess an organization's economic performance and impact on society and the environment and make informed decisions. Policymakers, regulators, investors, and consumers recognize the importance of sustainability disclosures in evaluating organizations' long-term viability, sustainability, and resilience. Effective, robust, and comprehensive sustainability reporting involves communicating an organization's economic, governance, environmental, and social impacts accurately, reliably, and transparently to all its stakeholders. Management should design, implement, and maintain proper sustainability reporting processes and strategies that provide a common ground for the integration of sustainability into the corporate culture, business environment, strategic plans, and supply chain that consist of:

- Utilizing all capital from strategic to financial, reputational, manufactured, social, environmental, compliance, and human creates accountability and stewardship for all capital and stakeholders.
- Presenting environmental disclosure, including the carbon footprint of reporting on greenhouse gas emissions and efforts to reduce them and reporting natural resource usage of water and energy consumption.
- Disclosure of social issues, including labor practices, human rights, and community impact.
- Disclosure of governance matters, including board composition and diversity, risk management, and ethical business practices.
- Engaging with stakeholders, including investors, customers, employees, suppliers, and communities, to understand their sustainability concerns and expectations.

- Integration of continuous improvement strategies for both financial ESP and non-financial ESG sustainability performance into the business environment, corporate culture and investment analysis, supply chain management, and decision-making process.
- Establishing tone at the top commitment by the company's board of directors and executives to the effective and robust application of sustainability best practices in managing sustainability issues, including environmental, human rights, and social issues across the operations and supply chains.
- Establishing robust and measurable sustainability targets and goals aligned with the profit-with-purpose mission and presenting progress toward achieving these goals and targets.
- Development of a long-term and sustainable relationship with all stakeholders. Collaboration among all stakeholders to enhance the effectiveness of implementing sustainability programs and development, including strategies for creating shared value for all stakeholders, is important in developing such relationships.
- Identifying, assessing, managing, and disclosing material sustainability risks and opportunities that could affect the present and future performance.
- Identifying and prioritizing relevant material ESG issues through a materiality assessment by focusing on sustainability matters that are likely to substantially impact business operations.
- Engagement of all stakeholders, including shareholders, to discuss the company's sustainability strategies and progress, including environmental and social initiatives. Engaging all key stakeholders, including customers, employees, investors, and suppliers, is vital to understanding material sustainability issues (e.g., human rights, societal, and environmental) to ensure ongoing communication and responsiveness to their evolving expectations.
- Development of sustainable supply chain management strategies for identifying and selecting suppliers that focus on achieving their sustainability performance.
- Communication of the company's sustainability strategies, practices, and expectations to major stakeholders, suppliers, and customers to mitigate risks and foster corporate values and culture. Failure to address sustainability issues (e.g., human rights, social, and environmental) can create the risk of litigation and damage to brand value and reputation, particularly as supply chains relevant to materials and labor have shifted to emerging markets.
- Integration of sustainability into all aspects of business, including the supply chain from purchasing and inbound logistics, production design, and manufacturing processes to marketing, distribution, outbound logistics, and customer services.
- Continuously assessing the company's sustainability performance to monitor and improve business sustainability and identify challenging areas needing further improvement.

- Linking business sustainable performance to the corporate culture, company strategy, and business model by focusing on the effects of sustainability issues (environmental, social, and human rights) on all aspects of business and corporate activities.
- Communicating the company's sustainability success stories to all stakeholders, including shareholders and trading partners.
- Compliance with mandatory and voluntary sustainability reporting regulations, standards, and frameworks, including those of the GRI, SASB, TCFD, ISSB, and CSRD, to enhance credibility, consistency, and comparability in sustainability reporting.
- Integrating ESG sustainability reporting with financial reporting to provide holistic corporate performance reporting and articulating the linkage between financial ESP and non-financial ESG performance in creating shared value for all stakeholders.
- Periodic disclosures of both financial and non-financial key performance indicators (KPIs) relevant to sustainability performance, including disclosing information on greenhouse gas (GHG) emissions policies and procedures, social activities as well as renewable energy resources, and climate change that are designed to address the associated challenges, opportunities, and risks that affect the business environment.
- Preparing an integrated sustainability report reflecting both material ESP and ESG sustainability performance and obtaining assurance statements on the sustainability report from third-party assurance providers to enhance the reliability and credibility of sustainability information.
- Telling sustainability stories in plain language to ensure the report is understandable and comprehensive, providing valuable and relevant information.

IV. CONCLUSION

An ever-increasing interest in and demand for business sustainability in the past several decades has led to a growth in issuing integrated sustainability reports on both financial ESP and non-financial ESG sustainability performance. Business sustainability focuses on corporate activities, including supply chains that generate long-term financial ESP in creating shareholder value, as well as other activities that result in the achievement of non-financial ESG sustainability performance that protects the interests of all stakeholders. Human capital disclosure in the aftermath of the COVID-19 pandemic is gaining much attention as organizations are required to ensure the safety, health, and well-being of their employees, suppliers, and customers. Investors want their companies to have proper policies and processes for employee layoff, retention, health, and safety.

Business organizations worldwide are now recognizing the importance of sustainability factors of planning, performance, disclosure, and risk. Proper business sustainability implementation requires companies to fulfill their stewardship responsibilities to all stakeholders, including shareholders, creditors, the community, society, and the environment. Disclosure of ESP and ESG dimensions of sustainability performance while signaling management commitments to sustainability and establishing legitimacy with all constituencies poses a cost–benefit trade-off that has implications for investors and business organizations. In creating shared value for all stakeholders, management should identify potential financial, human, social, environmental, governance, and ethical issues of concern and integrate them into its decision-making, strategic planning, and managerial processes, including supply chain management.

Business sustainability indicates that the main objective function for business organizations is to create shareholder value by maximizing firm financial performance through continuous improvements and reporting of both financial ESP and non-financial ESG sustainability performance. The ESP and ESG sustainability performance dimensions are interrelated and complement/complete each other, and thus, they should be integrated into the business environment and corporate culture. The focus of business sustainability should be on creating long-term and sustainable shared value for all stakeholders. This suggests that management realizes the importance of integrating sustainability into business operations. Companies should effectively and transparently communicate their business sustainability performance with all stakeholders by periodically releasing their sustainability reports. It is a management responsibility to use sustainability reporting to disclose sustainability information to all stakeholders and signal good business sustainability practices. The four sustainability factors of planning, performance, disclosure, and risk are the cornerstone and foundation of integrated sustainability reporting.

V. TAKEAWAYS

- Integrated sustainability reports should reveal both financial ESP and non-financial ESG information on sustainability performance to all stakeholders.
- Sustainability reporting should be aligned with the company's communication strategy and improve relationships with all key stakeholders.
- Sustainability risks should be assessed and managed to minimize the negative impacts on financial performance and sustainability reporting.
- Sustainability key performance indicators can create a benchmark for the company's sustainability success and reporting.
- Identify and disclose material sustainability risks and opportunities relevant to business operations that create shared value for all stakeholders.
- Present sustainability information in a clear, concise, and accessible manner by using plain language and visual aids, charts, and infographics to enhance readability, accessibility, and engagement.

Notes

1 Ernst and Young (EY). 2014. *Disclosure Effectiveness: What Investors, Company Executives and Other Stakeholders are Saying*. Available at https://www.eyjapan.jp/library/issue/us/gaap-weekly-update/pdf/GAAP-2014-11-25-03.pdf

2 Much of the discussion in this chapter comes from Rezaee Z. 2021. Business Sustainability Factors of Performance, Risk, and Disclosure, Business Expert Press, February 2021.

3 Rezaee, Z. 2015. *Business Sustainability: Performance, Compliance, Accountability and Integrated Reporting*. Greenleaf Publishing Limited, Sheffield, UK.

4 European Commission. 2014. Disclosure of Non-financial Information: Europe Information: Europe Council, the European Economic and Social, Environmental Issues. Available at *http://ec.europa.eu/internal_market/accounting/non-financial_reporting/index_en.htm*, (accessed March 29, 2016).

5 Hong Kong Stock Exchange (HKEx). January 13, 2015. *Environmental, Social and Governance Reporting Guide*, Appendix 27. Available at http://www.hkex.com.hk/eng/rulesreg/listrules/mbrules/documents/appendix_27.pdf (accessed July 28, 2015).

6 US Securities and Exchange Commission (SEC). 2022. SEC Proposes Rules to Enhance and Standardize Climate-Related Disclosures for Investors. Available at https://www.sec.gov/news/press-release/2022–46 (accessed March 21, 2023).

7 Securities and Exchange Commission (SEC). 2024. The Enhancement and Standardization of Climate-Related Disclosures for Investors. 17 CFR 210, 229, 230, 232, 239, and 249, [Release Nos. 33-11275; 34-99678; File No. S7-10-22]. Final Rules, March 6, 2024. Available at https://www.sec.gov/files/rules/final/2024/33-11275.pdf

8 European Union (EU). September 2014. "Directive 2014/95/EU of the European Parliament and of the Council amending Directive 2013/34/EU as Regards Disclosure of Non-financial and Diversity Information by Certain Large Undertakings and Groups." Available at: https://eur-lex.europa.eu/legal content/EN/TXT/PDF/?uri=CELEX:32014L0095&from=EN

9 European Commission (EC). January 5, 2023. "The Corporate Sustainability Reporting Directive (CSRD)." Available at https://finance.ec.europa.eu/capital-markets-union-and-financial-markets/company-reporting-and-auditing/company-reporting/corporate-sustainability-reporting_en

10 The International Financial Reporting Standards (IFRS). September 2020. *Consultation Paper on Sustainability Reporting*. https://cdn.ifrs.org/-/media/project/sustainability-reporting/consultation-paper-on-sustainability-reporting.pdf

11 Global Reporting Initiative. (n.d.). Global Reporting Initiative: Standards. Found at https://www.globalreporting.org/standards/

12 International Sustainability Standards Board (ISSB). 2021. Available at https://www.ifrs.org/groups/international-sustainability-standards-board/

13 International Financial Reporting Standards (IFRS). June 26, 2023. "ISSB Issues Inaugural Global Sustainability Disclosure Standards." Available at https://www.ifrs.org/news-and-events/news/2023/06/issb-issues-ifrs-s1-ifrs-s2/#:~:text=The%20ISSB%20Standards%20are%20designed%20to%20ensure%20that,be%20used%20in%20conjunction%20with%20any%20accounting%20requirements

14 Rezaee, Z. 2016. "Business Sustainability Research: A Theoretical and Integrated Perspective." *Journal of Accounting Literature* Vol. 36, 48–64.

15 Governance and Accountability Institute, INC. (G&A). 2020. *2020 Flash Report S&P 500*. Available at https://www.ga-institute.com/research-reports/flash-reports/2020-sp-500-flash-report.html

Chapter 9

Sustainability Assurance and Ratings

I. INTRODUCTION

External auditors have historically audited financial statements of public companies and, –since 2004, audited internal control over financial reporting (ICFR) for public companies in the United States and many other countries. Audits of financial statements and ICFR have played a significant role in protecting investors from receiving materially misstated financial reports and ensuring the efficiency of financial markets by lending more credibility and reliability to the financial information used by investors. The reliability and credibility of sustainability reports can also be enhanced by assuring such reports. The 2017 survey conducted by Ernst & Young (EY) indicates that (1) investors are increasingly considering the important role that non-financial ESG sustainability dimensions play in their investment decision-making; (2) management should present annual long-term board reviews of sustainability strategies; (3) a majority of surveyed companies have not considered environmental and social issues, their related risks, and the opportunities they present as core to their business; (4) generating sustainable financial ESP returns over time requires a sharper focus on non-financial ESG sustainability performance, and (5) non-financial ESG issues have a real and quantifiable impact on financial ESP sustainability over the long term.[1] According to the World Economic Forum, a coordinated set of ESG guidelines should be under four metrics: governance principles, planet, people, and prosperity.[2]

A growing number of public companies worldwide are issuing sustainability reports on various financial and non-financial dimensions of their sustainability performance. The credibility, objectivity, and reliability of sustainability reports could be significantly improved if they were accompanied by assurance statements.

DOI: 10.4324/9781003437949-9

As investors show more interest in using non-financial ESG in their investment decisions, an emerging move is toward having ESG sustainability reports assured by a third-party assurance provider. This chapter presents existing auditing and assurance standards and guidelines and presents an integrated framework of assurance on both financial ESP and non-financial ESG sustainability performance information. This chapter also presents several ESG sustainability rating agencies that rank companies based on their sustainability performance and disclosure.

II. ESG SUSTAINABILITY ASSURANCE GUIDELINES AND PRACTICES

More than 6,000 public companies in Europe are now required to disclose information on their sustainability performance for the 2017 fiscal reporting year and onwards.[3] The mandatory sustainability reporting is expected to continue worldwide as the 2023 EU Corporate Sustainability Reporting Directive (CSRD) requires mandatory sustainability reporting for European companies that could apply to their counterparts and trading partners worldwide.[4] These sustainability reports' reliability, objectivity, and credibility can be substantially improved by obtaining assurance. The American Institute of Certified Public Accountants (AICPA) has released sustainability attestation and materiality guides to assist practitioners in providing assurance statements on sustainability reports.[5] Sustainability assurance is not currently regulated in many countries; different types of entities provide assurance services using different scopes, methodologies, and assurance statements, and sustainability initiatives are not currently integrated with external financial reporting.

Assurance statements on sustainability reports ensure the accuracy, reliability, and credibility of both ESP and ESG information presented in a company's sustainability report and should be guided by a set of processes and standards. These guidelines promote accuracy, transparency, and accountability in reporting ESG performance. Currently, several international auditing standards provide assurance guidelines on sustainability reports. Two standards have been released by the International Auditing and Assurance Standards Board (IAASB): (1) International Standard on Assurance Engagements 3000, (Other than Audits or Reviews of Historical Financial Information), (ISAE 3000); and (2) ISAE 3410 (Assurance Engagements on Greenhouse Gas Statements).[6] The IAASB assurance standards guide covers assurance engagements relevant to sustainability reporting. It presents principles for the conduct of sustainability assurance engagements, including planning, evidence-gathering assurance procedures, executing, and reporting on the assurance process. Specifically, ISAE 3410 deals with assurance engagements for an organization reporting greenhouse gas (GHG) statements.

Global Reporting Initiative (GRI) standards typically present frameworks for sustainability reporting and also include specific provisions for business organizations to obtain external assurance statements to enhance the credibility of their sustainability reports.[7] Other assurance standards are the AICPA's Attestation Standards (AT Section 101), Canadian Institute of Chartered Accountants (CICA) section 5025, and AA1000 Assurance Standards (AS), issued in 2008 by AccountAbility.[8] These assurance standards guide non-financial dimensions of sustainability, including principles and guidelines for conducting assurance on sustainability reporting with a keen focus on accountability, inclusivity, and responsiveness to stakeholders. The PCAOB issued Auditing Standard No. 17 in 2013, which provides guidelines for auditors engaged to perform audit procedures on supplemental information that can include sustainability information accompanying audited financial statements.[9] The AICPA released its Exposure Draft (ED): "Proposed Statement on Standards for Attestation Engagements" on July 11, 2018, to harmonize its attestation standards with ISAE 3000 (Revised).[10] In September 2020, the AICPA issued a Statement on Standards for Attestation Engagements, which no longer requires the practitioner to request a written assertion for the responsible party reporting on the subject matter.[11] In August 2019, the AICPA released a discussion paper on materiality considerations for sustainability-related attestation engagements, which assures material disclosures about an entity's sustainability efforts, including an entity's internal control system or instances of noncompliance.[12] In August 2020, the AICPA issued its guidelines "Materiality Considerations for Attestation Engagements" that are designed to be performed on various subject matters, particularly when a practitioner conducts a review engagement of a narrative presentation of an entity's sustainability information.[13]

III. SUGGESTED FRAMEWORK FOR SUSTAINABILITY ASSURANCE STATEMENT

The credibility of sustainability reports can be improved when assurance statements from reputable assurance providers accompany them. Assurance reports are most effective when assurance providers are provided with globally accepted and standardized assurance standards. The existing sustainability assurance standards are often applied in an isolated fashion for several reasons, including divergence in the application of assurance standards. There is a choice between reasonable and limited assurance, a perceived credibility gap in sustainability assurance reports, diversity in the robustness of the assurance process and the quality of assurance reports, and improper use of materiality in the assurance process. Overall, business organizations often engage external assurance providers, including auditing firms, to review the accuracy and completeness of their sustainability-reported information. The assurance engagements typically consist of reviewing data collection methods, assessing the reliability of reported sustainability data, and verifying compliance with relevant assurance standards. Business organizations should consider the specific guidelines and standards relevant to their industry and sustainability reporting requirements when obtaining assurance on sustainability reports.

An integrated sustainability assurance framework should be developed by using several existing auditing standards (AICPA, PCAOB, IAASB) to audit the financial ESP reports and (2) the application of several sustainability-related standards (AA Accountability 1000, ISAE 3000, ISAE 3410, GRI, IIRC, SASB and AICPA), PCAOB and IAASB attestation standards on non-financial ESG sustainability performance reports. The effectiveness of assurance reports can be achieved when assurance providers are provided with globally accepted and standardized assurance standards. Different levels of assurance are rendered by assurance providers on both financial and non-financial dimensions of sustainability performance based on the extent of assurance procedures performed and assurance evidence gathered. Specifically, the sustainability assurance framework can be developed to provide sustainability assurance on both financial ESP and non-financial ESG sustainability performance reports and can be classified into distinct sections or reports based on the degree of assurance and content as follows:

1. Positive and reasonable assurance on financial statements reflecting financial economic sustainability performance (ESP).
2. Positive and reasonable assurance on internal control over financial reporting (ICFR), as related to the economic dimension of sustainability performance.
3. Negative and limited assurance on sustainability reports pertaining to the non-financial ESG dimensions of sustainability performance.
4. Materiality assessment of both financial ESP and non-financial ESG sustainability performance disclosures.

IV. ASSURANCE STRATEGY AND PROCESS FOR SUSTAINABILITY REPORTS

Effective sustainability assurance strategies are essential for ensuring sustainability reports' accuracy, transparency, reliability, and credibility. As sustainability reporting is gaining global acceptance as a common corporate reporting practice, its credibility must be assured by assurance providers. The practitioners in providing assurance services should identify and assess sustainability risks discussed in Chapter 7 for both financial and non-financial misstatements and the materiality of such misstatements in compliance with the GRI and SASB materiality guidelines in forming an opinion on sustainability reports on all dimensions of sustainability performance. Understanding the client's business and industry is important in assessing the risks associated with both financial ESP and non-financial ESG dimensions of sustainability performance. Practitioners can provide separate risk assessments and thus separate assurance levels on the financial ESP and non-financial ESG dimensions of sustainability performance by using the GRI, IIRC, and SASB's materiality map relevant to all stakeholders. Sustainability-related risks of strategy, operations, compliance, finance, security, and reputation, as discussed in Chapter 7, should be assessed, managed, and controlled. These risks and their impacts on the achievement of overall sustainability performance in creating shared value for all stakeholders, as well as the reliability of sustainability reports and the extent, timing, and nature of assurance procedures, should be evaluated by assurance providers. The risk assessment can be performed at both the high and low levels of assurance (calculating performance materiality based on the SASB guide) to generate materiality relevant to financial impacts, compliance with legal and regulatory measures, and other considerations.

Sustainability assurance providers should consider providing both limited and reasonable assurance on various dimensions of sustainability performance. Reasonable assurance can be rendered on the financial statements, whereas the review of the non-financial ESG dimensions of sustainability performance can offer only limited assurance. Practitioners should apply the AICPA and IAASB existing attestation standards, which address examination, review, agreed-upon procedures, and engagements to governance, social, ethical, and environmental reports and engagements that address subject matter other than historical financial statements. This suggested sustainability assurance framework enables assembling multidisciplinary teams with both the assurance and subject matter competencies necessary to complete sustainability assurance engagements and mitigates the perceived assurance gap by combining assurance frameworks and coordinating amongst various assurance providers. Sustainability assurance providers can develop separate audit frameworks for each financial ESP and non-financial ESG dimension of sustainability performance.

Sustainability assurance statements accompanied by sustainability reports can be made public, for use by external stakeholders, to lend more credibility to the published sustainability reports; or they can be kept private, for internal users, to suggest improvements and give confidence to the board and executives that the firm is doing the right thing in ensuring improvements in all financial and nonfinancial dimensions of sustainability performance. In providing assurance statements on sustainability reports, assurance providers (e.g., external auditors, internal auditors, and other assurance providers) should conduct their assurance services by performing the audit procedures summarized below:

1. Identify all stakeholders interested in the sustainability assurance statements, including the externally designated and internally intended use and distribution of sustainability assurance statements.
2. Determine the objectives of the assurance process by articulating what stakeholders expect from the sustainability report and identifying key focus areas (e.g., environmental, social, and human capital).
3. Select the reporting criteria, guidelines, and frameworks to be applied to various dimensions of financial ESP and non-financial ESG sustainability performance reports.

4. Choose relevant and most applicable assurance standards and frameworks based on the nature and type of the sustainability report on ESP or ESG sustainability performance. Common frameworks include ISAE 3000, GRI Standards, SASB, AICPA, and AA Accountability1000 Assurance Standard.
5. Determine the objective, extent, and scope of assurance engagements, information, and processes to be assured, including reasonable/positive assurance on financial ESP and limited/negative assurance on non-financial ESG dimensions of sustainability performance.
6. Identify auditing and assurance standards, guidelines, and frameworks applicable in forming audit opinions on financial statements and ICFR and assurance statements on non-financial ESG sustainability performance reports.
7. Communicate with stakeholders to identify their expectations and concerns regarding sustainability reporting, assurance, and material issues to ensure the report addresses key stakeholder interests.
8. Establish comprehensive and robust evidence-gathering procedures to collect data to ensure sustainability reports' accuracy, integrity, and completeness.
9. Evaluate sufficiency and competency audit evidence gathered to use it as a basis for forming an audit opinion of financial ESP and assurance statement on non-financial ESG. The audit and assurance evidence can be supplied to and/or gathered by the assurance providers to support the provider's conclusion report.
10. Decide on the expected form and content of the sustainability assurance report, the intended users, and the process for feedback to the reporting entity.
11. Maintain the objectivity and independence of the sustainability assurance reports.
12. Consider integrating independent assurance on both financial ESP and non-financial ESG sustainability performance reports.
13. Assess internal controls relevant to ESG performance to monitor and validate sustainability disclosures.
14. Use a risk-based approach to identify and prioritize material issues and areas for assurance that significantly affect the organization's sustainability reporting.
15. Adopt continuous auditing by leveraging technology to improve data management validation and streamline assurance procedures and reporting processes.

V. BEST PRACTICES OF SUSTAINABILITY ASSURANCE STATEMENTS

Business sustainability has extended the type and amount of financial ESP and non-financial ESG information business organizations provide to their stakeholders regarding their sustainability performance. As sustainability reporting is gaining acceptance as a common corporate reporting practice, its credibility must be assured by assurance providers. A sustainability assurance framework should be developed for the management of public companies to disclose their dimensions of sustainability performance, by auditors in providing assurance services on sustainability reports, and by stakeholders assessing the effectiveness of companies in achieving their sustainability performance. Professional organizations, standard setters, and regulators should consider whether public companies have established (1) the tone at the top (directors and executives) in issuing integrated sustainability reports, (2) the reporting framework for producing sustainability reports, (3) the process of obtaining assurance statements of their sustainability reports; and (4) a platform of performing the cost–benefit trade-offs of issuing reasonable versus limited assurance on financial ESP and non-financial ESG dimensions of sustainability performance. Business organizations can adopt several best practices to ensure effective sustainability assurance and enhance their sustainability reports' credibility, reliability, and transparency. Below are several sustainability assurance statements provided by the big four auditing firms.

According to a recent corporate responsibility report, Ernst & Young Netherland have reported several ways they have contributed to ESG activities and sustainability. They have reduced their CO_2 emissions by almost 30%. EY Netherland has reported results surrounding several materiality issues, including integrity and independence, process effectiveness and efficiency optimization, and customer satisfaction. They reported a 97% engagement quality rating of 1 or 2. They have supported 87 social start-ups. They have recognized a 17% increase in operational profit margin and a 3% growth in turnover. They have assured 29 clients regarding their sustainability information. They have outlined implementing sustainable development goals into their company through a six-step process: (1) Identify and Commit, (2) Develop targets and KPIs, (3) Synchronize sustainability and business strategy, (4) Create business opportunities, (5) Work with Stakeholders, and (6) Measure, evaluate, report, and communicate.[14] The EY Global Chairman and CEO, Mark Weinberger, stated how the company encourages its member firms to develop in business travel, continuous improvement and reporting, office operations, and procurement.[15]

PwC Singapore has reported several aspects of their sustainability surrounding key aspects of ESG strategies for FY20. In terms of their community, they saw a 37% increase in skill-based volunteer hours, a 56% increase in monetary donations, and a 23% increase in beneficiaries reached. Regarding the environment, PwC is committed to achieving net zero emissions by 2030. They have achieved 100% renewable electricity, maintained a 100% offset of air travel emissions, and saw a 33% reduction in total carbon emissions. In terms of people, PwC was active in activities such as World Mental Health Day, the "Be Well Work Well" challenge, the Employee Assistance Program, International Women's Day, and the "Lunch with a Stranger" campaign.[16]

In 2020, KPMG released the results of their survey on global sustainability reporting. They found that 80% of companies worldwide now report on sustainability, with North America accounting for the highest regional sustainability reporting rate. In Japan and Mexico, 100% of the top 100 companies report on sustainability, with a surge in integrated reporting in France, Japan, India, and Malaysia. GRI is the dominant global standard for sustainability reporting. In terms of climate risk, 40% of companies worldwide recognize the financial risks of climate change, with 1 in 5 companies reporting climate risk in line with TCFD recommendations.[17]

In its latest global report, Deloitte has reported several key metrics related to ESG for FY2021. They have reported a 41% reduction in gross emissions. They have purchased 70% renewable electricity toward their 100% goal. They plan to reach net zero greenhouse gas emissions by 2030 by reducing business travel emissions, sourcing renewable energy, and switching fleets to 100% electric or hybrid vehicles. In May 2021, Deloitte launched the World*Class* Education Challenge to assist professionals in promoting solutions to access quality education. They hope to expand opportunities, empower individuals, and engage ecosystems through this. Deloitte has made $223 million in societal investments and provided 1.1 million hours of volunteer and pro bono time. They also made clear in the report how much they value gender equality, with 25% of their partners, principals, and directors being female. They have sought ways to be involved in LGBT+ inclusion, mental health awareness, racial and ethnic inclusion, disability support, and pandemic support. In economics, they have seen a 5.5% growth in annual revenue, and 3.5% of their aggregate global revenue going to innovation investments. Deloitte has around 22,000 cyber professionals worldwide and 15 alliance relationships with leading technology partners.[18]

VI. SUSTAINABILITY DISCLOSURE METRICS

Sustainability disclosure metrics are measures and critical indicators that organizations can use to communicate their ESG factors of planning, performance, risk, and impacts to all affected stakeholders. These metrics are essential for disclosing accuracy, transparency, accountability, and sustainability practices. Sustainability disclosure metrics should apply to companies in all industries and demonstrate a commitment to achieving a comprehensive methodology that applies to all companies and can be suitably adapted for each industry. Sustainability disclosure metrics should use a combination of quantitative-structured and qualitative-unstructured data in developing ESG sustainability rankings and scores. Non-financial ESG and financial ESP metrics should be used as benchmarks against which ESG sustainability performance is evaluated and designed to be disclosed by a company to both internal and external stakeholders. Some of these metrics can be industry-specific, others relate to socioeconomic factors or macroeconomic matters and can vary across businesses and industries. Sustainability disclosure metrics tend to vary from business to business and from industry to industry. The existing management discussion and analysis (MD&A) disclosures are the starting point for developing sustainability disclosure metrics. However, they may need adjustment for industry specifics or sustainability matters unrelated to finances.

The International Business Council (IBC), a community of global business leaders worldwide, in January 2020, launched an initiative to identify a core set of material ESG metrics and recommended ESG disclosures that could be integrated into corporate annual reports consistently across industry sectors and countries.[19] These metrics and disclosures are organized into several pillars of principles of governance, planet, people, and prosperity, aligned with the UNSDGs and principle ESG domains. The pillar of the principles of governance deals with themes and dimensions such as governing bodies, their composition, executive compensation, and the process of setting purposes. It also involves stakeholders in key issues, promoting ethical business practices, policies, and practices to prevent corruption, compliance with anti-corruption laws and regulations, code of conduct, ethics training, whistleblower protection, and integrating risk and opportunity. The pillar of the planet deals with issues such as climate change, greenhouse gas emissions, energy consumption, loss of nature and land, consumption of fresh water, and waste management. The pillar of people deals with gender equality, diversity, inclusion, wages, employee well-being, community engagement, labor practices, and health, safety, and employee training. The pillar of prosperity encompasses job creation, investments, contributions, innovation, and community investment.[20] There are several other sustainability-related metrics, including (1) economic metrics of revenue, gross value added, taxes paid in different jurisdictions, research and development expenditures, and innovation initiatives; (2) supply chain metrics of supplier code of conduct, supplier diversity, emissions from the supply chain, and proper sourcing; (3) product and service impact metrics of product safety records, customer health and safety, social and environmental impacts of products and services; (4) metrics of initiatives taken to protect and promote biodiversity and efforts to preserve ecosystems and habitats; (5) metrics of adopting human rights policies, respect for the rights of indigenous communities, and efforts to prevent child and forced labor; and (6) technology and data privacy metrics including cybersecurity measures, and other efforts to protect customer, suppliers, and employee data.

These metrics disclosed in sustainability reports can be prepared using appropriate voluntary and mandatory frameworks discussed in Chapter 8 and this chapter, including those of GRI), SASB, Task Force on Climate-related Financial Disclosures (TCFD), and ISSB, among others. Business organizations should select metrics relevant to their industry, organizational priorities, business environment, and stakeholder expectations. For years, investors have advocated for public companies to disclose key ESG metrics that investors view as comparable, decision-useful, reliable, and verifiable, whether in SEC mandatory filings, voluntary sustainability reports, or MD&A. All the leading voluntary ESG frameworks require disclosure of various key ESG performance indicators and metrics. The SASB framework and related ESG matrices are intended to be used in SEC filings and encourage the inclusion of ESG disclosures in the MD&A. Public companies, however, typically include their ESG disclosures in voluntary sustainability reports as opposed to their SEC filings (10K, 10Q reports) for a variety of reasons, including concerns regarding (1) whether ESG metrics are material to an understanding of the company's business and require disclosure; (2) whether the internal or external review of ESG metrics (e.g., by internal audit or disclosure teams) is adequate to disclose such metrics appropriate in SEC reports; (3) the risk that inclusion of ESG metrics in SEC filings would unnecessarily increase the financial and accounting burdens associated with periodic reporting; and (4) potential liability risk associated with disclosure of ESG metrics in materials filed under the Exchange Act or incorporated by reference in registration statements filed under the Securities Act of 1933.

Sustainability ESG disclosure metrics should be normalized and need to be standardized. For example, the rating scale that Sustainalytics uses is based on a generally mixed ESG outcome ranging from negligible, low, medium, high, to severe. The rating scale used by MSCI ranges from AAA, AA, A, BBB, BB, B, to CCC. However, no specific guidelines exist for how each ESG factor contributes to the attributed rating when searched in the respective website's research engines. Nonetheless, the MSCI ESG ratings are also available in Bloomberg terminals in addition to the proprietary ESG ratings developed by Bloomberg itself.[21]

In September 2020, the World Economic Forum, the International Business Council (IBC), and the big four accounting firms (Deloitte, EY, KPMG, PwC) announced a new initiative to synthesize company sustainability reporting by attempting to establish commonly accepted metrics for ESG sustainability reporting.[22] According to the latest WEF *Global Risks Report*, several results are based on perception surveys surrounding economic, environmental, geopolitical, societal, and technological issues.[23] Some of the top results presented as clear and present dangers include infectious diseases, livelihood crises, and extreme weather events based on the results of over 50% of respondents. Some of the top results for knock-on effects, which are risks that can be seen in 3–5 years, include asset bubble bursts, IT infrastructure, price instability, commodity shocks, and debt crises. Some of the top results of existential threats are weapons of mass destruction, state collapse, biodiversity loss, and adverse tech advances. The top five risks by likelihood are extreme weather, climate action failure, human environmental damage, infectious diseases, and biodiversity loss. The top five risks by impact are infectious diseases, climate action failure, weapons of mass destruction, biodiversity loss, and natural resource crises.[24] The WEF framework encourages disclosure on a "comply or explain" basis, with the proper explanations and acceptable reasons (e.g., materiality, confidentiality, and legal constraints) for not disclosing a particular disclosure metric.

VII. SUSTAINABILITY RATINGS/RANKINGS

Sustainability factors of planning, performance, risk, and disclosure should be identified, evaluated, and implemented to ensure their effectiveness and proper use by professional organizations, regulators, investors, the business community, and society. Sustainability ratings and rankings are assessments of companies' ESG performance that are intended to assist stakeholders, including investors and the public, in evaluating their sustainability practices. Many organizations and agencies provide these ratings and rankings using different methodologies and criteria and presenting different ESG metrics. Sustainability ratings are opinions of and insights from professionals, organizations, and individual experts on the relative standing of a company's sustainability factors to peers and are intended to serve as a benchmark in assessing ESG sustainability performance. Due to the various agencies provided in the marketplace, the sustainability rating industry lacks a clear definitional foundation and criteria used in their ratings; therefore, the term corporate sustainability systems (CSS) is used.[25] The Corporate sustainability systems represent methods and avenues to grade the performance of corporations related to sustainability, and the common characteristics of the CSSs are grouped into three typologies: indexes, rankings, and ratings.[26] These three metrics are used to identify the most sustainable corporations throughout the world.

Examples of indexes are DJSI World, ECPI World ESG, Equity Index, and ESI Excellence Global. Global CR RepTrak 100, The Sustainability Yearbook, and the World's Most Sustainable Corporations – Global 100 are examples of rankings. Examples of ratings are ISS-oekom Corporate Rating and Supplier CSR Rating. According to research conducted by MPDI, most indexes are overseen by stock exchange operators or ESG rating agencies. In addition, ratings and rankings have been found to have a wider multi-stakeholder approach and a higher level of economic financial bias.[27] The most current list of CSS ranking and ratings includes the following:

- **CDP climate, water, and forests scores –** CDP evaluates companies' environmental impact in areas of carbon emissions, water usage, and deforestation. Companies disclose their environmental data and CDP scores and rank them based on environmental impacts. CDP has collected and disclosed information and environmental impacts to investors, companies, and cities. It has been essential in disclosing weather information and business practices worldwide. After a catastrophic year in 2020 with the coronavirus pandemic, several companies worldwide made the A list in issues involving climate change, forests, and water security. The climate change A list comprised 277 companies. The forests A list had 16 companies, and 106 companies made the water security A list.[28] In addition, 88 cities were added to the A list.[29]
- **SAM (Sustainable Asset Management)** – This group describes itself as a "global investment boutique" that directs its efforts toward investing in sustainability efforts. SAM is a leader in sustainable applications through an alliance with Robeco, a Rabobank Group subsidiary. SAM uses metrics and criteria in order to analyze ESG measures and has launched the SAM Sustainable Water Fund. The sectors that are under sustainability theme

investing include smart energy, smart materials, sustainable climate, and sustainable water. RobecoSAM publishes an annual *Sustainability Yearbook* highlighting top-performing companies in sustainability by ranking their sustainability performance based on industry and region. The sustainability services that SAM provides to consumers include benchmarking and climate assessments.[30]

- **Sustainalytics** – This Morningstar company assesses and reports important environmental, social, and governance research to companies and shareholders worldwide. Sustainalytics provides ESG risk ratings that evaluate companies' exposure to industry-specific ESG risks by covering a wide range of industries and enables investors to assess potential risks in their portfolios. Sustainalytics currently serves over 1,000 clients, has over 1,200 team members, utilizes over 500 research analysts, and covers 172 countries. It provides high-quality ESG environmental data research and ranking to investors and institutional companies.[31]
- **MSCI ESG ratings** – The MSCI ESG ratings are developed to assess a company's ability to respond to risks associated with ESG measures. MSCI presents ESG ratings for thousands of companies by assessing their exposure to ESG risks and opportunities and whether they are used by investors to integrate ESG factors into their decision-making processes. The MSCI ESG rating is a comprehensive measure of a company's long-term commitment to socially responsible investment and environmental investment standards and ESG initiatives. This ranking is based on a company's exposure to financial risks associated with ESG initiatives. The ratings used to measure a company's resiliency range from leader, average, to laggard. Leader ratings get AAA or AA. Average ratings get a score of A, BBB, or BB. Laggard ratings get a score of B or CCC. Leader-rating companies do well in overseeing the management of ESG opportunities. Average ratings have mixed experiences in overseeing the management of ESG opportunities. Laggard ratings are slow in their oversight of the management of ESG opportunities. These ratings are used for fundamental/quant analyses, portfolio construction/risk management, benchmarking/index-based product development, disclosure/reporting for stakeholders and regulators, and engagement and thought leadership.[32]
- **Bloomberg ESG scores** – Bloomberg's ESG data offers metrics and disclosures for over 11,000 companies and over 80 countries. The topics surrounding Bloomberg's metrics and disclosures include air quality, climate change, waste management, compensation, diversity, and shareholder rights. They have a wide range of ESG topics in the form of 600 key performance indicators.[33] Overall, Bloomberg is a data platform that provides sustainable investment data to financial analysts. Bloomberg is also working with the United Nations Global Compact to achieve the UNGC Sustainability Goals.
- **ISS-Oekom** – This subsidiary of the Institute of Shareholder Services (ISS) company provides the best investment options surrounding sustainability and

corporate governance. The ISS analyzes the actions of key stakeholders and investors in their efforts to implement environmental, social, and governance performance measures and how they contribute to the well-being of society.[34] ISS provides ESG rankings and data and sustainable investment research by combining socially responsible investment (SRI) with a high rate of return, and this is a competitive advantage that offers investment solutions and services. ISS provides an overall rating of sustainability solutions and more detailed information and data points related to specific sustainability goals.

- **FTSE Russell ESG ratings** – FTSE Russell establishes FTSE Russell ratings; the FTSE4Good index series includes companies that meet specific ESG criteria. It is widely used by investors looking for socially responsible investment options and provides investors and stakeholders with a comprehensive model and breakdown of ESG dimensions. Their model comprises 3 pillars, 14 themes, and over 300 indicators. The features of this model include promotion of materiality, alignment of UN Sustainable Development Goals, strong oversight, and an emphasis on rules and data. This ranking and data give investors insight into the management of ESG issues and how to deal with them from several perspectives. These ESG ratings consist of a total rating that includes columns, topics, and different scores. This classification, consisting of 300 indicators, is implemented for each company in unique conditions. The model is often used to assist in portfolio management, research, risk management, stakeholder management, and benchmarking practices.[35]
- **Eco Vadis** – This is an organization that helps companies the management of their networks, both in upstream and downstream value chains. They currently cover over 75,000 companies, 160 countries, and 200 industries. Their objectives include having better performance, greater impact, achieving efficiency, developing brands, and inspiring innovation. Their major clients include Johnson & Johnson, Nestle, and Centrica.[36] They also have a sustainability scorecard on four themes: environment, labor and human rights, ethics, and sustainable procurement.[37] This Eco Vadis rating ranks each company based on material issues, size, location, and industry. This assessment is presented with scorecards from zero to one hundred or medals. For the sustainability of the global supply chain, large multinational companies partner with Eco Vadis, and the ranked company can compare itself according to the ranking in its industry; as a result, these scores lead to a competition called Race to the Top, in which companies compete for best global performance.
- **Refinitiv** – The London Stock Exchange group business provides financial markets data and infrastructure.[38] Their sustainability efforts surround transitioning to a low-carbon economy, being responsible for the environment, and improving investment decisions and market transparency. In the next few years, Refinitiv hopes to reduce travel, help their suppliers set emission targets, improve community service, and provide long-term financial and analytical solutions.[39]

- **Vigeo-Eiris** – This is an affiliate of Moody's, and they exist to provide worldwide solutions for environmental, social, and governance issues to investors and their respective communities. Their key values include transparency, ambition, responsibility, and team spirit. They have 10 offices, 350 people, 28 nationalities, and 4 partners. They comprise an executive committee, which carries out strategies, projects, and organizational objectives, and a scientific committee to evaluate the quality of their work and conclusions related to their research.[40]
- **Standard Ethics** – This self-regulated company assigns a rating system to environmental, social, and governance using ratings collectively known as standard ethics ratings (SER). The company assigns these ratings to companies, sovereign issuers, and bonds. The templates and sources that help guide these ratings come from standards and ideals published by organizations such as the United Nations, the European Union, and the Organization for Economic Cooperation and Development. The ratings pride themselves on being "solicited, standard, and independent."
- **Dow Jones Sustainability Indices (DJSI)** – The DJSI was launched in 1999 and managed by S&P Dow Jones Indices. They were designed to assess the ESG sustainability performance of leading global companies across various industries. These indices consist of an economic sustainability dimension of about 50%, environmental (20%), social (20%) and governance (10%).[41]
- **Thomson Reuters ESG data** – Thomson Reuters presents ESG data and rankings for companies to enable investors to assess their sustainability performance based on various criteria, including economic, social, environmental, and governance data.[42]

These agencies offer a variety of ranking services to the market. For example, Bloomberg, FTSE Russell, the CDP, and MSCI offer sustainability rankings on the composite ESG and each component of environmental (E), social (S), and governance (G). Alternatively, EcoVadis offers specialized raking on supply chain sustainability. Thomson Reuters and BlackRock initially created Refinitiv in 2018 and sold it to the London Stock Exchange. Vigeo-Eiris, a rating agency, was recently acquired by Moody's, whereas Morningstar acquired a 40% stake in Sustainalytics in 2017. Obtaining sustainability ratings and rankings by disclosure of financial ESP and non-financial ESG sustainability performance information is very relevant and beneficial to shareholders in comparing sustainability standings of public companies and in making sound investment and voting decisions. Other stakeholders also benefit from public disclosures of sustainability rankings and scores.

Companies typically use these ratings and rankings to showcase their sustainability efforts to attract socially responsible investors. Sustainability ranking organizations use methodologies that can vary among rating agencies, and thus, companies may be assessed based on different criteria depending on the evaluations that emerge over time. However, several costs associated with public disclosure of sustainability information should be considered by public companies and their directors and officers. First, the direct cost of producing sustainability reports, obtaining assurance on sustainability reports, and submitting these reports to the sustainability rating organizations. The second cost is the opportunity cost of managerial time and efforts spent on sustainability disclosures and their public rankings. Finally, proprietary costs of submitting sustainability information to external ranking organizations and the disclosure risk when the firm reveals valuable information, such as information about profitable customers and markets, the revelation of trade secrets, or the exposure of operating, organization, or reporting weakness to competitors, unions, regulators, investors, customers, suppliers and/or other stakeholders.

VIII. CONCLUSION

Business organizations worldwide recognize the importance of sustainability factors of planning, performance, disclosure, and risk, particularly related to sustainability disclosure metrics. Business sustainability indicates that the main objective function of business organizations is to create shareholder value by maximizing firm financial performance through continuous improvements of both financial ESP and non-financial ESG sustainability performance. A growing number of public companies worldwide are issuing sustainability reports on various financial ESP and non-financial ESG dimensions of their sustainability performance. Sustainability reports' credibility, objectivity, and reliability would significantly improve when assurance statements accompany them. The sustainability reporting framework and assurance standards for sustainability assurance statements are evolving. Practitioners providing assurance statements on sustainability reports should develop a framework that suits their practice based on the suggestions presented in this chapter. This chapter presents existing auditing and assurance standards and guidelines and an integrated framework of assurance on ESP and non-financial ESG sustainability performance information. The ESP and ESG sustainability performance dimensions are interrelated and complement/complete each other, and thus, they should be integrated into corporate reporting. Establishing sustainability indexes, rankings, and ratings enables investors to compare ESG sustainability performance across all companies in different industries. Companies should effectively and transparently communicate their business sustainability performance with all stakeholders by periodically releasing their sustainability reports and providing rating organizations with sufficient information to develop appropriate, relevant, compatible, and comparable ESG sustainability metrics, as explained in this chapter.

IX. TAKEAWAYS

- Integrated sustainability reports should reveal both financial ESP and non-financial ESG information on sustainability performance to all stakeholders.

- Sustainability reporting should be aligned with the company's communication strategy and improve relationships with all key stakeholders.
- Public companies should provide professional rating organizations with sufficient and relevant ESG sustainability information to establish their sustainability disclosure metrics.
- Sustainability rankings can create a benchmark for the company's sustainability success.
- The accounting profession should take more initiative to provide assurance standards on voluntary non-financial ESG sustainability information.
- There is a need for integrated and comprehensive global assurance standards on both financial ESP and non-financial ESG sustainability performance reports.
- Sustainability assurance statements lend more credibility, objectivity, and independence to sustainability reports.
- Sustainability assurance services allow auditing firms to expand their practices.

Notes

1 Ernst & Young (EY). 2017. "Is Your Non-Financial Performance Revealing the True Value of Your Business to Investors?" Available at http://www.ey.com/gl/en/services/assurance/climate-change-and-sustainability-services/ey-nonfinancial-performance-may-influence-investors (accessed August 1, 2017).

2 World Economic Forum (September 2020). Measuring Stakeholder Capitalism Towards Common Metrics and Consistent Reporting of Sustainable Value Creation. Available at https://www3.weforum.org/docs/WEF_IBC_Measuring_Stakeholder_Capitalism_Report_2020.pdf (accessed October 6, 2021).

3 European Commission. September 29, 2014. Disclosure of Non-financial Information: Europe Information: Europe Council, the European Economic and Social, Environmental Issues. Available at http://ec.europa.eu/internal_market/accounting/non-financial_reporting/index_en.htm.

4 European Commission (EC). January 5, 2023. The Corporate Sustainability Reporting Directive (CSRD). Available at https://finance.ec.europa.eu/capital-markets-union-and-financial-markets/company-reporting-and-auditing/company-reporting/corporate-sustainability-reporting_en

5 American Institute of Certified Public Accounting (AICPA). August 15, 2019. Discussion Paper: "Materiality Considerations for Attestation Engagements Involving Aspects Of Subject Matters that Cannot Be Quantitatively Measured." https://www.aicpa.org/content/dam/aicpa/interestareas/frc/assuranceadvisoryservices/downloadabledocuments/exposuredrafts/materiality-discussion-paper.pdf

6 International Auditing and Assurance Standards Board (IAASB). January 1, 2005. *International Framework for Assurance Engagements*. Available at http://www.ifac.org/system/files/downloads/b003–2010-iaasb-handbook-framework.pdf. And International Auditing and Assurance Standard Board (IAASB). 2015. International Standard on Auditing (ISA) 720 (Revised). The auditor's responsibilities relating to the other information and related conforming amendments. April 2015.

7 Global Reporting Initiative (GRI). 2013. The Global Standards for Sustainability Impacts. Available at https://www.globalreporting.org/standards

8 AccountAbility 2008. Guidance for Reporting Organizations Seeking Assurance to AA1000AS. Retrieved from https://www.accountability.org/standards/aa1000-assurance-standard/ And The Canadian Institute of Chartered Accountants (CICA). 2000. "Standards for Assurance Engagements," in *CICA Handbook*, v.II, S5025. The Canadian Institute of Chartered Accountants, Toronto.

9 Public Company Accounting Oversight Board (PCAOB). October 10, 2013. Auditing Supplement Information Accompanying Audited Financial Statements. Auditing Standard No. 17. Retrieved from https://pcaobus.org/oversight/standards/archived-standards/pre-reorganized-auditing-standards-interpretations/details/AS17

10 American Institute of Certified Public Accounting (AICPA). July 11, 2018. Exposure Draft (ED): "Proposed Statement on Standards for Attestation Engagements." Available at https://www.aicpa.org/content/dam/aicpa/research/exposuredrafts/accountingandauditing/downloadabledocuments/20180711a-ed-ssae-18-revisions.pdf

11 American Institute of Certified Public Accounting (AICPA). 2020. Statement on Standards for Attestation Engagements, Direct Examination Engagements. Available at https://us.aicpa.org/content/dam/aicpa/research/standards/auditattest/downloadabledocuments/ssae-21.pdf

12 American Institute of Certified Public Accounting (AICPA). August 15, 2019. Discussion Paper: "Materiality Considerations for Attestation Engagements Involving Aspects of Subject Matters that cannot be Quantitatively Measured." https://www.aicpa.org/content/dam/aicpa/interestareas/frc/assuranceadvisoryservices/downloadabledocuments/exposuredrafts/materiality-discussion-paper.pdf

13 American Institute of Certified Public Accounting (AICPA). August 5, 2020. "Materiality Considerations for Attestation Engagements." Available at https://www.aicpa-cima.com/resources/download/materiality-considerations-for-attestation-engagements

14 EY Netherland. 2020. *Corporate Responsibility Report 2019–20*. Available at https://assets.ey.com/content/dam/ey-sites/ey-com/nl_nl/topics/corporate-responsibility/cr-reports/2019–2020/ey-corporate-responsibility-report-2019–2020-en-v1.pdf(accessed October 6, 2020).

15 Ernst & Young. 2019. *EY Global Environmental Statement*. Available at https://assets.ey.com/content/dam/ey-sites/ey-com/en_gl/topics/purpose/purpose-pdfs/ey-global-environmental-statement.pdf (accessed October 5, 2021).

16 PwC Singapore. 2020. *Sustainability Report*. Available at https://www.pwc.com/sg/en/publications/assets/sustainability-report-fy20.pdf (accessed October 6, 2021).

17 KPMG. December 2020. *The Time Has Come: The KPMG Survey of Sustainability Reporting 2020*. Available at https://assets.kpmg/content/dam/kpmg/xx/pdf/2020/11/the-time-has-come.pdf (accessed October 5, 2021).

18 Deloitte. 2021. *A Year of Connection, Action, and Impact: 2021 Global Impact Report*. Available at https://www2.deloitte.com/il/en/pages/about-deloitte/articles/global-report-home-2021.html .

19 World Economic Forum. January 2020. *Toward Common Metrics and Consistent Reporting of Sustainable Value Creation*. Available at https://www3.weforum.org/docs/WEF_IBC_ESG_Metrics_Discussion_Paper.pdf

20 Ibid

21 https://www.bloomberg.com/company/press/bloomberg-to-offer-msci-esg-research-data-on-the-bloomberg-terminal/ (accessedJune 11, 2020).

22 World Economic Forum (WEF). 2020. White Paper. *Measuring Stakeholder Capitalism Towards Common Metrics and Consistent Reporting of Sustainable Value Creation*. Available at http://www3.weforum.org/docs/WEF_IBC_Measuring_Stakeholder_Capitalism_Report_2020.pdf (accessed September 22, 2020).

23 World Economic Forum (2021). *The Global Risks Report 2021: 16th Edition: Insight Report*. Available at: https://www3.weforum.org/docs/WEF_The_Global_Risks_Report_2021.pdf
24 Ibid.
25 Daniel Cash. 2020. "Sustainable Rating Agencies" in Magdalena Ziolo, *Sustainable Financial Systems: The Global Context, Risks, and Responsibility*. Routledge.
26 Borja Diez-Cañamero, Tania Bishara, Jose Ramon Otegi-Olaso, Rikardo Minguez, and José María Fernández. 2020. "Measurement of Corporate Social Responsibility: A Review of Corporate Sustainability Indexes, Rankings and Ratings." Sustainability Vol. 12, 2153.
27 Diez-Canamero, Borja, Bishara, Tania, Otegi-Olaso, Jose Ramon, Minguez, Rikardo, and Maria Fernandez, Jose. March 10, 2020. "Measurement of Corporate Social Responsibility Indexes, Rankings and Ratings." MPDI: Sustainability. November 2,+ 2021.
28 CDP. 2021. *The A List 2020*. November 3, 2021. Available at https://www.cdp.net/en/companies/companies-scores
29 CDP (2021). Cities A List 2020. 3 November 2021. Found at https://www.cdp.net/en/cities/cities-scores
30 Sustainable Asset Management (SAM) Group. December 11, 2012. Sustainability HQ. Found at https://www.sustainabilityhq.com/subscriber-only-pages/asset-managers/sam-group/ (accessed November 3, 2021).
31 Sustainalytics: A Morningstar Company. 2021. "About Us." Available at https://www.sustainalytics.com/about-us (accessed November 3, 2021).
32 MSCI. 2021. ESG Ratings. Available at https://www.msci.com/our-solutions/esg-investing/esg-ratings (accessed November 3, 2021).
33 Bloomberg Professional Services. 2021. Global Environmental, Social & Governance – ESG Data: Content and Data. Found at https://www.bloomberg.com/professional/dataset/global-environmental-social-governance-data/ (accessed November 4, 2021).
34 3BL CSRWire. April 27, 2018. "Oekom Corporate Responsibility Review 2018: Ongoing Upwards Trend in Sustainability Management." About ISS-oekom. Available at https://www.csrwire.com/press_releases/40986-oekom-corporate-responsibility-review-2018-ongoing-upwards-trend-in-sustainability-management
35 FTSE Russell. 2020. *ESG Ratings and Data Model: Integrating ESG into Investments*. Product Overview. Available at https://research.ftserussell.com/products/downloads/ESG-ratings-overview.pdf (accessed November 4, 2021).
36 EcoVadis. n.d. "The World's Most Trusted Business Sustainability Ratings." Available at https://ecovadis.com/ (accessed November 4, 2021).
37 Ecovadis. n.d. "About Us." Available at https://ecovadis.com/about-us/ (accessed November 4, 2021).
38 Refinitiv. n.d. "We Are Refinitiv. About Us." Found at https://www.refinitiv.com/en/about-us
39 Refinitiv. n.d. "Sustainability. About Us: Sustainable Leadership." Available at https://www.refinitiv.com/en/about-us/sustainable-leadership (accessed November 4, 2021).
40 Vigeo Eiris: Part of Moody's ESG Solutions. n.d. "About Us." Available at https://www.developmentaid.org/organizations/view/135238/vigeo-sas (accessed November 9, 2021).
41 Dow Jones Sustainability Indices, DJSI Index Family. Available at https://www.spglobal.com/esg/performance/indices/djsi-index-family
42 THOMSON REUTERS INSTITUTE. ESG Resource Center. Available at https://www.thomsonreuters.com/en/institute/esg-resource-center.html

Chapter 10

Contemporary Issues in Business Sustainability

I. INTRODUCTION

Business organizations are being criticized for primarily focusing on profit maximization and, thus, shareholder value creation with minimal attention to the impacts of their operations on society, communities, and the environment and the creation of shared value for all stakeholders. The corporation's purpose has evolved in recent decades from profit maximization to shareholder wealth maximization to creating shared value for all stakeholders with the mission of profit-with-purpose.[1] The profit-with-purpose mission can be achieved when corporations focus on generating desired financial returns for their shareholders and achieving social and environmental impacts while protecting the interests of other stakeholders, including customers, employees, suppliers, communities, society, and the environment. This chapter focuses on several emerging aspects of business sustainability, including sustainability investment strategies, workplace diversity, inclusion, and equity; focus on product and service quality; supply chain sustainability; and sustainability and mergers and acquisitions, biodiversity accounting and finance.

II. INVESTOR INTEREST IN SUSTAINABILITY INFORMATION

A growing number of investors is now considering impact investing with a keen focus on financial, economic sustainability (ESP) and non-financial, environmental, social, and governance (ESG) sustainability performance and integrating non-financial ESG sustainability factors of planning, performance, risk, and disclosure

DOI: 10.4324/9781003437949-10

into their investment strategies. Business sustainability factors and ESG criteria are now more commonly integrated into executive incentive plans of S&P 500 firms, witnessing a 23% surge this year, bringing the overall prevalence to 70%.[2] Diversity and inclusion and carbon footprint metrics have experienced the most substantial expansion. Investors place high importance on human capital management and environmental concerns, prompting companies to include these metrics in their plans to demonstrate their dedication to ESG objectives. Human capital management metrics currently hold the most vital position, but environmental metrics are also gaining traction, primarily due to pressure from institutional investors and growing awareness of climate change implications.[3]

The impact investing concept suggests that investors demand a desired rate of return on their investment while they would like to see their companies have social and environmental impacts as well. Existing research provides mixed results regarding the link between financial/market performance and ESG factors of performance, risk, and disclosure.[4] The quality and reliability of public information, both financial ESP and non-financial ESG sustainability performance, improve the integrity and efficiency of capital markets. The quality of sustainability disclosures also improves market liquidity by reducing information asymmetry across traders. Sustainability disclosures are expected to affect market liquidity when such disclosures cause information asymmetry that induces adverse selection into share markets. Non-financial ESG sustainability disclosures are expected to be value-relevant to both external and internal users of such disclosures. Investors and other stakeholders, including employees, suppliers, customers, the environment, governments, and society, can have more transparent information about ESG performance, which enables them to make more informed decisions. ESG sustainability disclosures can also improve internal management practices by enabling companies to implement their strategic sustainability planning and establish better relationships with investors, customers, suppliers, employees, regulators, society, and the environment.

The relationship between financial ESP and ESG performance has been extensively yet inconclusively debated in the literature in the past decade, which has caused investors not to pay enough attention to sustainability factors of performance risk and disclosure. However, global regulators are attempting to make ESG information more value-relevant to investors. For example, the raids on Deutsche Bank and DWS Group in Germany and the SEC's proposed rules worry US asset managers about increased scrutiny. The SEC aims to boost transparency and fair marketing of ESG products, but compliance costs may discourage ESG investments. Despite challenges, the regulatory focus on ESG investing and corporate disclosure will persist, and companies should prepare to comply and reinforce their ESG strategies.[5] A growing number of investors has considered impact investing with a keen focus on financial return and ESG sustainability factors, regulators now mandate ESG sustainability performance disclosure, and public companies prepare and disseminate sustainability reports. In this era of sustainability-oriented investors, directors, and executives, a major challenge is determining whether management's optimistic expectations about future financial performance are associated with better ESG disclosure and higher ESG performance as investors continue to consider opportunities and risks associated with ESG investing.

The two measures of firm value, namely the economic value and market value, may diverge, and this divergence can be caused by many factors, including the quality and quantity of earnings and other financial ESP and non-financial ESG sustainability performance information disseminated to the market. Investors may trade shares based on expectations about the company's future growth and performance and on short-term considerations of quarterly earnings guidance that may cause changes in stock prices independent of changes in the company's true condition and long-term performance. Management, asset managers, equity analysts, and even shareholders are motivated by obtaining short-term gains, and thus, their behaviors are biased toward short-term financial performance. The enlightened value maximization concept of sustainability performance suggests that non-financial ESG sustainability can provide both opportunities and challenges for investors. More sustainability information can lead to a better understanding of the link between investor expectations, management actions, and sustainable performance. It could reduce noise in the corporate reporting process, divert attention from short-term outlooks, and thus enable investors to make more informed investment decisions.

Investors expect to receive financial ESP information to ensure the desired rate of returns on their investment and non-financial ESG sustainability information to obtain social and environmental impacts. Based on standardized sustainability reporting and assurance, investors consider sustainability information value-relevant when it is relevant, reliable, and transparent. Investors prefer to receive sustainability ratings, rankings, indexes, and matrices assured by independent third parties and often consider them when making investment decisions. Investors seek these standardized and assured sustainability disclosures when assessing a company's strategic planning for securing sustainability and its drivers of long-term economic growth and prosperity. The content and format of sustainability disclosures and metrics have been debated and considered among public companies, investors, regulators, and standard setters. Transparent, qualitative, and quantitative sustainability metrics that are measurable, meaningful, verifiable, generally acceptable, and applicable are value-relevant to retail and institutional investors.

More than 1,300 institutional investors worldwide, representing $59 trillion in assets under management, have signed on to the UN Principles of Responsible Investing, which seek to integrate sustainability factors of planning, performance, disclosure, and risk into their investment objectives.[6] Asset managers, such as BlackRock, State Street, and Vanguard, are now investing in sustainability-centric companies. Business organizations play a vital economic role by creating jobs, fostering innovation, and providing essential goods and services. Investors buy their shares and expect desired financial returns when they invest in business organizations. Shareholders are better off when their companies are economically sustainable and generate earnings and cash in the long term. Business sustainability is important to investors in obtaining sustainable returns on their investment, and companies maximize firm value and, thus, shareholder wealth. Shared value creation for all stakeholders can be promoted within the wealth-maximization framework for shareholders in pursuing the goal of profit-with-purpose for corporations. Corporations can balance wealth maximization for shareholders under the shareholder primacy concept while achieving welfare maximization for all stakeholders under the stakeholder primacy concept.

According to the agency theory, there is an inherent information imbalance (III), better known as asymmetric information risk (AIR), between management, investors, and their representative board of directors. It is a critical governance and accountability reporting challenge for many public companies and their stakeholders.[7] To mitigate the AIR, the board of directors and investors should receive transparent and relevant information on both financial ESP and non-financial ESG dimensions of sustainability performance. There are two aspects of ESG investment and expected returns.[8] The first aspect is the traditional "shareholder value maximization," where management attempts to improve earnings for shareholders under the shareholder primacy concept. Second, the broader "stakeholder/society value creation" where management maximizes the sum of the various stakeholders' surpluses (e.g., creditors, employees, customers, suppliers, society, and the environment) under the stakeholder primacy concept. Given that ESG information is typically provided voluntarily, investors should be interested in opportunities and risks associated with ESG disclosures by focusing on managerial incentives, the assumed level of agency conflicts between management and shareholders, and the value-relevance of such information.

The agency theory focuses on risk sharing and agency problems between the principal (owner) and agent (management), and thus, three agency costs (monitoring, bonding, and residual) are assumed by principals to align their interests with those of the agent. The agency theory, by ignoring the consideration of all corporate stakeholders, views a business organization as being accountable only to its shareholders, and its sole ESG is to maximize firm value under the shareholder primacy model. Thus, any levels of ESG beyond firm value maximization would lead to reduced levels of financial performance. The stakeholder theory asserts that firms have relationships with many constituencies (stakeholders) who both affect and are affected by the actions of the firm.[9] Thus, a focus on stakeholder interest is vital to a firm's success, and management must pursue rational and optimal actions for all stakeholders rather than those that seek only to maximize shareholder interests. The concept of profit-with-purpose suggests that while the main purpose is to maximize shareholder wealth, proper attention should be given to social and environmental impacts.

Investor perception regarding the relative importance of ESP and ESG sustainability performance with respect to each other and their contribution to the overall firm's long-term value maximization is affected by whether ESP and ESG are viewed as complementary or conflicting factors. Sustainability performance dimensions (ESP and ESG) can be considered complementary since firms must be financially prominent in the long run to perform well in other sustainability activities (e.g., social and environmental). Economically viable and financially profitable firms are in better positions financially, have more resources to create jobs and wealth, and better fulfill their social and environmental responsibilities. In addition, firms that are committed to corporate social responsibility (CSR), environmental obligations, and effective governance can also be sustainable in generating long-term financial performance. However, it is also possible that investors view these dimensions as conflicting, and a tradeoff exists between investing in environmental, CSR, and corporate governance initiatives or business activities that maximize economic profits. Focusing on ESP and ESG sustainability performance enables long-term firm value maximization by creating value for shareholders while meeting the claims of other stakeholders. Sustainability performance pertaining to ESG could improve the relevance and precision of the performance signal and thus result in more informationally efficient stock prices.

In the context of sustainability, current earnings contribute limited useful information for predicting future dividends, and thus, investors must rely on alternate information to secure expected returns on investment in their valuation model. Impact investing, focusing on both financial returns on investment and social and environmental impacts, becomes more critical to investors. However, a growing number of investors are switched on to impact investing with a keen focus on financial return and ESG sustainability factors and integrating non-financial ESG sustainability factors into their investment strategies.[10] Institutional investors and socially responsible investors have a growing interest in business sustainability. Thus, management should recognize this continuous interest in sustainability and its possible impact on the cost of capital. The 2021 survey conducted by the Institutional Shareholder Services (ISS) reveals that:[11]

- The majority of respondents (62.5%) report that environmental, social, and governance (ESG) factors of performance risk and disclosure have been more relevant to them since the beginning of the COVID-19 pandemic.
- The governance dimension of ESG sustainability is considered the most important ESG factor (86% of respondents) in their investment analysis and stewardship activities.
- The most important drivers of focus on ESG investments in response to the COVID-19 pandemic are client and stakeholder demand, racial inequality and diversity, and regulatory changes.
- Fewer than half of the respondents (44.1%) expect future ESG ratings to integrate sustainability factors of diversity and inclusion, workplace safety, treatment of employees, and supply chain labor dynamics into sustainability rating disclosures.
- More than one-third (37.5%) of respondents have either already added or intend to add new staff to manage ESG-related issues during and in the aftermath of the COVID-19 pandemic.

Long-term sustainability investment strategies can be achieved when:

1. Investors, both retail and institutional investors, focus on the achievement of long-term and sustainable investments rather than short-term market movements.
2. Investors are attentive by setting a sustainability tone at the top, engaging in sustainability initiatives, and practicing in socially responsible investing strategies through their proxy proposals. There is a need to elect at least one director with sustainability interests and skills.
3. Investors demand the creation of a board sustainability committee consisting of directors with adequate sustainability expertise.
4. Investors require the entire board of directors to engage in sustainability issues and initiatives, being held accountable for achieving sustainability performance and providing sustainability leadership.
5. Investors demand executive commitments to business sustainability and the proper implementation of strategic sustainability planning by seeking active oversight function of the board of directors by including a sustainability performance target clause in executive compensation contracts and by enabling the labor market to reward sustainability executive leadership and punish managerial short-termism.
6. Investors utilize sustainability investment initiatives and innovation.
7. Investors demand sustainability performance reporting and assurance be integrated into corporate reporting.

In summary, investors' interest in and the use of sustainability information by investors has been a growing trend because they increasingly recognize the importance and relevance of ESG factors in assessing the opportunity for long-term performance and risk of their investments. Sustainability disclosures relevant to a company's environmental and social impacts and governance structure can be used by investors to assess the risks and opportunities associated with ESG initiatives and make more informed decisions. Investors use sustainability ESP and ESG information in many ways including: (1) opportunity for investment in long-term ESP and ESG performance as reported by public companies about their long-term financial viability, management of environmental and social issues, and ability to generate sustainable returns over time; (2) risk assessment of analyzing ESG factors to identify potential risks that may impact a company's financial performance including assessing climate-related risks, regulatory compliance, and supply chain vulnerabilities; (3) impact investing of achieving desired rates of returns on investment while obtaining some social and environmental impacts of aligning financial goals with positive societal or environmental outcomes; (4) investors prefer to engage with companies to promote better sustainability practices including communicating with company directors and management, voting on ESG-related issues during annual meetings and involving shareholders in resolutions on sustainability matters; (5) comparing and evaluating companies' ESG factors with peers and industry norms based on consistent metrics; (6) compliance assessment of companies' compliance with sustainability-related applicable laws, rules, regulations and standards; and (7) stakeholder engagement, relationships, and influence that could affect companies' long-term performance, sustainable success, growth, and prosperity.

III. BOARD OF DIRECTORS AND BUSINESS SUSTAINABILITY

In today's dynamic world, corporate boards face new challenges and expectations. They are now expected to address climate change and workforce wellness while navigating technology's opportunities and risks. Adaptability and change are key to success in this dynamic landscape. Priorities include impact investing, stakeholder engagement and relationships, ESG factors and considerations, risk assessment and management, growth and innovation, diversity, equity and inclusion, transparent communication, and fostering a responsible corporate culture. These are important and can impact the board of directors' effectiveness. A company's board of directors is essential in overseeing and impacting business sustainability practices and performance. The board is responsible for providing strategic direction and governance overseeing sustainability efforts, and its decisions can significantly affect a company's sustainability initiatives and accomplishments.

The board of directors, as representatives of shareholders, has traditionally been responsible for protecting the interests of shareholders by overseeing corporate governance, financial reporting, and auditing processes under the shareholder primacy model presented in Chapter 2. The only fiduciary duty of the board of directors under the shareholder primacy model has been to shareholders. Under the emerging stakeholder primacy model and with recent events of perceived social injustice and a move toward diversity, inclusion, and environmental initiatives, the board of directors has assumed fiduciary responsibility to all stakeholders. The current move toward the stakeholder primacy model and recent events encourage public companies and their board of directors to: (1) renew interest in the company's mission of profit-with-purpose in defining its purpose in society in providing the goods and services that are not detrimental to society and meet basic needs and innovation; (2) hold the board of directors fiduciary responsible to all stakeholders; (3) focus the board's interest in both financial ESP and non-financial ESG sustainability performance; (4) address the value of human and social capital and related changes in the nature of work and the workplace; (5) explore social matters, including issues of racial and gender equality and social justice; and (6) focus on environmental initiative and climate change; (7) oversee the assessment and management of all sustainability riskes presented in Chapter 7; and (8) hold management responsible for managing all sustainability capitals (financial, human, social, environmental) presented in Chapter 6.

The emerging modification in the board of directors' oversight function in protecting the interests of all stakeholders with strategic sustainability planning is to:

- Set a tone at the top, accepting fiduciary responsibilities to all stakeholders.
- Set sustainability strategy and strategic oversight of defining the company's overall strategy, including setting sustainability goals and objectives and overseeing the implementation of the profit-with-purpose concept.
- Ensure that sustainability efforts and considerations align with the company's long-term vision, values, and financial goals.
- Oversee the process of integrating both ESP and ESG initiatives into the corporate culture and business environment.
- Promote business sustainability and engage in sustainability initiatives in both financial ESP and non-financial ESG sustainability performance.
- Define the corporate purpose of the profit-with-purpose mission.
- Encourage socially responsible investors to place a need to elect at least one director with sustainability interests and skills in proxy proposals.
- Create a sustainability board committee like the audit committee to oversee sustainability activities and initiatives.
- Address a corporate culture of responsibility, accountability, and fairness to all stakeholders by focusing on long-term, value-creation activities that influence ESG efforts' business decisions and the company's sustainability.
- Oversee workforce and human capital matters by investing in training and building expertise among directors, executives, and employees to ensure they have adequate knowledge to make informed decisions and perform their activities regarding sustainability.
- Establish strategic planning for achieving long-term sustainable performance and value.
- Require the board of directors to engage in sustainability issues and initiatives, implement strategic sustainability planning, be held accountable for achieving sustainability performance, and provide adequate sustainability leadership.
- Conduct active oversight function of demanding sustainability performance from executives.
- Include a sustainability performance achievement target clause in the executive compensation contract. Hold the executive accountable for achieving both desired financial ESP and nonfinancial ESG sustainability performance by linking executive compensation to sustainability performance to encourage senior executives to prioritize and drive sustainability initiatives.
- Accept ESG initiatives and strategic sustainability planning for major and mainstream corporate governance issues ranging from financial performance to climate change and other environmental risks and impacts, human capital management, labor standards, consumer and product safety, resource management, social justice, and fair labor.

- Recognize that the board's role in these ESG areas is generally one of stakeholder protection, partnership with management, and appropriate oversight.
- Understand that ESG matters often have important image and reputational impacts and significant consequences for public, investor, and stakeholder relations.
- Receive regular briefings on relevant ESG matters from executives and the company's strategic sustainability planning to ensure that the company adheres to relevant and applicable sustainability regulations, standards, and guidelines.
- Create an ethical and collegial work environment that promotes diversity, inclusion, and equity.
- Consider how the risk oversight role specifically applies to various ESG-related risks by assessing ESG factors to identify potential risks and opportunities that may impact the business, including regulatory changes, cybersecurity, climate change, supply chain disruptions, and reputational risks associated with sustainability issues.
- Focus on corporate strategy and evaluating the effectiveness and quality of management's sustainability factors of performance, risk, and disclosure by working with management to develop and implement strategies for capitalizing on opportunities and mitigating sustainability-related risks.
- Understand the company's approach and response to investor requests for ESG-related engagement, external disclosure and sustainability reporting, and assurance by understanding stakeholder expectations and ensuring transparent communication of sustainability initiatives, performance, progress, and regular reporting on key ESG metrics.
- Align the company's sustainability reports with best practices in the industry and peers and compliance with the globally accepted sustainability standards to ensure that the company provides accurate, reliable, and comprehensive sustainability disclosures in annual reports and other communications to stakeholders, including shareholders.

In recent years, shareholders have shown interest in obtaining financial returns on their investments and achieving social and environmental impacts. Theoretically, business organizations and their board of directors' engagement in ESG activities, performance, risk, and disclosure can be viewed as value-increasing or value-decreasing for investors. On the one hand, companies that effectively manage their business sustainability improve ESG performance, enhance their reputation, fulfill their social responsibility, and promote a corporate culture of integrity and competency. On the other hand, companies can only survive and generate sustainable performance when they continue to be profitable and can create shareholder value. Nonetheless, ESP and ESG sustainability performance disclosures supplement each other and are not mutually exclusive. Companies that conduct themselves ethically are governed effectively, are socially and environmentally responsible, maintain a good reputation and employee and customer satisfaction, are typically more sustainable in the long term, and generate more value for their shareholders. In this context, sustainability focuses on business activities that generate long-term ESP of firm value maximization and voluntary activities that achieve ESG sustainability performance that concerns all stakeholders.

The board of directors should oversee the managerial function of focusing on long-term sustainability performance and communicating sustainability performance information to all stakeholders. The board should be informed about and understand the stakeholders' objectives and rationales for focusing on sustainability factors of performance, risk and disclosure, managerial, strategic planning, sustainable operational performance, and executive compensation in promoting long-term corporate value. The board should also provide oversight, insight, and foresight function on achieving both financial ESP and non-financial ESG performance driven by financial, human, social, and manufacturing capitals, innovation, culture, corporate governance, and ESG initiatives.[12] The financial and non-financial key performance indicators (KPIs) should be identified, measured, and disclosed through metrics reflecting corporate value, long-term investment, and innovation on ESG initiatives. In general, the four sustainability oversight functions of the board of directors are:[13]

1. Refocusing on long-term strategic sustainability planning: The board of directors should focus on long-term sustainable goals and achievements rather than short-term gains that may discourage them from investing in research, technology, innovation, and ESG initiatives.
2. Identifying, measuring, and disclosing key long-term value drivers, including employee talent and skills, innovation and consumer preferences, environment and society factors, and corporate governance measures.
3. Developing company-specific sustainability metrics on both financial ESP and non-financial EGS sustainability performance tailored to the companies' mission, purpose, culture, strategy, objectives, and operating activities.
4. Identifying sustainability issues that drive value by identifying, measuring, reporting, and managing sustainability factors of planning, performance, risk, and disclosure. These value drivers can be tailored to a particular company in a specific industry culture and operations that can have long-term material financial impacts.

The board of directors should set a tone at the top by defining the statement of purpose for a business organization beyond maximizing profit for shareholders. A purpose-driven organization should not be limited to not-for-profit organizations and extended to for-profit business organizations. The board of directors should promote the concept of profit-with-purpose and design and oversee the implantation of the long-term strategy of achieving the profit-with-purpose mission. The board's priority should be set for defining the statement of purpose, establishing strategic planning to achieve the purpose, and overseeing managerial decisions and actions in implementing the statement of purpose by focusing on the current environmental issues of climate change, social justice, diversity, and other emerging forces that drive business purposes and impacts. To effectively and vigilantly oversee managerial strategy and monitor management's performance in achieving the profit-with-purpose mission, the board of directors should consider the emerging business environment and conditions and the changing expectations of stakeholders' that affect the business environment and corporate culture. The board of directors should evaluate and redirect how the company does business in the post-COVID-19 pandemic in response to the new norm for conducting business, changing customer behaviors, reliability in the supply chain, consumer demand, and global economic conditions. The board should be prepared to adapt the corporate strategy.

Diversity in terms of expertise, knowledge, ethnicity, and gender for directors, executives, and employees is gaining the attention of policymakers, regulators, standard-setters, investors, and society. Investors prefer recruitment, development, promotion, and retention policies and procedures for a well-diversified workforce with fairness, equity, and justice. The company's strategic sustainability planning, human capital strategy, goals, resources, and management should support these policies and procedures. Investors demand disclosure of the board's diversity across gender, ethnicity, and race. However, diversity includes more than ethnicity, gender, or race and should include expertise, knowledge, and experience to build human capital and improve human resource management. In recent years, increasing diversity, inclusion, and representation at the board level has gained the attention of policymakers, regulators, and the business community. Better corporate governance measures and performance are expected to stem from enhanced diversity as public companies face greater pressure from their stakeholders to improve gender, social, and ethnic diversity at the board level. The best practices suggest that companies include a separate section in their annual reports presenting the board's policy on diversity, related policies, and procedures to implement the policy effectively. Diversity should extend beyond board representation to the entire corporate structure, including the top management team and key employees. Business organizations should also attempt to implement a diversity policy in their compliance function to improve their corporate governance. Demands are growing for the board of directors and executives to set an appropriate tone at the top to ensure the safety, health, and well-being of employees, suppliers, and customers by promoting effective practices to treat them with respect and taking affirmative steps to ensure diversity, inclusion, and equal opportunity. The board of directors should evaluate the commitments to diversity, inclusion, and equity and implement effective policies to sustain diversity, inclusion, and equity. Companies with good diversity, inclusion, and equity practices are expected to add to their bottom-line earnings and avoid adverse, legal, regulatory, worker, community, and consumer consequences. In addition, business judgment rules protect and support directors and executives who commit to good diversity, inclusion, and equity practices.

Board accountability can be addressed from regulatory, legal, investors', shareholders', stakeholders', societal, and media perspectives. From the legal perspective, the board of directors is accountable for all important strategic decisions that affect the company's operation and bottom-line earnings. Directors usually make decisions based on the information available to them using their expertise, experience, and judgment. However, the "business judgment rule" is intended to protect directors from unjustifiable lawsuits for making incorrect business decisions as long as they provide evidence that those decisions were duly considered. Many believe that the financial scandals of Enron, WorldCom, and others prove that the business judgment rule can be misinterpreted in holding directors accountable to investors for engaging in activities detrimental to investors and thus protect them from accountability to shareholders and stakeholders. However, recent court cases suggest that courts have begun to raise the minimum standards for a board to fulfill its fiducial duties by expecting them to take a more proactive approach to their oversight function of effectively overseeing managerial decisions and actions.

In recent decades, investors in general and investor activists such as hedge funds have been very active in holding the board of directors accountable for governance and board activities. Through exercising their legal voting rights as shareholders or by launching public pressure campaigns, these informed and sophisticated investors have taken proactive initiatives to influence corporate governance and hold boards accountable for their actions. Pension funds for public employees and organized labor have effectively exercised their legal rights to vote out and replace directors who did not fulfill their fiduciary duties or engaged in activities detrimental to society and communities. In the past several years, three asset managers of BlackRock, State Street, and the Vanguard Group have focused on ESG sustainability and accountability of the board of directors. These asset managers have been adamant about their expectations of boards on various corporate governance, social, and environmental issues, including diversity inclusion, social justice initiatives, and climate change. As employees are also becoming shareholders by investing in their company's stock directly or through pension funds, they have held the board of directors accountable for ensuring and protecting human capital and addressing human rights. Policymakers and regulators have held the board of directors accountable by establishing laws (SOX 2002) and related applicable rules, regulations, and standards.[14]

In 2018 Senator Warren introduced a bill entitled the Accountable Capitalism Act, proposing that corporate boards be more accountable to all stakeholders, not just shareholders, and that employees be able to elect directors.[15] To ensure effective accountability for directors, the board of directors should get sufficient, reliable, and transparent information from different groups and corporate gatekeepers, including management, auditors, legal counsel, and financial advisors, apply proper methods and procedures in making data-driven sound decisions, and be vigilant in overseeing managerial decisions, actions, and performance, be proactive in response to crises. In response to and in the aftermath of the 2020 COVID-19 pandemic, the board of directors should have regular meetings with top executives to consider corporate scenario planning and contingencies to deal with the continuous challenges of the pandemic. The board should oversee human capital needs and focus on employees, customers, and suppliers'; safety, health, and well-being.

The board of directors should oversee the company's climate change initiatives. Investors are typically concerned about climate change and the associated risk, and they expect the directors and officers to focus on minimizing the negative impacts of climate change and global warming. Investors expect company disclosures in compliance with the recommendations of the Task Force on Climate-related Financial Disclosures (TCFD).[16] TCFD recommendations include disclosures relevant to climate-related risks, opportunities, and threats and their governance, strategy, key performance indicators, risk assessment, and management policies and procedures, including the adoption of science-based GHG reduction targets aligned to the goal of the Paris Agreement, the commitment to net-zero greenhouse gas (GHG) emissions by 2050, the performance of climate-related scenario analysis and adoption of renewable energy targets. Investors are also concerned about the negative impacts of the COVID-19 pandemic on climate change and possible systemic risks relevant to exogenous events and shocks to the economy and business.

The audit committee's involvement in business sustainability is important at the board level. The audit committee is a committee of the board of directors typically overseeing financial reporting and auditing processes. In the post-SOX act of 2002, the audit committee took a more extensive role overseeing internal controls, risk assessment and management, whistleblowing policies and procedures, and compliance with all applicable laws, rules, regulations, and standards. In recent years, the audit committee has overseen the reliability, relevance, and transparency of financial economic sustainability performance (ESP) and non-financial environmental, ethical, social, and governance (ESG) sustainability performance. Specifically, the audit committee should ask the following relevant sustainability-related questions.

- Has the board of directors defined the company's purpose statement?
- Does the statement of purpose specify the profit-with-purpose mission?
- Does the profit-with-purpose mission focus on achieving the desired rate of returns on investment for shareholders and obtaining social and environmental impacts?
- Is management focusing on achieving financial ESP while generating non-financial ESG sustainability performance?
- Is the company preparing and disseminating integrated financial ESP and non-financial ESG sustainability performance information?
- Have managerial and financial control policies and procedures affected non-financial ESG sustainability information?
- Is there sufficient focus on profit-with-purpose of achieving both financial ESP and non-financial ESG performance?
- Is the board effectively reviewing and assessing sustainability risks (strategic, financial, compliance, reputational, operational) discussed in Chapter 7?

- Is the board's culture suitable and strong enough to initiate direct dialogue with all stakeholders who are affected by sustainability efforts and activities?
- Does the board set the tone for addressing and advancing ESP and ESG initiatives and efforts?

IV. MANAGEMENT AND BUSINESS SUSTAINABILITY

The substantial growth in the use of both financial ESP and non-financial ESG by investors in making investment decisions encourages business organizations and their board of directors, as explained in the previous section, and management, to pay attention to sustainability strategies. Proper attention to all four sustainability factors of planning, performance, risk, and disclosure and effective practices of sustainability strategies enable management to communicate sustainability success stories to all stakeholders, including shareholders. Lack of focus on business sustainability and poor sustainability practices causes management to miss opportunities to adopt robust and comprehensive sustainability strategies to create shared value for all stakeholders. Business organizations and their boards of directors and executives should develop financial ESP and non-financial ESG sustainability performance and continuous improvement, consisting of board oversight, strategic alignment, executive monitoring, risk assessment and management, and performance evaluation in promoting and advancing business sustainability. One way to improve the transparency and quality of corporate reporting is through voluntary disclosures on ESG information and related key performance indicators (KPIs). Requests for sustainability KPI information on products, strategies, plans, forecasted performance, and non-financial ESG are gaining momentum. Management plays an important role in corporate reporting, and stakeholders, including shareholders, can view its engagement in both financial ESP issues and non-financial ESG activities. Management is willing, able, and capable of producing integrated sustainable performance reporting for all stakeholders.

Management plays an important role in ensuring the effective implementation of sustainability strategic planning and whether the company operates economically, environmentally, and with social responsibility, including integrating sustainability principles and factors into the core business strategy, corporate culture, decision-making processes, and daily operations. The top management team in the C-suite is led by the chief executive officer (CEO) in collaboration with other executives, including the chief financial officer (CFO), the controller, the treasurer, and other senior executives who are responsible for managing the organization for the benefits of its stakeholders. Management's primary responsibilities are to achieve operational efficiency and effectiveness, comply with all applicable laws, rules, regulations, and standards, conduct proper assessment of risk, and give fair and true disclosure of both financial ESP and non-financial (ESG) sustainability performance information.

Management under the oversight function of the company's board of directors is primarily responsible for operational efficiency and effectiveness, compliance with all applicable laws, rules, regulations, and standards, and preparation of reliable information. The effective fulfillment of management responsibility creates sustainable performance in protecting the interests of all stakeholders, including shareholders. Management is responsible for achieving financial ESP and non-financial ESG sustainability performance, effectively assessing the related risks, and properly disclosing sustainability financial and non-financial information. Those in the C-suite, including the CEO, chief financial officer (CFO), chief operating officer, chief compliance officer, chief human resources officer, chief legal office or general counsel, and chief sustainability officer (CSO), should coordinate their efforts and activities to address the emerging move toward business sustainability. To effectively address the company's sustainability initiatives and factors, the board of directors may form a new executive position of "chief sustainability officer" to be responsible for (1) promoting achievement of both ESP and ESG sustainability performance; (2) assessing and managing COVID-19-related risks; (3) ensuring compliance with all applicable rules, regulations, and standards to protect the safety and well-being of all stakeholders, particularly customers, suppliers, and employees; (4) managing business continuity; (5) preventing possible disruption in supply chain; (6) effectively communicating sustainability information to all stakeholders; and (7) complying with all the growing government guidelines and regulations.

Management plays a crucial role in effectively implementing business sustainability strategic plans under the oversight function of the company's board of directors and producing robust and comprehensive integrated sustainability reports. Integrated sustainability thinking and reporting by management consists of:

- **Value creation:** Generate a profit-with-purpose mission of creating shared value for all stakeholders. The main objective of integrated reporting is to reflect the company's stakeholder value creation.
- **Knowing the strengths and concerns of sustainability performance:** Identify and assess the positive and negative impacts of trends shaping your organization's five economic, governance, social, ethical, and environmental (EGSEE) dimensions of sustainability performance.
- **Navigating current and future trends:** An organization should be familiar with the current environments in which it operates and the environment in which it will operate in the future.
- **Understanding non-financial metrics:** Determine what non-financial measures may be in play for the organization, study them, and report them to the stakeholders as a main point, not just an annex to the financial statements. Environmental, social, and governance (ESG) are typical non-financial dimensions of sustainability performance.

- **Demonstrating the link between non-financial measures and long-term financial success:** Show the stakeholders the importance of the above non-financial measures to the organization's long-term financial stability.
- **Leading with tone at the top commitments to sustainability performance reporting:** Give evidence to the board that all parts of the organization are linked to each other through financial and non-financial information.
- **Publishing holistic and integrated sustainability reporting:** Be extensive when it comes to reporting. While few would read a report with every piece of sustainability information an organization has made available, readers should be able to get a good overview of the measures the organization puts forth to create sustainable value.

Management under the oversight function of the board of directors should prioritize a proper balance between investing in human capital and physical and financial capital and oversee managerial strategic plans in implementing investment in and allocating resources to various capitals. In collaboration with other executives and oversight of the board of directors, the CFO should consider all possibilities and scenarios under which an organization can survive, recover, and continue sustainable performance. Business risk assessment and supply chain management can play important roles in recovery. Particularly, the finance function led by the CFO should reevaluate the critical finance processes, including working capital and cash flows, accounts receivable, accounts payable, investment activities, operation cycle, financing activities, financial reporting, filing with regulators, and financial communications with investors.

Management should assess and manage sustainability risk by considering:

- Enterprise Risk Management (ERM) is vital in turning challenges into opportunities.
- The move toward sustainability reporting underscores the importance of an adequate ERM in improving the effectiveness of all five EGSEE dimensions of sustainability performance.
- *ISO 31000: Risk Management – Principles and Guidelines* (2009), which provides principles and guidelines on risk management.

An integrated sustainability report reflecting both financial ESP and non-financial ESG sustainability performance information prepared by the CSO in collaboration with other executives under the board of directors' oversight function can improve the quality and quantity of the firm's communication and financial reporting with all inside and outside stakeholders. First, ESG sustainability disclosures and ratings can improve transparency, enabling more effective monitoring of management to act in the best interest of all stakeholders. Second, increased ESG sustainability disclosure can enable stakeholders (e.g., institutional investors, analysts, creditors, government, suppliers, society, and employees) to develop their own independent and informed views on firms' sustainable performance in all areas of economic, environmental, social, ethical, and governance activities. Third, focus on sustainability performance encourages management to pursue firm value maximization that benefits all stakeholders, and disclosure of sustainability performance and ratings affect stock prices. Fourth, more transparent sustainability disclosures on long-term economic and ESG performance create opportunities to identify and correct operational inefficiencies and reputational and financial risks that would improve economic performance and thus increase firm value. Finally, market-wide effects of firm sustainability disclosures are also important if the net benefits of issuing sustainability reports at the firm level affect the entire market or if the net benefit is ignored or not fully internalized by firms. Market-wide effects of voluntary sustainability disclosures can be measured regarding impacts on cost of capital, liquidity, and firm valuation.

Business sustainability enables management to establish synergy and congruence between cost and performance management and integrate sustainability into the business environment, corporate culture, and supply chain processes. The concept of cost management suggests that management maximizes the utilization of scarce resources in generating revenue and delivers high-quality value to customers in improving performance. The concept of performance management suggests that management strikes a proper balance between short-term and long-term ESP and accepts a tradeoff between financial/quantitative ESP and non-financial/qualitative ESG sustainability performance. The integrated cost management and performance management concepts under business sustainability suggest that a firm must extend its focus beyond maximizing short-term shareholder profit by considering the impact of its operations on the long-term interests of all stakeholders, including shareholders, creditors, customers, employees, the community, society, and the environment.

Best sustainability practices for management suggest the integration of cost management and performance management in promoting the following aspects of sustainability performance:

- Design and implement a company-specific statement of purpose that defines goals and mission and how the operations are conducted in producing goods or services.
- Focus on policies and procedures that promote the achievement of financial ESP and non-financial ESG sustainability performance.
- Establish managerial policies and procedures to deal with issues of diversity, social justice, and treatment of complaints from employees, customers, and suppliers.
- Assess and manage all sustainability risks from reputational to operational, financial, environmental, and compliance, as presented in Chapter 7.
- Prepare and disseminate an integrated sustainability report presenting both financial ESP and non-financial ESG sustainability performance information to all stakeholders.

- Follow developments and trends in both financial ESP and non-financial ESG disclosure, including guidelines by professional organizations and standard-setters (GRI, IIRC, SASB) and regulators.
- Ensure employees, customers, and suppliers' safety, health, and well-being after the COVID-19 pandemic.
- Focus on a long-term sustainable strategy to create shared value for all stakeholders.
- Assess how current crises can be addressed to minimize their long-term impacts.

Proper management of both financial ESP and non-financial ESG can contribute to sustainability success, and a lack of commitment to sustainability by directors and officers can result in an unsustainable business environment and ongoing concern. The most challenging and problematic practice of sustainability success is the lack of a profit-with-purpose mission and strategy for achieving sustainability. Management should engage in both financial ESP and non-financial ESG sustainability issues by:

- Establishing sustainability initiatives and goals by setting clear goals aligned with the company's values and corporate culture, business environment, and industry standards to achieve economic stability, environmental conservation, and social responsibility.
- Developing robust and comprehensive sustainability policies that guide the company's practices covering areas such as climate change, human capital resource use, waste reduction, environmental and social impacts, and ethical business conduct.
- Allocating resources, including financial and human resources such as budget and personnel, to support sustainability initiatives and invest in technology training programs that contribute to the sustainability goals and objectives.
- Monitoring the level of disclosure by establishing accountability systems to track the company's sustainability performance and corporate reporting on key sustainability metrics.
- Responding to third-party information requests from emerging ESG-ratings services and existing providers (e.g., the proxy advisory firm ISS' new "Environmental & Social Quality Score" and accompanying list of 300-plus questions for companies to complete).
- Developing expertise in ESG by encouraging innovation for sustainability in product design, manufacturing processes, or service delivery.
- Focusing on the company's key ESG issues and conversing comfortably on those issues that matter or present significant risks by ensuring compliance with environmental regulations to mitigate sustainability-related risks.
- Developing specialized in-house expertise and updating internal reporting and business unit structures to have greater capacity in ESG areas by fostering a culture of sustainability within the company and educating and engaging employees.

IV.1 Chief Sustainability Officer (CSO)

Effective achievement of both financial ESP and non-financial ESG dimensions of sustainability performance demand "tone at the top" commitments to business sustainability strategies and actions. Commitment by the board of directors and top executives is essential in effectively coordinating all sustainability strategies and activities and successfully implementing sustainability strategies. Businesses are more likely to achieve their ESG targets when their sustainability leader reports directly to a CEO committed to sustainability initiatives. A chief sustainability officer (CSO) is a top-level executive responsible for leading and overseeing sustainability initiatives, efforts, and strategies. The role of a CSO has become increasingly important as businesses integrate sustainability into their overall business strategy, corporate culture, business environment, and operations. Chief sustainability officers (CSOs) who are empowered and report to CEOs can drive positive organizational change. They have better access to resources, which enhances the company's chances of meeting its sustainability goals. Having alignment with the CEO and setting comprehensive ESG targets are crucial factors that contribute to impactful sustainability transformations.

There is an urgent need for the establishment of the position of CSO in C-suite executives of business organizations. The role of the CSO includes:

- Participation with other executives in preparing the "statement of purpose" for the company.
- Managing the development and implementation of sustainability strategies across all aspects of the business, including operations, supply chain, product development, and corporate social responsibility.
- Developing and implementing the organization's sustainability strategy by working with other top executives to set goals, define key performance indicators (KPIs), and align sustainability initiatives with the company's overall business goals and objectives.
- A profit-oriented mentality and practice establishing and implementing sustainability policies and procedures to achieve economic viability and prosperity, environmental impact, social responsibility, governance effectiveness, and ethical business conduct.
- Implementing the concept of profit-with-purpose by focusing on allocating resources more wisely, managing waste and CO_2 emissions responsibly, acting as a good citizen, and celebrating diversity among workers to support sustainability initiatives and investing in technologies, infrastructure, and programs that contribute to sustainability goals.
- Engaging with various stakeholders, including shareholders, employees, customers, suppliers, and communities, by building relationships, understanding stakeholder expectations, and finding ways to reach out to new stakeholders or increase participation and communication with existing ones.

- Demonstrating flexibility in new endeavors that seek to increase the company's future growth aspects.
- Communicating effectively to other officers and employees about best practices in sustainability and enforce compliance with the same.
- Learning to leverage company strengths, such as technology, manpower, expertise, resources, and market positions, by evaluating the effectiveness of existing initiatives, identifying areas for improvement, and staying informed about emerging sustainability initiatives, trends, and best practices.
- Engaging in long-term strategy and performance by discussing and shaping long-term business strategies within corporations and having an open, transparent dialogue with investors when developing a strategy.
- Establishing a relationship with shareholders to understand their perspective on the company's strategy, performance, and governance by leading efforts to assess and improve sustainability performance continuously.
- Implementing sustainability standards into strategic and operational plans by collaborating with other executives and external advocacy and partnerships to promote sustainability within the company, the industry, and broader society.
- Ensuring compliance with environmental regulations and managing sustainability-related risks are part of the CSO's responsibilities by staying informed about evolving regulations and proactively addressing potential risks to the company.
- Benchmarking a baseline risk appetite for a corporation, setting standards to comply with legal and regulatory initiatives, creating a culture of risk awareness, and implementing that into the decision-making process.
- Maintaining a relationship with top executives and employees to increase the chances of long-term success by monitoring and improving the execution of long-term strategies by fostering a culture of sustainability within the organization, including educating employees about sustainability goals, encouraging their participation in initiatives, and integrating sustainability into training and development programs.
- Setting a tone at the top by creating an environment that values high ethics to guide business practices and a commitment to balancing economic success with environmental and social responsibility.

Chief Sustainability Officers (CSOs) usually possess a set of skills, traits, and qualifications that enable them to effectively lead sustainability initiatives and actions within an organization including (1) passion for sustainability that demonstrates their commitment to making a positive impact and driving change towards a more sustainable future; (2) leadership skills to effectively drive sustainability initiatives across various departments and levels of an organization; (3) the ability to develop long-term sustainability strategies aligned with the organization's goals and values by integrating sustainability into core business practices and driving innovation to achieve sustainability objectives; (4) analytical skills to analyze data, trends, and metrics to inform decision-making to assess the environmental and social impacts of business operations, track progress towards sustainability goals, and identify areas for improvement; and (5) communication skills for engaging stakeholders, building partnerships, and advocating for sustainability initiatives both internally and externally.

V. DIVERSITY, INCLUSION, AND SOCIAL JUSTICE

The year 2020 was very challenging, with significant issues of perceived systemic inequality exacerbated by the 2020 COVID-19 pandemic and other events which highlighted the deep divisions within society worldwide. The environmental, economic, social, and political challenges are expected to continue to affect all aspects of organizations of all types and sizes, from oversight by the board of directors to management and corporate gatekeepers to monitoring by investors and other stakeholders. In response to reported global racial and social injustice and to the detrimental effects of the 2020 COVID-19 pandemic on people of color, business organizations are reemphasizing their commitments to diversity, inclusion, and social justice. The renewed recognition of the importance of and commitment to diversity, inclusion, and social justice in boardrooms and the C-suite is evident since 2020. Policymakers, regulators, and business organizations worldwide are establishing and implementing initiatives to address improving gender and racial diversity in the workplace.

Diversity in the corporate boards and among executives has recently gained attention from regulators as they address the importance of diversity in the upper echelons of public companies. Two initiatives (mandatory and voluntary) have recently been taken to address gender diversity in the workplace in general and the boardroom. Mandatory initiatives, such as California Legislation (SB 824) and quotas in Europe, are required by regulators. Voluntary initiatives are actions taken by corporations to increase the number of female directors and officers. The decision as to whether public companies should voluntarily or be required to increase the percentage of female directors/executives (FDE) is an important issue that should be addressed by policymakers, regulators, investors, and the business community. Companies may be more inclined to voluntarily increase the percentage of FDE if they believe that FDE would improve financial performance and corporate governance effectiveness. The importance, relevance, and value of female directors and executives can no longer be ignored because about half of the workforce in the United States is composed of females. Women represent more than half of the population, and the majority of United States College graduates in business are steadily moving up the ladder of corporate success. Undoubtedly, female directors and executives are underrepresented on the boards and in the C-suites of public companies worldwide. Diversity in the corporate boards and executives has recently gained attention from regulators as they address the importance of diversity in the upper echelons of public companies.

Business organizations differ in their mission, goals, policies, and procedures for workplace diversity, inclusion, and justice. However, regardless of their challenges and opportunities for diversity, inclusion, and justice, the board of directors and executives should set the right tone at the top in promoting diversity and inclusion. Public companies should also communicate their commitment to diversity, equity, and inclusion to investors and other stakeholders and provide relevant and adequate disclosures on workforce diversity activities and other equity and inclusion-related issues, including gender pay gaps. Corporations should continue to assess and make progress on diversity, equity, and inclusion matters by (1) developing and strengthening diversity commitment by the board of directors and top executives, (2) assessing diversity-related risks and effectively managing such risks of pay inequity among diverse groups; (3) disclosure of workplace diversity, inclusion, and equity.

On December 17, 2020, the UK's Institute of Business Ethics (IBE) released its report *The Ethics of Diversity*, which provides guiding principles and a practical guide to why diversity matters to business organizations and their boards, executives, and stakeholders.[17] The IBE report addresses important ethical dimensions in the context of diversity. It provides business organizations, their boards, and executives with guiding principles and a framework for understanding diverse ethical dimensions and addressing their relevance and importance to corporate strategic planning, decisions, and actions. The report also addresses the possible impacts of the COVID-19 pandemic on systemic risks related to inequalities and perceived racial injustices with a keen focus on the diversity agenda. Business organizations should develop and implement strategies to promote and value diversity, inclusion, and equity of thought and experience. The IBE report suggests the following 10 recommendations regarding the board's consideration of diversity and the challenge of groupthink:[18]

1. Promote diversity on the board of directors and for top executive positions.
2. Ensure that the company's diversity, equity, and inclusion mission is integrated into corporate culture and business environment and becomes a strategic and business imperative.
3. Assess the diversity culture in the boardroom and workplace and the acceptance of diversity, equity, and inclusion purpose.
4. Review nomination, selection, and succession planning processes for all the board of directors and executive committee appointments.
5. Periodically review the individual roles assigned to board members in understanding the three elements of diversity: cognitive diversity, identity diversity, and experiential diversity.
6. Follow best practices of diversity, including the experience of improving gender balance, and learn from the experience of other sectors.
7. Communicate, engage with, and understand the company's stakeholders and respond to their diversity matters.
8. Communicate the diversity policies and practices to all stakeholders internally and externally.

9. Address all relevant challenges related to board evaluation of diversity matters and issues.
10. Recognize inequalities, racism, and social injustice as systemic risks to the economy and business operations and thus consider diversity, equity, and inclusion opportunities for long-term change and business sustainability.

In summary, diversity, equity, and inclusion (DEI) refers to a set of principles, policies, and practices intended to create workplaces and communities that are diverse, equitable, and inclusive. Diversity reflects various backgrounds, identities, and perspectives within an organization, including differences in race, age, ethnicity, gender, sexual orientation, abilities, socioeconomic status, and expertise. Equity refers to ensuring fairness and impartiality in treating all individuals by creating conditions that allow everyone equal access to resources and opportunities and enable them to reach their full potential, considering their unique needs and circumstances. Inclusion represents all efforts to ensure a sense of belonging for all individuals within an organization or community where everyone feels respected, valued, heard, and given the opportunity to achieve their best performance. Organizations and communities should prioritize DEI initiatives intended to build an environment that is diverse, inclusive, and equitable and can contribute to enhanced employee engagement, improved organizational performance, increased innovation, increased employee effectiveness and productivity, and create positive impacts on social and community relations.

VI. BUSINESS SUSTAINABILITY AND SUPPLY CHAIN MANAGEMENT

Supply chain sustainability refers to the integration of environmentally and socially responsible practices throughout the entire supply chain, from sourcing raw materials to distributing finished products. It involves minimizing the negative environmental and social impacts associated with producing and distributing goods while maximizing positive contributions. Technological advances, globalization, and the move toward business sustainability have disrupted traditional supply chain models and created the evolving landscape of supply chain strategies, emphasizing the shift from focusing solely on cost and efficiency to considering risk and resilience. A sustainable supply chain requires companies to contemplate more localized sourcing, increased transparency, and digital technology to enhance supply chain visibility and resilience. Developing the right balance between efficiency and resilience is a complex task, requiring data-driven decision-making and human judgment. The role of boards in overseeing and guiding supply chain strategies is crucial in achieving a sustainable supply chain management system.

Business sustainability has become a strategic imperative for corporations worldwide in integrating financial (ESP) and non-financial ESG sustainability performance into their business environment, corporate culture and supply chain management, and operational models, for creating shared value for all stakeholders. Global public companies are adopting proper supply chain sustainability (SCS) strategies and practices to respond effectively to the move toward integrating non-financial ESG sustainability performance and financial ESP and creating shared value for their shareholders. The transition towards clean energy has heightened awareness of critical minerals like cobalt, copper, lithium, and nickel and their use in SCS strategies and practices. Management should assess the control over critical mineral supply chains. Using critical minerals in SCS requires understanding of ownership structures, governance issues in producer countries, and economic/geopolitical risks.

Business sustainability has moved from the periphery, greenwashing and branding to the mainstream as a strategic imperative for global companies for generating sustainable revenues, optimizing costs, enhancing brands, attracting the best talent, mitigating risks, promoting innovation and growth, and adequately disclosing sustainability information in creating shared value for all stakeholders. The 2013 *Global Business Sustainability Report* released by the United Nations Global Compact states that supply chains are a roadblock to improved sustainability performance and encourages companies to engage their suppliers in establishing more sustainable practices and integrating sustainability into their supply chain processes.[19] Integrating business sustainability into supply chain management (SCM) should be consistent with cost management and performance management concepts discussed in the previous section, sustainable continuous improvement, and sustainability best practices. This integrated SCS model focuses on both financial ESP in creating shareholder value and non-financial ESG sustainability performance dimensions in protecting the interests of all stakeholders and their integration into supply chain management (SCM). The integration of business sustainability into SCM is becoming more relevant and important in the aftermath of the 2020 COVID-19 pandemic, as business organizations are required to protect the safety, health, and well-being of their employees, customers, suppliers, and other stakeholders.

Supply chain management (SCM) is defined in the context of business sustainability as managing the flow of products and services in the supply chain and converting raw materials into final products with a keen focus on maximizing customer value and earnings while achieving social and environmental impacts. The 2015 United Nations Global Compact defines supply chain sustainability (SCS) as "focusing on effective governance practices to ensure delivery of high quality of goods and services with utmost economic, social and environmental positive impacts."[20] The focus on SCS during and in the aftermath of the COVID-19 pandemic is relevant and important for several reasons.[21] First, the implementation of SCS with a keen focus on performance management and cost management enables companies to set a tone at the top by their board of directors and to top executives in managing all business capital, including financial, strategic, operational, human, reputation, social, and environmental. Second, SCS can improve the corporate environment, business culture, infrastructure, and business models that could achieve desired financial returns for shareholders while generating positive social and environmental impacts. Third, integration of business sustainability and continuous improvement into SCS provides opportunities for corporations, their boards of directors, and top executives to maximize customer value and improve product and service quality. Fourth, public companies can integrate both financial ESP and non-financial ESG sustainability performance dimensions into their supply chain management, from purchasing and inbound logistics and production design and manufacturing to outbound marketing distribution, delivery, logistics, and customer services. Finally, the focus on continuous improvement, cost management, performance management, and SCS strategies enables companies to comply with all applicable laws, rules, regulations, standards, and best practices to improve the overall quality and quantity of SCS.

The best practices of SCS are evolving as more business organizations integrate cost management, performance management, lean management, and continuous improvements of financial ESP and non-financial ESG sustainability performance into their business environment, corporate culture, and supply chain. These best practices recommend integrating the sustainability continuous performance improvement concept presented in the next section, focusing on both financial ESP and non-financial ESG sustainability performance into SCS strategies, policies, and procedures. Management should design, implement, and maintain proper SCS strategies that provide a common ground for integrating both financial ESP and non-financial ESG into their supply chain management. Key attributes and aspects of SCS are: (1) supply chain transparency that facilitates understanding and improving the sustainability of the supply chain and provides visibility into manufacturing processes, suppliers, and the potential impacts of the supply chain on the environment and communities; (2) ensuring that raw materials and components are sourced ethically and factors such as human rights, and fair labor practices are considered, while avoiding the use of materials that can cause environmental harm; (3) identifying, evaluating and mitigating potential risks associated with sustainability issues in the supply chain, and assessing the impact of regulatory initiatives, climate change, and other factors that could impact the stability and sustainability of the supply chain; (4) adopting SCS practices that minimize the environmental footprint of the supply chain, minimizing waste, using renewable energy sources, reducing greenhouse gas emissions, and optimizing logistics and transportation to lower energy consumption; (5) designing products and packaging for reuse, recycling, or repurposing that could reduce waste and encourage a more sustainable use of resources throughout the supply chain; (6) collaborating and working closely with suppliers to set and achieve sustainability goals, provide support, and encourage the adoption of sustainable practices; (7) complying with relevant sustainability standards and regulations, and adhering to fair trade standards, environmental certifications, and other industry-specific guidelines; (8) focusing on social responsibility issues within their supply chains to create positive impacts on the communities, ensure fair labor practices, safe working conditions, and respect for human rights; (9) conducting an ongoing process of improvement, regular assessments, audits, and feedback mechanisms; and (10) leveraging technology and innovation, using data analytics, blockchain, and other technologies to address the environmental and social impact of products throughout the supply chain.

Supply chain sustainability challenges should be identified, evaluated, and turned into sustainable opportunities by business organizations and their boards of directors and executives. Examples of these challenges are the following:

1. Lack of proper definition of the profit-with-purpose mission that contributes to the creation of shared value for all stakeholders.
2. Inadequate focus on lean management and continuous improvement strategies.
3. Lack of integration of supply chain sustainability into business sustainability for the achievement of both financial ESP and non-financial ESG sustainability performance.
4. Ineffective communication and disclosure of the importance and relevance of supply chain sustainability to all stakeholders, including investors, customers, employees, and suppliers.
5. Insufficient guidelines and robust policies and procedures for achieving supply chain sustainability.
6. Disconnection of supply chain sustainability with continuous improvement and other sustainability-related strategies.
7. Nonexistence of tone at the top by the board of directors and failure of executives to commit to supply chain sustainability and related strategies.
8. Ineffective and inadequate assessment and management of risks associated with supply chain sustainability.
9. Lack of monitoring of the progress toward achieving supply chain sustainability.
10. Lack of focus on 10 key aspects of supply chain sustainability discussed in the previous pages.
11. Insufficient use of continuous improvement strategies, cost management, and performance management in the supply chain sustainability system.

Digital technology provides visibility, data-driven decision-making, and risk management. Digital supply networks, risk-sensing technologies, and automation are leveraged to enhance resilience. Digital tools also enable companies to consider environmental, social, and governance (ESG) factors in their supply chain decisions. Ultimately, the supply chain equation is complex and requires a balance between data, technology, and human judgment. Boards play a crucial role in overseeing and understanding these complexities. They need to assess supply chain resilience, balance efficiency, and resilience, consider performance metrics, and promote collaboration across tiers of the supply chain. Boards should also evaluate investments in supply chain management to position the company for success in the future.

In summary, supply chain strategies are evolving from focusing on cost and efficiency to resilience in the face of unexpected disruptions, with digital technology playing a pivotal role in enabling this transformation. Boards must actively oversee these changes to ensure the company's supply chain aligns with its mission and strategy. Companies prioritizing SCS can contribute to environmental and social well-being and benefit from cost savings, enhanced brand reputation, and increased customer loyalty.

VII. BUSINESS SUSTAINABILITY OF MERGERS AND ACQUISITIONS

Mergers and acquisition (M&A) deals have increased substantially in recent years as worldwide M&A deals in 2021 reached $6.2.00 trillion, were higher in global volume in 2022 and reached $3 trillion in 2023, marking it the second-weakest year in a decade.[22] The ESG sustainability factors of planning, performance, risk, and disclosure and their effects on investment and M&A decisions are becoming increasingly important to businesses and investors. Disclosures of ESG performance can provide value-relevant information about investment risks and opportunities pertaining to M&A transactions. However, how the M&A dealmakers, including the boards of directors and executives of acquirer and target firms, consider the ESG factors need to be examined. A survey of corporate executives and asset managers found that ESG factors are relevant and important to M&A decision-makers as they perform ESG due diligence on ESG assessment for investment opportunities and risk.[23] The 2022 M&A trends survey conducted by Deloitte reveals that more than 70% of respondents report that their organizations consider ESG metrics in the valuations of target firms and portfolio reassessment.[24] The 2023 Deloitte poll results indicate that about 50% of private equity investors (PEIs) and 44% of corporates use ESG clauses in deal contracts and conduct some form of ESG pre-deal due diligence.[25] The ESG issues critical to the M&A due diligence processes are climate change, greenhouse gas emissions (GHG), labor standards, and human rights. M&A deals significantly impact stakeholders, suppliers, customers of both acquirers and targets, and the economy. It is expected that ESG factors of planning, performance, risk, and disclosure have a significant impact on M&A deal-making in several ways:

1. **Expansion of ESG-oriented M&A:** Companies are considering ESG factors when evaluating potential acquisitions and looking for synergies in ESG profiles. ESG-related risks and opportunities drive some transactions, especially in response to climate change and transition risks.
2. **Financial sector involvement:** Financial institutions are expanding their ESG services and analytical capabilities, helping businesses incorporate ESG into M&A decision-making.

3. **Valuation, due diligence, and contracts:** ESG performance increasingly affects company valuations, due diligence processes, and contract terms. Investors are willing to pay premiums for companies with strong ESG records.
4. **Financing:** ESG risks impact creditworthiness, with credit rating agencies integrating ESG into ratings. Sustainability-linked financing is emerging, potentially lowering the cost of capital for companies to improve their ESG performance.
5. **Investor and stakeholder engagement:** Companies are addressing ESG synergies and opportunities in investor communications, engaging stakeholders on ESG matters, and demonstrating how ESG will impact long-term performance.
6. **Regulatory risks:** Evolving ESG, human capital, and cybersecurity disclosures may introduce new regulatory risks affecting M&A. Recent legislation and potential new regulations could create opportunities in renewables and impact supply chains.
7. **ESG activism:** Activist investors use ESG issues to rally shareholder support for broader strategic changes, including M&A. Regulatory changes may encourage activism against companies slow to adapt to new ESG standards.
8. **Post-merger governance and integration:** ESG considerations are shaping post-acquisition governance structures, with oversight responsibilities being transferred and delegated. Integration efforts must align with ESG goals and policies to avoid negative impacts.

The full impact of ESG on M&A is still unfolding, and it will depend on ongoing developments in regulations, disclosures, and the evolving priorities of companies, investors, and regulators. Using ESG considerations in M&A deals has become increasingly important as businesses recognize the relevance of integrating sustainability and responsible business practices into their strategic planning. Sustainability ESG factors of planning, performance, risk, and disclosure are now considered critical elements that can impact the success and long-term value of M&A transactions. Some of the ESG considerations that should be incorporated into M&A deals are (1) due diligence of the target company's environmental practices, including its waste management, carbon footprint, resource usage, compliance with environmental regulations, social practices, diversity and inclusion, employee relations, community engagement, board composition, internal controls, executive compensation, and adherence to ethical business practices; (2) risk assessment and management of potential ESG-related risks (regulatory compliance, litigation risks, and reputational risks) that could affect the target company's financial performance and reputation. This includes assessments associated with ESG issues: (3) setting targets and milestones for incorporating sustainable practices, ensuring a smooth transition that preserves or enhances ESG performance, aligning cultures, engaging employees from target and acquired organizations to promote a culture of sustainability, diversity, and ethical business conduct; (4) post-merger monitoring and reporting of tracking progress on sustainability initiatives, diversity metrics, and other relevant indicators, enhancing stakeholder confidence and supporting long-term value creation; (5) ensuring that the combined entity complies with ESG-related regulations; and (6) considering the interests of various stakeholders including investors, employees, customers, suppliers, and communities. Integrating ESG considerations into M&A deals requires understanding that sustainable and responsible business practices contribute to long-term business success. Companies should incorporate planning, performance, risk, and disclosure sustainability factors into their M&A strategies to enhance resilience, reputation, and overall business value.

VIII. BUSINESS SUSTAINABILITY AND BENEFIT CORPORATION

Benefit corporations (BCs) have recently been incorporated under corporate law in many states in the United States to provide flexibility to social entrepreneurs to achieve the dual objectives of doing well and doing good by focusing on creating shared value for and protecting the interests of all stakeholders. A BC is a for-profit entity legally required to meet specific social and environmental goals and achieve financial returns for its shareholders. The primary goal of corporations has evolved from maximizing profit to increasing shareholder wealth. The goalpost has recently been advanced to create shareholder value while protecting the interests of other stakeholders, including employees, customers, suppliers, society, and the environment. It is expected that BCs will gain more acceptance as business organizations pay more attention to their continuity and sustainability in addressing their financial position and ensuring the safety, health, and well-being of their employees, customers, and suppliers. This section presents the evolution, relevance, status, and future of BCs.

The BC is an alternative legal entity that addresses the requirements of entrepreneurs and investors for creating shareholder value while protecting the interests of identified stakeholders, including society, by filling a gap between conventional corporations (CCs) and non-profits and giving social entrepreneurs flexibility to achieve the dual objectives of doing well and doing good. BCs have recently emerged in the United States as an alternative business entity for entrepreneurs who want to make a profit and give back something to society. In CCs, the primary goal is to create shareholder value, and the main fiduciary duty of their boards of directors is to protect shareholders' interests, oftentimes without regard for the needs of other stakeholders (social or environmental). In contrast, the fiduciary duty of the boards of directors of BCs is to protect the interests of all identified stakeholders. However, BCs are still taxed under the same corporate taxation laws and held to the same level of accountability and transparency as CCs. The existence and persistence of high-profile corporate scandals triggered by greed on the part of corporate directors and officers have caused the investment community and society to embrace the creation of BCs that protect the interests of all stakeholders.

Benefit corporations, "BCs" were formed initially as legal entities by legislation in nine states.[26] The Delaware General Corporation Law, since August 1, 2013, has authorized the formation of public BCs.[27] As of this writing, more than 40 states have adopted the establishment of BCs.[28] Pursuing a mixed commercial and social mission creates a unique research opportunity for business organizations to obtain desired financial returns for their shareholders while achieving social and environmental impacts. Benefit corporations are a new business structure that enables for-profit-seeking organizations to earn profits for their owners while considering society, the environment, employees, customers, and suppliers in decision-making. Benefit corporations are legally for-profit entities incorporated as CCs under state law that have also chosen to adopt other ESG missions in their articles of incorporation. BCs are intended to minimize the conflicts between corporations and society caused by differences between private and social costs and benefits and to align corporate goals with those of society under both the state corporate model and the benefit statute. Examples of conflicts between corporations and society are related to environmental issues (pollution, acid rain, global warming), wages paid by multinational corporations in poor countries, and child labor in developing countries. BCs, in pursuing their mission of protecting the interests of all stakeholders, can raise companies' awareness of the social costs and benefits of their business activities.

Benefit corporations represent a paradigm shift in conventional corporate governance by focusing on a broader and more inclusive approach to business success aimed at extending a corporation's purpose beyond maximizing shareholder value to a more sustainable and socially responsible business ecosystem. BCs should be viewed in a broader framework of the free enterprise system by considering firms as a nexus of contracts between the company and its stakeholders with often conflicting interests. Potential conflicts of interest can create information asymmetries and unique empirical settings to investigate differences among three groups of firms: (1) those with mandatory disclosures of their financial reports under the legal doctrine of "shareholder primacy and wealth maximization" and no disclosure of their environmental, social and governance (ESG) sustainability performance beyond financial reporting disclosures (CCs); (2) those with mandatory disclosures of financial performance as well as voluntary disclosures of their ESG disclosures (HCs); and (3) those with mandatory disclosures of both financial and non-financial sustainability key performance indicators (KPIs) under benefit corporation law (BCs).

The major characteristics of the BC form are (1) the requirement of a corporate purpose to create a material positive impact on society and the environment with a commitment to pursuing a social and/or environmental mission and profit-making objectives; (2) this mission is integrated into governing documents that are legally obligated to consider the impact of its decisions on various stakeholders; (3) an expansion of the duties of directors to require the consideration of non-financial stakeholders as well as the financial interests of shareholders; (4) the main objective is to balance profit-making with positive impacts on society and the environment; (5) impact investing that focuses on generating financial returns for investors while having social and environmental impacts; (6) as legal entities in many jurisdictions their legal structure incorporates the requirement to consider the interests of stakeholders beyond shareholders with specific requirements and reporting obligations; (7) requirements to meet their social and environmental goals and to publish regular reports presenting their performance in fulfilling their mission; (8) requirements to consider the impact of their decisions on various stakeholders including investors, employees, customers, communities, and the environment; (9) independent third-party assessments to verify and validate their social and environmental performance through certification from organizations like B Lab to demonstrate commitment to high standards; (10) flexibility in their governance structures enabling them to adopt governance practices that align with their mission and values; (11) creation of trust among investors and consumers who are increasingly interested in supporting businesses that prioritize social and environmental impacts; and (12) an obligation to report on overall social and environmental performance using a comprehensive, credible, independent, and transparent third-party standard.

Expected benefits of BCs include (1) the attention and market share of socially conscious investors; (2) the power of business resources to solve social and environmental challenges; (3) more trust in businesses by the public, shareholders, potential employees, and customers; (4) improved business, operational, and investment efficacy; (5) generating desired financial returns for investors while protecting interests of other stakeholders including employees, customers, suppliers, social and environmental; and (6) disclosure requirements that will improve assessing, managing, and minimizing strategic, operational, financial, reputational, and compliance risks.

IX. BIODIVERSITY ACCOUNTING AND FINANCE

Companies worldwide face risks from biodiversity loss, regulators require and highly encourage multinational firms to increase attention to biodiversity, and companies have a powerful incentive to view biodiversity as a key business issue. Biodiversity accounting and finance are gaining the attention of businesses and investors. These fields of business address the integration of biodiversity, including natural resources, environmental considerations, and ecosystem services, into accounting and finance disciplines, as well as accounting, business, and finance decisions. Biodiversity accounting and finance focus on business sustainability, including protecting nature and biodiversity, ensuring sustainable use of natural resources, and preserving the environment while achieving economic prosperity, growth, and development.

Biodiversity accounting, also known as natural capital accounting or ecosystem accounting, is an approach that seeks to measure, monitor, and account for the value of biodiversity and ecosystems in economic and policy decision-making. This concept recognizes that biodiversity and healthy ecosystems provide a wide range of benefits and services to society, often referred to as ecosystem services. These services include clean water, climate regulation, food production, recreation, and cultural values. Biodiversity accounting evaluates, measures, and quantifies the value of biodiversity and ecosystem services in financial terms and reporting biodiversity performance. Biodiversity accounting provides value-relevant financial information pertaining to the natural capital generated by ecosystems to better understand the contributions of biodiversity and natural systems to the global economy, businesses, and investment decision-making.

Biodiversity finance enables the financial resources, mechanisms, and instruments to support biodiversity conservation and sustainable resource management. It involves various financial approaches to generate funds for conserving ecosystem services such as clean water, pollination, climate regulation, and genetic resources and integrating biodiversity considerations into financial decision-making. Sources of biodiversity finance are socially responsible investments, including social stocks, green and sustainable bonds, government budgets, philanthropic donations, international aid, ecosystem service payments, biodiversity offset programs, sustainable business practices of impact investing, risk assessment, and sustainable supply chain management.

Biodiversity accounting and finance can have several implications for regulators, investors, businesses, and academics, including the following:

1. Policymakers, regulators, and standard-setters should be concerned about ecosystems, nature, climate change, and the environment and provide guidelines for regulatory compliance to preserve nature, protect the environment, and set standards for businesses to integrate biodiversity in their corporate culture, supply chain, operations, performance, and reporting.
2. Investors should assess biodiversity risks and opportunities by identifying and mitigating risks associated with climate change, environmental changes, regulatory pressures, and reputational issues. Investors should also consider the opportunities associated with biodiversity and ecosystems, new markets, sustainable and green investments, and governmental grants and incentives.
3. Businesses should take advantage of the benefits provided using natural resources, biodiversity, and ecosystem services to maintain the sustainability of ecosystem services for future generations.
4. Research should be conducted in the areas of ownership and depletion of natural resources, valuation methods for green and sustainable development, bonds and stocks, examination of stakeholder expectations, social trust, the preservation of biodiversity and ecosystems, and the sustainable use of natural resources.

X. CONCLUSION

Business organizations worldwide integrate financial ESP and non-financial ESG sustainability performance into their business operations and activities, including social responsibility, customer satisfaction, work environment, maintaining a good reputation, ensuring sustainability, environmental conscientiousness, engaging in supply chain sustainability (SCS), and creating stakeholder value. In creating shared value for all stakeholders, corporations should identify potential social, environmental, governance, and ethical issues and integrate them into their strategic planning and supply chain management. Integrating supply chain sustainability into the business environment and corporate culture enables organizations to be responsible stewards in generating both financial ESP and non-financial ESG dimensions of sustainability performance in creating shared value for all stakeholders. Continuous improvement and lean management strategies enable organizations to prioritize their activities by improving operational effectiveness and efficiency, promoting employee engagement, customer satisfaction, and social and environmental activities. This chapter examines the integration of business sustainability into supply chain management by continuously improving both the financial ESP and non-financial ESG dimensions of sustainability performance in generating shared value creation for all stakeholders. This chapter also suggests several ways management can focus on sustainable and long-term performance, including providing financial/quantitative and non-financial/qualitative sustainability information to investors, communicating sustainability performance and SCS information to all stakeholders, and focusing on long-term performance and its continuous improvements. In this context, sustainability focuses on business activities that generate long-term financial ESP to ensure firm value maximization and non-financial ESG sustainability performance that protects the interests of all stakeholders.

Currently, the benefit corporation universe is dispersed across state databases and subject to a wide range of certifying entities. However, the B corps dataset can be collected from the nonprofit B Lab, which requires its certified companies to seek benefit corporation status in the states with relevant laws and holds the remaining firms to the same certification standards in other states. BCs are established to implement initiatives to advance some social good beyond their own interests and be in compliance with applicable laws, rules, and regulations. BCs are intended to maximize positive impacts, minimize negative effects and harm on society and the environment, and create positive impacts on the community, environment, employees, customers, and suppliers. The true measure of success for BCs should not only be determined by reported earnings but also by their governance, social responsibility, ethical behavior, and environmental initiatives. BCs have received considerable attention from policymakers, regulators, and the business investment community during the past decade, and they are expected to remain the main theme of the twenty-first century.

XI. TAKEAWAYS

- Integrate SCS into the business operation and environment, corporate culture, and sustainability strategies.

- Incorporate lean management and continuous improvement for both financial ESP and non-financial ESG sustainability performance into the business and investment analysis, supply chain management, and decision-making process.
- Establish tone at the top commitment by the company's board of directors and top management team to enable effective and robust SCS.
- Develop a long-term and sustainable relationship with suppliers and other stakeholders.
- Integrate sustainability performance into all aspects of SCS, from purchasing and inbound logistics, production design, and manufacturing processes to marketing, distribution, outbound logistics, and customer services.
- Continuously assess the company's sustainability performance to monitor and improve supply chain sustainability and identify challenging areas that need further improvements.
- Promoting corporate culture consists of many shared attributes that influence the behaviors and actions of individuals as a group within the organization that enable the creation of sustainable performance.
- Address diversity, equity, and inclusion in the workplace and their integration into the business environment and corporate culture and practices.
- Promote a profit-with-purpose mission to create shared value for all stakeholders.
- Consider moving away from the shareholder primacy model and moving toward the stakeholder primacy model.
- Achieve impact investing for the purpose of generating desired financial returns for shareholders while achieving social and environmental impacts.
- In the past several years, more than 40 states, including Delaware, New York, New Jersey, Tennessee, and California, have enacted laws creating a new hybrid type of corporation designed for businesses that want to simultaneously pursue profit and benefit society.
- Benefit corporations (BCs) are intended to fill a gap between traditional corporations and non-profits by giving social entrepreneurs flexibility to achieve the dual objectives of doing well and doing good.
- The justification for BCs is that existing law prevents boards of directors from considering the impact of corporate decisions on other stakeholders, the environment, or society at large.
- Boards of directors of BCs are required to consider the impact of their decisions on specific corporate constituencies, including shareholders, employees, suppliers, and the community, as well as on the local and global environment.

Notes

1 Much of discussion in this chapter comes from Rezaee, Z. and T. Fogarty. 2019. *Business Sustainability, Corporate Governance, Organizational Ethics*. John Wiley and Sons, Inc., New Jersey.

2 Bebchuk, L. and R. Tallarita. 2022. "The Perils and Questionable Promise of ESG-Based Compensation." *Journal of Corporation Law* Vol. 48, 37–75.
3 Ibid.
4 Rezaee, Z. 2016. "Business Sustainability Research: A Theoretical and Integrated Perspective." *Journal of Accounting Literature* Vol. 36, June, 48–64.
5 Strine, Jr. L. E. 2021. "Restoration: The Role Stakeholder Governance Must Play in Recreating a Fair and Sustainable American Economy – A Reply to Professor Rock." *Business Lawyer* Vol. 76, Spring. Available at https://papers.ssrn.com/sol3/papers.cfm?abstract_id=3749654
6 Rezaee, Z and N. Rezaee. August 2021. "Business Sustainability: Investor, Board and Management Perspective." *Business Expert Press* .
7 Ibid.
8 Rezaee, Z. and T. Fogarty. 2019. *Business Sustainability, Corporate Governance, and Organizational Ethics.* John Wiley and Sons, Inc. New Jersey.
9 Ibid.
10 Ibid.
11 Sounders, Maura. 2020. *Survey Analysis: ESG Investment Pre-and Post-Pandemic*. Institute of Shareholder Services (ISS). Available at https://www.issgovernance.com/file/publications/ISS-ESG-Investing-Survey-Analysis.pdf
12 Klemash, S., J. C. Smith, and R. Doyle. 2019. "Stakeholder Capitalism for Long-term Value Creation." *Harvard Law School on Corporate Governance and Financial Regulation* June 13. Available at https://corpgov.law.harvard.edu/2019/06/13/stakeholder-capitalism-for-long-term-value-creation/
13 Ibid.
14 Sarbanes-Oxley Act (2002). H.R.- Sarbanes-Oxley Act of 2002. Available at https://www.congress.gov/bill/107th-congress/house-bill/3763
15 Warren, E. 2018. "Warren Introduces Accountable Capitalism Act." Available at https://www.warren.senate.gov/newsroom/press-releases/warren-introduces-accountable-capitalism-act/
16 Task Force on Climate-related Financial Disclosures (TCFD). 2017. Recommendations of the Task Force on Climate-related Financial Disclosures. Available at https://www.fsb-tcfd.org/publications/?gclid=Cj0KCQiA962BBhCzARIsAIpWEL0Ku-jqsvMGQMGgsg6YFbrnhU0PihQI0k1jOLR02ywktgpHBcOiLIPAaApHWEALw_wcB
17 Institute of Business Ethics (IBE). December 17, 2020. *The Ethics of Diversity*. Available at https://www.ibe.org.uk/uploads/assets/98157842-65c6–43fb-84145c19ff8e03d0/ff71757c-eb3d-439d-b8c834dba2e9ac26/IBE-Report-The-Ethics-of-Diversity.pdf
18 Ibid.
19 United Nations Global Compact (UN Global Compact). 2013. *Global Corporate Sustainability Report 2013*. Available at https://www.unglobalcompact.org/docs/about_the_gc/Global_Corporate_Sustainability_Report2013.pdf (accessed September 3, 2020).
20 United Nations Global Compact (UN Global Compact). 2015. *Supply Chain Sustainability: A Practical Guide for Continuous Improvement*, Second Edition. Available at https://www.unglobalcompact.org/library/205 (accessed September 3, 2020).
21 Rezaee, Z. 2018. "Integrating Business Sustainability into Supply Chain Management." *International Journal of Finance and Managerial Accounting* Vol. 3, No. 9 (Spring), 1–15.
22 PitchBook. 2024. *Global M&A Report.* Available at https://pitchbook.com/news/reports/2023-annual-global-ma-report

23 HIS Markit. 2019. *ESG on the Rise: Making an Impact in M&A*. Available at https://cdn.ihsmarkit.com/www/prot/pdf/1120/Mergermarket-ESG.pdf
24 Deloitte. January 2022. *The Future of M&A: 2022 M&A Trends Survey*. Available at https://www2.deloitte.com/content/dam/Deloitte/us/Documents/mergers-acqisitions/us-deloitte-2022-mna-trends-report.pdf.
25 Deloitte. March 2023. *ESG's Evolving Role in Corporate M&A Decisions*. Available at https://www.slideshare.net/DeloitteUS/private-equity-leads-corporate-deal-teams-on-esg-in-ma?from_action=save
26 Hiller, J. S. 2013. "The Benefit Corporations and Corporate Social Responsibility." *Journal of Business Ethics* Vol. 118, 287–301.
27 Delaware Law Series. August 14, 2013. "DGCL Amended to Authorize Public Benefit Corporations ." Available at http://blogs.law.harvard.edu/corpgov/tag/delaware-law/
28 Northwest Register Agent. 2020. *Benefit Corporations AKA the "B Corp."* Available at https://www.northwestregisteredagent.com/benefit-corporation.html#:~:text=You%20can%20currently%20form%20a%20benefit%20corporation%20in,Island%2C%20South%20Carolina%2C%20Vermont%2C%20Virginia%2C%20and%20Washington%20DC.

Index